TOVARISCH,
I AM NOT DEAD

TOVARISCH, I AM NOT DEAD

Garri S. Urban

Weidenfeld and Nicolson London

Copyright © Garri S. Urban 1980

First published in Great Britain by
George Weidenfeld & Nicolson Limited
91 Clapham High Street, London SW4 7TA

ISBN 0 297 77740 8

Printed in Great Britain by
Willmer Brothers Limited, Rock Ferry, Merseyside

To those who died, and those who live
in suffering under dictatorships

Garri S. Urban

Contents

The author has changed some names in order to protect the privacy of individuals who are still alive

I express my gratitude to Josephine, my beloved wife,
for translation and help with the English language

Garri S. Urban

Preface

When I first decided to write the story of my early life I had no idea how difficult and how moving it would be. As I recalled those vivid scenes the old feelings I had experienced as a young man came flooding back. Was it such a good idea after all to have listened to my friends who after hearing only a fraction of my adventures and misadventures had told me I must write them down? The work is finished, and now I ask myself what made me carry out this project. It is the story of the struggle of one individual against a system, the Soviet system, and the reason that made me write this autobiography is that I feel that it is an evil system, a threatening one that has hardly changed since Stalinist days.

It will be clear from the story that I am very proud of being a Jew, but at the same time not anti-Russian. I have always been more in sympathy with the ordinary Russian people than with the Germans, Ukrainians, or Poles among whom I was brought up and of whom I have childhood memories of anti-semitism.

The part played by Jews in the Russian Revolution was something we all knew about: such men as Lazar Kaganovitch, Zinovieev, Litvinoff, Kamenov, Chernikov and Jerzov built the Soviet state with a willing heart, with love and patriotism. By the time the Revolution had ended nearly all the bourgeoisie had emigrated while most of the Russian Jews had stayed on. They stayed because the new state, as envisaged by Marx, Engels, Lenin and Trotsky, would offer absolute equality to all without regard to religion. Such ideals perished with those leaders. In order to conclude his pact with Hitler in August 1939 Stalin had been obliged to rid himself of the Foreign Minister Litvinoff who was a Jew. The tradition of anti-semitism in Tsarist Russia which had led to pogroms and atrocities against the Jews began to rear its ugly head again. Ever since there has been a systematic campaign, planned and carried out in almost Nazi style, to oust the Jews from all positions of authority in the Soviet state.

There is a dangerous tendency toward believing that the Soviet Union has relaxed its aggressive policies, when in fact the threat is more immediate than ever. From Yalta onwards the Soviet empire has been expanding. At Yalta Stalin managed to obtain everything he wanted by insisting upon secure borders for the Soviet motherland and the division of Germany. A deep rift developed between Churchill and Roosevelt, who capitulated to Stalin's demands. In consequence the Soviet empire spread across half Europe. During the last decade the Russians have extended their influence across South East Asia, Central Asia, Africa, the Middle East and the Caribbean by posing as the protectors of the Third World nations and the Arab peoples. What they want from the Arabs is their oil and their lands, and among other nations they have similar objectives in order to occupy strategic points in preparation for war. Jews and Arabs have a common forefather, and sooner or later must learn to live and work together. This will only come about when Soviet leaders have ceased to agitate the Arab states against Israel. Why should the continued existence of Israel, with its ancient people, be the subject of discussion and bargaining?

The enormous growth in Russia's armed forces, particularly with regard to the Navy and space technology, has outstripped the military capabilities of the Western powers. On the one hand their policy is to talk of peace and Salt agreements, and on the other they proceed with the installation of offensive weapons and even send combat troops to Cuba. Perhaps nuclear warheads are already pointing at the cities of the United States.

I fear a new spirit of appeasement and credulity in the West – another Munich? The one organization that might have been able to stand up to the Soviet threat has become weak and unreliable – the United Nations. Its achievements have lagged sadly behind its failures and it is now manipulated, directly and indirectly, by the Soviet Union. Soviet leaders respect only force and determination. Until the free world stands up to them they will gain on every front, making a Third World War inevitable.

PART ONE

Blood and Death

1

Blood in the Snow

September 1939. The war caught up with me in the little town of Stryy, in what was then south-east Poland. Around me the screams of the injured, crying for help, filled the air: screams that became more agonized still when a massive bomb exploded near the centre of the town, killing and wounding scores of people.

I ran to the edge of the enormous crater it had made and eyed the scene with horror. Parts of bodies were scattered here and there: arms, legs and dismembered trunks – while those still living screamed and moaned in distress. I scrambled down and managed to clear the debris from a man who was still alive. Getting him back up the steep side of the crater was not easy, but by clawing at the rubble and dragging him through I managed it.

Others had run to the crater too and were desperately locating and freeing casualties. Standing on the edge was a Polish army officer, hands on hips, shouting instructions to the civilians working below. There were two seriously injured men still down there: one was a bearded Jew, a Chasid, with his arm blown off, crying for help in Yiddish. The Polish officer had seen them too; and, although he had not gone forward to save anyone himself, he continued to shout out his commands. One of the passers-by jumped into the crater and was trying to free the other victims. The officer shouted to him and pointed to the two badly injured men who were lying close to each other. When the man went over to them and was about to start freeing the one with his arm blown off, the officer cried out:

'*Zostaw Zyda!* Leave the Jew! Take the other one!'

I can still hear those words today. But the man, a Jew himself, took no notice and continued to clear the wreckage.

Once we had rescued all the injured we could find we returned to the top of the crater, looked at one another, and saw the same instinctive rage in each other's eyes. We turned on the Polish officer, snatched his gun away, and threw him down into the crater. Stains of blood, not his own, seeped across his uniform as he lay wedged between the corpses.

'Get me out of here! Help!' he whimpered.

I stood where I was. But the other man went back into the crater again, pulled the officer to his feet, and got him to the top. Then I waved my clenched fist in his face.

'You see!' I cried. 'A Jew has saved you!'

He was shaken and humiliated.

'*Tak, tak*. Yes, yes,' he snuffled.

A food truck had been hit by the blast of a bomb, and people were looting and carrying off the food. As the three of us stood watching another plane flew in very low, strafing the street with machine-gun fire. When it had passed I picked myself up and looked at the destruction around me. To my horror I saw that, of the three of us, I was the only one alive: the other two were lying on the ground, both riddled with bullets. I could feel a warm trickle of blood running down my back: there was a shrapnel wound in my neck.

But, wounded or not, I had at least survived. No, I was not dead – though little did I guess, as I stood there in a semi-trance with my own blood gradually seeping all over me, how many dangers I would have to survive, how often I would have to thank not only luck but my own resourcefulness and sheer determination to go on living, and never never to give in over the next six years if, at the end of that time, I would be able to claim, proudly and gratefully: 'No, my friend, no, my enemies, despite everything – I am not dead!'

That summer had been one of the finest within memory. I had been spending the late summer holiday at the resort of Truskavice in south-eastern Poland, an idyllic break for a young medical graduate living in Warsaw, brought to an abrupt close by the German invasion and *blitzkrieg*.

Young men were hurriedly called up for military service by special radio announcements and instructed to report to the nearest military centre, but within days the German invasion had totally disrupted communications and it was impossible to comply. I was doing my best – Stryy was en route to Warsaw – when Poland was subjected to another, sudden blow. Two weeks after the German invasion, the Russians marched forward into eastern Poland and occupied all the territories east of the Curzon Line.

Were they justified? What must be said is that, despite the treacherous stab-in-the-back of the Soviet leaders, most of the inhabitants of eastern Poland looked upon the Russians as protectors. The Russian army did not fight the scattered remnants of the Polish forces; they simply rounded them up without fighting or killing; and to the Poles the Russians looked a better bet than the Germans, whose pretext for invasion had been the freeing of down-trodden German minorities. But the situation was not simple, for the Ukrainian Nationalists, who detested Russians and Poles alike, occasionally made forays from their forest hide-outs, heavily armed, and attacked the Russians. There were even, despite their status as official 'allies' since the infamous Nazi-Soviet pact that virtually partitioned Poland, some full-scale engagements between the Red Army and the Germans, with infantry, artillery, tanks and air support involved – a presage of things to come.

But in general, confused though the situation was, when the Russians did arrive the people welcomed them. The Red Army soldiers, from private to general, assured the populace that they had come to help them, to save them from the German fascists. Whatever their reservations about the sincerity of the motives the Russians expressed, the people knew they had no choice and in any case they preferred the Russians to the Germans. Very simply the Russians looked kinder, ordinary, more friendly and smiling, whereas the image created by the German soldier was a cruel, frightening one. And, naturally enough, we were afraid; all the news we heard concerning the Germans confirmed our fears. Consequently the Russians appeared to some extent as deliverers.

But then, very rapidly, things changed. The Soviet Government hurriedly organized a plebiscite in the occupied territories and incorporated them into the USSR. Their thirteen million inhabitants were declared to be Soviet citizens. As my place of birth was Warsaw, this new declaration did not apply to me and I was still legally a Polish citizen, technically a member of the satellite rump state the Germans had set up, the 'General Government' – though I remained in what had been the Polish province of Galicia which was now a part of the Soviet Socialist Republic of the Ukraine – as indeed it remains today.

The Soviet economic and administrative system was quickly introduced. This was not to the taste of many people. There were deportations and arrests. It was not to my own taste. I made up my mind, like countless other Polish citizens or ex-citizens, that I would have to get out. Obviously there could be no question of returning to Warsaw now – that would be out of the frying pan perhaps but into the fire with a vengeance. No, the obvious escape route was in the south-east, across the border to Hungary or, better still, to Roumania – both neutral countries, Roumania being pro-allied whereas Hungary was both pro-German and anti-semitic.

And fortunately I was in the south-east. Therefore my first move would be to go to the nearest large city, Lvov, and from there make my plans to cross into Roumania and go on to wherever I should decide. I was not alone. From all parts of Poland and the Ukraine people were converging on Lvov, each and every one with a fixed idea of how to get away and which country eventually to go to – Poles who wanted to continue the fight determined to get to France, others like myself with no reason for loyalty to the Polish state, wanting only to escape from the tyranny of the dictatorships and rebuild our young lives elsewhere in the wide world outside.

In November 1939 Lvov, the traditional gateway into Poland, was occupied by the Russians, and army personnel of all ranks, officers and soldiers, men and women, thronged the city. They sat in the cafes and crowded into the shops where most of them bought watches, silk stockings and luxuries to take home to Russia. They seemed quite jovial and had pleasant manners and appearances, especially the women who were good-looking.

I was a very young man full of the joy of life. She was an elegant woman, a doctor of medicine with the rank of major in the Soviet army. I was first attracted by her beautiful blue eyes which she fixed on me as we sat in the Palace Cafe. I moved straight to her table and started an entertaining conversation with her. Her military uniform rather intimidated me, but I was overcome by her eyes, and I could see she had fine breasts in spite of her uniform. I forgot she was a major in the Soviet army, and my state of excitement became obvious. It was around five in the afternoon. I told her that, since she was a doctor and I was too, we should go to my room to continue our conversation on medical matters. Kira (by now we were on first name terms) laughed and replied:

'Of course, but we can talk here too, it's so pleasant.'

I asked for the bill and stood up, holding my coat in front of me to hide my embarrassment. She reacted against this and blushed at the idea of leaving the cafe with me in front of all her brother officers. She must have been about thirty-five – I was much younger. I took her by the hand and said: 'Let's go!' There were no taxis to be had and my flat was some distance away, but we walked. I opened the door and followed her inside, took off her greatcoat and drew her to me.

I unbuttoned her tunic and put my hand on her breasts – I confess I have a weakness for firm breasts. She tried to resist but I gave her no time, she was helpless against my onslaught. As we embraced my hand touched an enormous pistol she was carrying and the touch of that cold metal momentarily cooled my desire. However I went on undressing her and, as I did so, she whispered, *'Niet, niet, proshu astabtye.'* No, no, please stop.'

But she continued to remove her clothes and, as she did so, I kissed every part of her body. She got on to the bed wearing nothing but her knickers – they were long red flannel ones, and I couldn't get them off quickly enough. Here we were on the bed, flaying around like two fish in water, she heightening my ardour by her continued resistance and cries of 'No, no', and now I was denied entry by her red flannels. Hard as I tried, I couldn't pull them down, so I tore a hole in them and finally reached my target. Her cries gradually changed from *'Niet, niet'* to *'Kak characho!* How wonderful!'

After some time Kira eventually confessed to me that it was the first time she had betrayed her husband and, to make matters worse, it was with a capitalist, myself. I replied that it was the first time I had had to make love through a tear in a pair of red flannel knickers. So our discussion of medical topics had become a practical demonstration. I might have repeated the attack but I caught sight of the offending underwear and lost the urge, and the pistol on the floor didn't help matters either.

She must have sensed how I was feeling and quickly pulled a sheet over her, saying:

'We Soviet women do not give such great importance to things like underwear as you in the capitalist world.'

I would have made love to her again, since she was beautiful, and I loved women older than I was; but those flannels were just too much, and the moment passed. That was my first, but not my last, sexual encounter with a Soviet female officer. War is, however, surprisingly inducive to love-making; and it was less than two months later that I found myself breaking a train journey towards the Roumanian border at the town of Stanislav in order to pay what I imagined would be a last visit to a very beautiful friend of mine, Cristina, a well-known singer with a most attractive voice.

We – I was with a little man, Manek, who had pleaded with me to help him to escape too – took a *droshky*, a horse-drawn cab, from the station. It was dark when we reached Cristina's house and I tapped on the window. She rushed out when I spoke, recognizing my voice: '*Kochanie!* My love!' she greeted me. She was completely oblivious of the presence of my friend Manek – at least till our first raptures were over – but then came the problem of where to put him for the night. Cristina had a girl-friend who usually slept in the same room, which was the largest in the house, but there was no second bedroom for Manek. This wasn't the only difficulty: Maruha, her friend, didn't like the look of him. We could have divided the room with a curtain, but it was obvious that he felt out of place, and so he said he would go to a hotel for the night. He gave me an envious look as he left and said he would come back in the morning.

Cristina was as lovely as ever, and she produced a large bottle of vodka which we proceeded to drink by the tumbler. Maruha joined in the drinking with us, but it soon became clear that her presence was not required, and she went into the bathroom. The poor girl must have stayed in there for two hours but, in the end, the noise and shouts she heard made her knock at the door and she came back into the room. She was a dark good-looking girl, and I encouraged her to come in. I love women too much to see them suffer. Old and young, one must treat them well. But I had not foreseen that Cristina would become jealous. She suddenly bit my lip and called me a 'Swine!' However, Maruha's instincts had been aroused and were not to be left unsatisfied. I did the best I could that night to satisfy both those Polish girls – the last, as it happened, I was to make love to for many years. They seemed to have no complaints.

Next morning, poor Manek returned. He wasn't bad looking, but he had no life in him, no personality. We knew a train would be leaving for Kolomyya at noon, and from there it would take about two hours to reach Novoselitsa on the frontier. It was late November and got dark early, around four o'clock, so I wanted to arrive in Novoselitsa in plenty of time to reach the River Prut, the actual border, by four.

We all sat down for a chat and a drink before leaving, and Cristina confirmed that the Russians were shooting people trying to escape across the frontier. She cried and begged me to wait, not to leave now; but once I have decided to do something I never go back – I have been like that since childhood. Manek however was shitting in his trousers with fear; and he decided he couldn't go on. He tried to make excuses and explain but I was only too pleased to be without him as I considered him a liability. So, saying a fond farewell to them all, I set out for the station by myself.

Hours later, about three thirty that afternoon, I was trudging through open country; snow-covered fields very close to the frontier. It must have been about twenty degrees below zero; I was lightly clad in a grey suit, blue coat and white scarf, all autumn-weight clothes. I breathed in deeply through my open mouth : it made my lungs ache. I was happy to be alone.

At first I walked fast past the notices which read : ENTRY STRICTLY FORBIDDEN EXCEPT TO RESIDENTS, OR TO THOSE WITH SPECIAL PERMISSION, but I felt I was being observed and purposely assumed a slow steady pace. Two Soviet guards were coming towards me wearing heavy winter great-coats and carrying rifles mounted with bayonets which flashed in the waning afternoon light.

I came to a little house. In front of it, on the opposite side of the road, rose a snow-covered bank about ten feet high. On the far side of the bank was my objective – the River Prut. Between the road and the river was a wide snow-covered expanse, tree-less, without cover of any kind. Lights began to twinkle on the opposite bank, almost half a mile away.

I walked up to the door and knocked. A girl of about twenty appeared and asked me inside.

It was invitingly warm and cosy. An orthodox Jew was sitting at a table. He looked up. 'We don't want you here,' he said in immediate alarm. 'You will get us into trouble. Get out. Now.' He would have said more, but the girl looked at him. Rather shamefacedly he repeated, more pleadingly : 'Get out of here!'

From the window I could see that the guards were retracing their steps and coming slowly back towards the house. The girl came forward and asked her father if she could give me a hot drink. He became agitated. I intervened and said : 'Look, I have come to visit your daughter. I have no intention of crossing the frontier,' and I winked at the girl.

She said : 'Yes, father, I asked him here.' He looked at us both, and we all looked at each other. He knew the girl was lying and that I had lied but he accepted it and for a moment it looked as though my situation had altered. After what seemed several minutes he asked me to sit down. I kept the road in view, and could see the heads of the guards and their bayonets as they walked along a dip in the road, their bodies obscured by a bank. They were still coming towards the house. The father saw them too, and shouted : 'Now there will be trouble! They're coming here!'

It was a desperate moment for him and the girl, and only later did I reflect that the fault was entirely mine. The room had three windows, hoary with frost on the outside. Through one of them I could make out the lights beckoning me across the river : behind us the empty fields stretched away into the distance. I pressed my nose against the window which overlooked the road – the guards were much closer, steadily approaching the house. It was dusk, but the clear skies and the snow gave good visibility.

The old man was getting whiter and whiter. His eyes stood out from his head. 'Oh my God! How shall we explain this?'

Before I could answer I saw that the guards had stopped and were standing only a few yards from the house. We all looked at each other, listening – 'He's inside the house. Let's go in,' said one. 'There's no need,' his companion replied. 'He'll have to come out sooner or later, and we've made fools of ourselves enough times before when they've had visitors. Let's wait outside.'

'Alright, but I don't like standing here in front. Let's go round the back.'

Without consulting the old man, I opened the front door and went out. 'What are you doing? Why don't you go about your business and move on? I asked the old man to make me some tea, but he's frightened. I don't know why, because I didn't come here to drink tea. I'm really interested in his daughter. Please, carry on . . . move away . . . you understand . . . she's a lovely girl. Do you want to see my papers?' – and I put my hand in my pocket for my non-existent papers. They looked a little nonplussed. 'There's no need for that,' the shorter of the two answered, 'but you must be gone from here before nightfall.'

He laughed and took out some cigarette papers and a tobacco pouch to fill himself a cigarette. I quickly reached for the long Belomorcanal cigarettes which I had loose in my pocket and offered one to him. At that time I was a heavy smoker.

He laughed and said : 'Thanks no, I prefer my Machorka.'

'Alright,' I replied, 'let me try one of yours.' He offered me a smelly cigarette which was not at all pleasant.

I turned with a cheerful wave and went back inside. The girl was full of gratitude but the father was still petrified :

'You may fool them, but you don't fool me. I know why you're here, and I want you to go now, immediately.'

I paced up and down the room looking from each window; the guards were walking away in a northerly direction. I could see the River Prut and even make out people standing on the opposite bank in Roumania. I had been there only twenty minutes, but to the old man it was obviously twenty minutes too long. I thanked the girl for the tea, and thanked him too. He with tears in his eyes – old men are very changeable – pronounced a blessing over me in Hebrew, which I didn't understand entirely, but I knew he had asked God to help me. I certainly needed God's help – but I also needed the girl's information.

'How deep is the water?' I asked her. She replied that it was very shallow at the edges, and about two yards deep in the middle with a very swift current. That didn't sound too good. But, as always in the most difficult moments of my life, I remembered my mother whom I loved very much and who had died very young. I called on her to help me and be with me.

A handful of *zlotys* had remained in my pocket, and I placed them on the table: 'If anything happens to me, honour the memory of my mother, she died in the month of December.' The old man pushed back the money: 'Please take it, we don't want it.' His daughter looked at me with woe-begotten eyes. I suppressed the urge to kiss her, squared my shoulders, walked out of the house, crossed the road, clambered cautiously over the bank, and started to wade through the snow which came up to the top of my thighs. I reckoned that for the first stretch the house would give me cover, and that I could be seen only from the Roumanian side. As the snow became less deep I started to run as quickly as I could, and broke into a sprint as I neared the river.

I had covered about four fifths of the distance and was only about a hundred yards from the river when the rifle shots began. The intervals between shots told me it was a sniper. I started to swerve and zig-zag, then other snipers opened up cross-fire from other directions. I knew they would get me, but I had to keep running. From the other side of the river I could hear the Roumanians shouting encouragement: 'Run! Run! We're here!'

The shots came faster and faster. I threw myself on the ground and started to crawl the last five yards to the water. I heard more shots: the pebbles jumped and split around me. My hat had gone; there were drops of blood on the pebbles. I lay there. Everything grew still around me. I could smell the spent bullets.

On the other side they shouted 'They've got him! He's dead!' My blood froze on the stones. I tried breathing deeply and, when I felt that there was no major injury, I crawled slowly to the river. I was still well within range: they had only stopped firing because they thought me dead. I moved imperceptibly so that they wouldn't realize I was still alive.

However, as I reached the river's edge, a burst of machine-gun fire spattered the water in front of me. If I moved they would finish me off.

One of my hands dangled in the icy water, and I could hear the Roumanians shouting to each other: 'Yes, he must be dead. They would have got him in any case, he would never have made it.'

As I lay there, I realized too late how I had made my mistake: I shouldn't have crawled towards the river. If I had stood up and run, the snipers could not have continued firing for fear of hitting the onlookers on the opposite bank where they were waiting for me with blankets.

I was weak from loss of blood, I could hear horses coming near, then two mounted officers circled me, armed with machine-guns and revolvers.

'He's dead.'

'You're wrong, Comrade,' I replied. '*Tovarisch*. I am not dead!'

They made no attempt to lift me out of the water.

'You are no comrade of ours. If you were you wouldn't be running away.'

One got down from his horse while the other covered me with the machine-gun. He tried to lift me but I resisted. 'Don't touch me, I can get up alone.' But when I stood up all I remembered was falling down again.

I fell face down. One of them turned me over, and I heard him shouting: 'Call for help. Get a stretcher.'

They put me on the stretcher. I vaguely remember soldiers moving about me and watching the steam of their breath in the cold air. The voices on the other side were raised in protest and sympathy as I was carried across the snow and on to the road in front of the house where I had started my attempt. They laboured up the steep, sloping bank and brought me to where an open army truck was standing on the road. As they lifted me on to it I saw the girl come out to the doorway, pale and panting. Perhaps she thought I was dead.

The officer in command shouted: '*Skoray, bistro!* Hurry!' As we moved off, soldiers jumped aboard and sat on the seats along the sides of the truck.

In spite of my weakness I knew my wounds were not serious, but the bumping movement of the vehicle made me feel worse. I told myself: 'Keep your mouth shut till you get to the hospital.' From time to time I opened one eye to look around me to see if there was any chance of escape, but all I could see were the vast grey skies above. I had the sensation of swimming, as though I was going under an anaesthetic in the old days when a mask was used over the mouth. The smoke of their Machorka cigarettes nauseated me. They held their weapons at the ready so that there was no possible chance of escape.

After about three miles we reached the barracks in Novoselitsa. The truck slowed down and came to a halt. I heard the noise of heavy doors being unbolted and the truck moved inside. The back flap was released and the soldiers piled out quickly: I counted four of them. My stretcher was lifted out and I was carried through a dark door. I kept looking about me every so often with one eye.

'*Ifpodval!* To the cellar!'

2

A Russian Joke

The steps down were very wide. There was a strong smell of gunpowder. They placed me on the floor in a dark windowless room lit by one naked electric light bulb. The four men quickly disappeared, and two officers stumped in. One of them placed his boot on my chest and pressed down while the other leant over me and opened my eyelids. Suddenly I caught the man's boot in my hand, pulled him to the floor, rolled over and up, and, taking advantage of the second one's astonishment, knocked him down too. They both lay on the floor. I dashed to the door. It was locked. I turned to see that one of them had got up and pulled out a revolver.

'You parasite – one move and I'll finish you!' he yelled.

The other officer was armed but made no move to reach for his revolver. He picked himself up from the floor, with a rather puzzled look, then started to laugh.

'After all, we brought him here to finish him off. He's wounded and bleeding. Put away the gun. There's no need for it.'

'You're right,' I said.

'We'll take you upstairs to see what you have to say for yourself,' said one of the NKVD men.

When we came down I had not noticed that the cellar was two floors below ground level. Upstairs was an infirmary and a few beds. So that was their system! Obviously they were afraid of taking wounded escapers to the properly equipped local hospital for fear of the rumours and speculation that that would trigger off. So they treated the lightly wounded themselves – the staff, as I soon observed, were local Ukrainians who had little sympathy for Poles or Jews and could be relied upon not to talk. As for the seriously wounded – well, this was my first actual personal contact with Soviet ruthlessness but I cannot pretend that it surprised me. Clearly they took the seriously wounded down to the cellars as I had been taken, and there, as the officer had said, 'finished them off'. After all they were all fugitives from the newly-imposed paradise!

We passed through several rooms, each one of them occupied by guards, both officers and soldiers. I recognized one of them, he had brought me in and had helped to carry me downstairs. When he saw me he took a bent cigarette, made with newspaper, from his lips and rolled it in his fingers. He couldn't believe his eyes. He had helped to bring in a fugitive, mortally wounded, and taken him downstairs to await his death, and now here I was walking past him.

The two officers brought me to a comfortable well-lit room. Through the barred windows I could see it had started to snow. They told me to sit down. Through the open door I could hear a voice:

'Let's have a look at this hero!'

I sat on a chair in the middle of the room. Suddenly my weakness overcame me and the faces in front of me seemed to turn upside down. My hand searched in my pocket for the loose cigarettes I always carried with me. They were frozen and fell in a wet heap to the floor. I felt pains in my abdomen, face and jaw. When I passed my hand inside my trousers it was covered in blood. My chin was caked with coagulated blood which fell off in lumps when I touched it and made red bloodstains on my trouser-leg. Down one side my trousers were soaked and shapeless where they had frozen to my leg.

The officer I had punched came forward and gave me a backhander across the face. The force of it tumbled me from the chair. I got up, grabbed the chair, and hit him over the head with it – I saw the blood come. Then they fell upon me kicking and punching until I lost consciousness.

When I came round there were three more officers in the room, looking at me curiously; and two soldiers, one a sergeant wearing many decorations and carrying my hat in his hand. I staggered dizzily to my feet and sat down. An enormously fat officer, a captain, took the hat, came near, and held it close to my face:

'This is yours.'

'Yes, it's mine,' I replied, glad that the atmosphere seemed to have changed and that instead of receiving blows I was receiving my private property back.

He showed me two three-cornered holes, one on each side of the hat:

'You have just been born!' he said. Then he took my hair between his fingers saying: 'His hair is singed.'

At that time I had a full head of chestnut hair of which I was very proud. A soldier came forward with a pair of scissors which he handed to the officer. I jumped to my feet and grabbed the chair again: 'Don't touch my hair,' I screamed.

'I only want to cut a small piece to show you something,' said the officer placatingly. He cut two locks of hair from different places, and showed me how they were singed – they still smelt of burning.

Then the sergeant with all the medals came up to me and asked if I knew what medals they were. When I replied that I didn't he told me:

'Four of them are first prizes for marksmanship, at various distances.' He laughed. 'You've got a steel head, but I don't mind telling you, I'm happy to see you alive.'

'Why?' I asked.

'Because I was shooting to kill. When you fell I fired again to be sure you were dead and I saw your hat come off. I thought it was enough. It wasn't only me you fooled: my comrade with the machine-gun thought that you were dead too. Well, your destiny is to live.'

Everyone around me was examining the hat, I don't remember how many there were in the room. I said:

'You'll have to send back all your medals and decorations for reclassification.'

It was very strange. There was this general atmosphere of excitement and I was the centre of attraction. I kept popping up and sitting down again, rather light-headed, until someone noticed blood running on to my shoe. The senior officer, a colonel, ordered that I should be taken to the infirmary. Another officer, a captain, a *politruk*, a party member, couldn't resist a parting dig:

'You wanted to get away to Roumania. Well, we will be getting you away to Siberia, and for a nice long spell too. You are an enemy and a parasite.'

Siberia! My feeling of euphoria disappeared in a flash. I stared at him but this time I had no ready answer. A guard tapped me on the shoulder and we left the room.

The infirmary was a small place, one floor down. I undressed and noticed a small wound in the abdomen, a couple of inches above my appendix scar. It was an open wound from which the blood seeped slowly. I opened the wound with my fingers and saw that it wasn't serious.

'I'll take care of myself, I'll dress it.'

But the male nurse made me lie down, washed and disinfected it, put four stitches in, then bandaged it. Next came my chin, which he showed me in the mirror. The jaw-bone had been slightly splintered. He attended to my chin which needed two stitches, then put a plaster on it. I suppose he must have used a sterile powder. When he discovered I was a doctor, he apologized and said it was all he could do for me.

I paced up and down the room, feeling much better and ready and eager for escape. I was young, impulsive, and thought my extraordinary luck would continue now the immediate danger had passed. Before I left the infirmary I asked the nurse for a drink and he gave me a small glass of pure surgical spirit. He told me to be careful of the officer I had beaten up. The two guards who had been waiting outside took me to a newly-constructed cell with no bed or chair. A dim light reflected from the passage on the dark walls.

The guard who opened the door for me said:

'Here's a nice place for you. Your wounds will heal quickly here.'

As he locked the door behind me I was left standing in what was no more than a cage. Now I felt broken and exhausted, but on reflection not unduly worried about what might happen next. I had committed no real crime, nothing to justify Siberia. An empty threat! It must be!

Many, many hours passed locked up like an animal. It was have been around eleven in the morning when I was called up for interrogation again and found the Colonel waiting for me. I sat down. He looked at me and offered me a cigarette. He proceeded to ask me many personal questions and wrote down my replies. It took two to three hours. Before he sent me back he offered me another cigarette. He seemed to be sympathetic.

'Don't worry. So you ran away. But we are human; if you have told me the truth you may get away with ten years in Siberia.'

I thanked him and asked if he would like to come with me.

'How do you mean?' He seemed astounded.

'If there is a law which can cause me to be sent to prison in Siberia for what I have done, I shouldn't be surprised to see you there for what you are doing.' I could still hardly take these Russians and their threats seriously.

I was sent back to my cell. The door banged shut, and I heard the loud grating noise of the key being turned in the lock, a noise I had already grown to hate. I was back in my cage again.

I paced up and down as far as I could in such a confined space, as prisoners in these circumstances will often do in order to tire themselves before attempting to sleep at night. But my walking was less purposeful, more instinctive: I strode up and down at speed as confused thoughts and fears raced through my head. I even took a run at the walls and tried to mount them, falling back, defeated by gravity. I was like a caged leopard, taken by force from a world in which I had ranged free.

Why had my captors mentioned such long terms of imprisonment or hard labour? Why all the fuss? Why? They could so easily have shot me and rid themselves of such an uncomfortable prisoner. The nearest point I had come to that was in the cellar. Even though I had proved to be very much alive, there had been nothing to prevent them from shooting me.

My brain remained in a whirl after hours of fruitless pacing and jumping in this terrible cage. I finally concluded that they were bluffing. If they had not done so already, they would not kill me now. After all, the war against Poland was over, and the Russians were at peace with all the world. As for years of hard labour, there could not be a lawful sentence of such severity in any country in the world for what I had attempted – the cross-ing of a peaceful frontier. There must be a reason. They would try to use me for some purpose. They were accustomed to hand-ling would-be escapers. They could see how determined I was.

Determined to do what? I longed to get as far away from Europe as possible and start a new life in a free country. Though I was young, I had travelled abroad a lot and could speak, well or badly, six languages. The world was open to me – in theory, at least. Not that I had anything against the Russians I had met. They seemed very good-hearted people and as such I much preferred them to the Nazi Germans – even at this very moment when they had nearly shot me and were threatening me so inexplicably with hard labour. But I had no wish to live under the Soviet regime, much as I might like individual Russians. Besides even someone as politically naïve as I then was could see that, though there might be peace in Poland for the moment, the Nazi-Soviet pact was an artificial one which would not hold. And what then? The three weeks of war we had lived through would have been just a tiny foretaste of the horrors to come. Besides, there was nothing to hold me back. I had left no one behind who would suffer because of my absence. My dearly-loved mother was dead. My sisters were all married with hus-bands and children. Mischa, my little brother? Yes, I had a moment's qualm about him; but he was living with my father and my father's new wife. No, there was nothing to keep me in Europe – nothing but these wretched Russians with their bluff and their infuriating delays.

On the third night I was awakened by the delicate touch of an NKVD guard.

'Get up. Your interrogator wants to talk to you.'

I jumped up quickly, dressed and was taken up to the officer with whom I had fought. He signed a form and gave it to the guard (this was routine Soviet procedure to confirm that the prisoner had been passed into his custody). He looked up.

'You have been lucky. You're being moved in fifteen minutes to a central prison. If I could have kept you here longer I would have taught you a lesson. As it is, I will recommend to my colleagues that you be sent to Siberia for twenty years, and I'm sure they'll take good care of you.'

First it had been just 'a nice long spell'; then ten years; now it was twenty. What would it be after I'd passed through the hands of another two or three officers? A century and a half? It really was impossible to take the Red Army seriously.

'You're a communist,' I said, with a very serious expression on my face, 'and do not believe in God.' I paused and raised my hand. He drew back in fright and reached for his holster. 'May God bless you for your kindness to me;' and, so saying, I made the sign of the cross over his dumbfounded head.

I was taken to a courtyard where an open truck was waiting. It was dark, about four in the morning. I was bundled in to join a few other prisoners. We were warned that we should not talk. Two guards sat at one end with machine-guns, and the driver had another soldier sitting next to him. Gates opened and closed behind us. I recognized the road to Stanislav – which I had left only a few days before in such different circumstances.

At Stanislav we disembarked and were herded into an enormous prison, and there we were separated and sent to different cells. I was put in a cell where there must have been around a hundred prisoners in a space constructed for thirty. They were a very mixed collection of individuals: Polish army officers, intellectuals, Ukrainian Nationalists and others, all pale and unshaven.

Five or six of the most privileged officers occupied the only mattresses there were. The rest of us all sat on the floor without room to stretch out.

The head man among the prisoners was a Pole called Marian, a bomber pilot, a tough, strong, aggressive type. They all gathered round to ask me questions: Where had I come from? What had I done? Why was I wearing bandages? Which was my home town? I was tired and told them to go to hell. Marian didn't like that. He said:

'If anyone is asked a question here he has to answer.'

There was one man there whom Marian respected and obeyed, an army captain. I think he must have made a sign behind my back that I should be left alone, because Marian looked away, then turned back, saying:

21

'You can sleep on there,' and pointed to the only toilet in the cell.

The Captain came near and said that I looked too ill and must have had a bad time; they should put a stronger man there. Marian concurred. In any case no one would have forced me to sit there or sleep there.

Night-time came quickly. All the inmates of the cell were in transit and remained there for a maximum of thirty days while decisions were made about their future. There were certain strict and unbreakable rules.

At mealtimes we formed a line, a long line; the elite Polish officers were first, then came the Ukrainians, then Jews. I discovered the reason for this strictly observed procedure in my first few days. The food was doled out through a hatch; the ration was one large spoonful, but the first portions were spooned up from the bottom of the pan and so were thicker. The last portions, those the Jews received, contained of course the least nourishment of all.

Until war had broken out in 1939 I had had nothing against the Poles but, in spite of the *blitzkrieg* they then suffered at the hands of the Nazis, I could not help but remark how they continued to practise their congenital anti-semitism. Every Jew who has lived through the Second World War in Eastern Europe came to know that the worst anti-semites were the Ukrainians, then the Poles and, lowest on the list, the Russians.

On one particular day a small, pale man was standing in front of me (whom I later discovered was the editor of the Jewish newspaper called *Chwila*, published in the city of Lvov). His name was Spund. He looked resigned, his eyes lifeless. When he received his spoonful of food he looked at it and saw that it was little more than water. He sighed and said to Marian: 'If you don't put me at the front sometimes, I think I'll die.' Marian jostled him brusquely out of the line, his plate fell to the floor and he reeled across the room, then crumpled to the ground. The saucepans which held the soup were enormous and I was lucky enough to arrive at the moment when a fresh pan was brought in. My portion contained a lot of thick, hot soup with barley. I took the soup plate with my right hand, grabbed Marian by the nape of the neck with my left hand, and plunged

his face forward into the scalding soup, at the same time bringing my knee up into his groin. I threw him to the ground and he rolled over and over until he found himself next to Mr Spund. A tremendous noise broke out in the room among the Polish officers; all eyes were on me, some pleased, most outraged. They wanted to lynch me. I took hold of a colonel whom everyone liked, and held him in a stranglehold:
'If you touch me, he will die,' I shouted.
Suddenly the door opened. An alarm whistle sounded, and guards came pouring in. Marian was holding his hands to his face, screaming in pain. They took him away to the infirmary. I was pulled away from the Colonel and taken directly to the office of an official who asked me what had happened. I told him. He was taken aback. No doubt he was wondering how I, in my weak condition, had been able to confront that animal Marian. After five minutes he went to a telephone in the next room, then I was sent to another cell, smaller, in another wing of the prison. There were nine Poles there, each with his own mattress.

As I sat on the filthy mattress provided for me I reflected that it appeared that the Soviet police had approved of what I had done. The Russians always know exactly what goes on in the prisons either through informers or by the constant watch kept through the peepholes in the doors by the guards who observed the prisoners' behaviour towards each other at all times. On occasions the interrogators and judges would also study and observe certain prisoners, the better to understand them. How can anyone lucky enough never to have been in prison or isolation understand the tragedy of an innocent human being locked in a cage?

Yes, my action against Marian had met with the tacit approval of my interrogators. As I sank on to the mattress, hungry and exhausted, I wondered what would happen next.

I did not have long to wait. Next day, in the evening, at dusk, I was brought out again for interrogation by a man in his early forties, an officer of the NKVD Special Branch, called Morozov. He was wearing glasses and had before him a file containing many papers.

'I'll be quick with you. I don't intend to see you here often. Your destination has been decided. You will travel to the Soviet Union, to a central prison where you will await the verdict of a court. You will be tried on three charges: counter-revolutionary activities, attempted illegal escape across a frontier, and assault on a Soviet officer. From these reports I see that you are an aggressive young man, lucky to be alive. Furthermore, you have here in this city a good-looking girl-friend. If you co-operate with us and behave yourself, you will receive certain privileges.'

I looked steadily into his eyes trying to fathom what it was he wanted from me. The bit about the girl surprised me. In one detail he was wrong: I had more than one girl-friend in that city. I remained silent. This evoked the question:

'Are you deaf?'

'No, just constipated.'

He got up quickly from the desk, and walked round it, put his boot on the rail of my chair and bent towards me:

'You're a Jew, aren't you?'

'Yes,' I answered, and tried to stand up.

'Stay where you are. There are high-ranking Polish officers in your cell. Some of them had government posts. They're all anti-semitic, and they have destroyed all their identity papers so that we are unable to try them for any of their crimes. I would like you to help us, especially with the man who sleeps next to you. He says his name is Dr Cilichowski. We know otherwise. He's the ex-Governor of the city of Poznan. I want you to become friendly with him and help us with our investigations.

I jumped up from the chair so quickly he shot across the room. There was a moment of silence. He was standing nervously a few yards from his desk. Finally I said:

'I am in agreement with you about one thing only. There are many anti-semites among those Poles, but you should learn that you can never expect a man of my dignity and guts to become an informer.'

He grew pale and tense, then he laughed ironically, went back to his desk saying:

'Well it's your choice.'

He rang a bell and I was taken away. The interview had only lasted a few minutes. I had been moved yet again. This time in my new cell there were only two other prisoners, and we all had beds.

Next morning I was called out again and marched by a route new to me to a small visiting room, divided across the middle by a metal grille. My curiosity was aroused, wondering who would be coming to see me. Then I saw Cristina, the beautiful singer with whom I had spent the night before setting out for the frontier. She looked well, and ran forward when she saw me. Her blue eyes were full of tears which made her long lashes stick together.

She told me she had become a friend of Morozov, who had allowed her to visit me. From her tone I could tell she thought I was in serious trouble. Lowering her voice and glancing at the guard, a young Tartar, she added that it was a last favour – for Morozov had told her that my case was hopeless and that I would be moved over the frontier into Russia within the next few days.

'And, *Garinka*,' she added with a break in her voice, 'you will probably never live to come back.'

I strained her against me, she pressed her body closely, warmly against mine. The Tartar's eyes seemed to be popping out of his head. I held her at arm's length to be sure it was she, then kissed her again. I had forgotten what it was like to touch a woman's body. Hers was like sculptured marble: high buttocks, pear-shaped breasts – and now it was down between them she pointed so urgently: she had concealed a gun wrapped in a handkerchief there and whispered to me to take it. All the pleasure I was feeling evaporated instantly. I was confused. I told her hastily I couldn't take it, thanked her for coming, and kissed her a passionate though fearful goodbye. Our farewells were rushed because the guard should only have allowed us five minutes and we had been talking for much longer. He had probably lost count of the time. When I got back to my cell I was given a parcel containing some packets of tobacco, some bread and sugar and was asked to sign that I had received these items intact.

I couldn't sleep that night. I was regretting not having taken the gun, couldn't understand why I had refused it. I was not in a state of despair: my wounds had healed, I had removed the stitches myself. I felt well now, although always hungry. The hours of boredom and idleness had given me the chance to reflect on my future. Cristina had been right to sound worried. I had been wrong to be so confident. This was no short-term arrest. The Red Army was not a pack of jokers. I faced many, many years of imprisonment.

In early December, hundreds of prisoners, myself included, were moved from Poland via Lvov to Chernikov. So this was Russia! As we sped through the streets in the truck I lifted the tarpaulin cover to look at the city, an undistinguished collection of snow-covered buildings. I was far from thrilled.

Once again I was taken before an officer of the NKVD, this time a Captain Niemkov Lebidyev. He told me to sit down as he examined my dossier which now appeared to have grown much fatter.

'I have been looking at your file for some hours now. A proposition was put to you which you refused; and, from what I read here, I understand that you are quite a character and a dangerous man. It is not my intention to break you ... excuse me one moment. ...'

He picked up the telephone.

'Yes. ... *Da*. ... Restaurant. ... Send me a few bitki with fried potatoes. ... Excuse me. ...' He covered the mouthpiece of the telephone with his hand:

'You like onion?' he asked.

'Yes,' I replied.

He continued speaking on the telephone:

'Yes, with fried onions, a cold beer and make it quick. How long will it take? Twenty minutes? That's too long. Alright.'

He put down the receiver, opened the drawer of his desk, took out a packet of cigarettes and offered them:

'Smoke? I know you're a heavy smoker.'

I took one and lit it with one of the matches he had put on the desk.

He stood up. He wore wide military breeches, not a tall man,

26

about forty. As he paced the room, he held his hands behind his back.

'Listen carefully. You will have to make up your mind in twenty minutes – either you tell me the truth, or you will have to face the consequences of your crimes.'

He opened the file and took out my passport:

'This document proves that you have moved around the world a great deal. We have other proofs that you are a spy. I understand that you refused to co-operate with us before, but now I am offering you the job of becoming a Soviet agent. You will be sent to Moscow to receive specialist training and preparation, then you will work for our Socialist motherland.'

As I listened I smoked one cigarette after another: my first cigarettes for some time. The effect of the smoke was to heighten my hunger. My head was swimming, I felt drunk. The meal arrived. He told me to sit down, relax, and eat. I enjoyed the meat balls and even more the beer that washed them down. As I ate, the telephone rang several times. Lebidyev answered it. During one of the conversations he said:

'. . . Yes, he's eating well. . . . Yes, quite a character. No, I don't agree with some of the opinions in the dossier. I find him pleasant. . . . Impulsive, very proud. He doesn't begin to realize what trouble he's in. Yes, I'll see you tonight.'

He hung up. The telephone business was probably a new method they had of provoking a reaction from the person interrogated. At that moment I was concerned, like a hungry dog, only with the food on the plate before me. I even had a strong urge to lick the plate but would not give my tormentor the satisfaction of watching me do so.

More questions, more persuasive arguments followed, but the basic choice remained: become a Soviet agent or go to Siberia.

I thanked him for the meal and for the humane treatment – I told him he was the first real person who had interrogated me.

'I respect you for it,' I told him. 'I am willing to work for you in the Soviet Union, but in my own profession. So, please, if it is in your power, set me free to do so.'

Without answering me yes or no he lifted the telephone to call a guard to take me back to my cell.

As I walked into the cell the door was swung closed behind me, the key grating in the lock : the noise of the key in the lock always made me uneasy. I paced up and down the cell trying to assess my position. What would they do next?

Three weeks passed without interrogation or news of any kind. It was late in January 1940, the door opened one day and a guard shouted:

'U!' (They always called prisoners by their initials.)

In the corridor outside the cell, Lebidyev reappeared, flanked by two armed guards. There were no meat balls or cold beer this time.

'You have been condemned by a court to five years' hard labour on various counter-revolutionary charges.'

The 'court' was the famous Moscow Troika, a court specially set up which automatically condemned millions of people, most of them innocent of any crime, to be sent to labour camps during Stalin's day and even afterwards. Those condemned were not tried by ordinary court, due to lack of evidence, but were normally set up by the NKVD and condemned to between five and twenty years of hard labour in the camps. At least my 'crime' had merited the minimum punishment.

'Will you sign a statement that you have heard the verdict as read out by me?'

I looked into his face closely and said quietly :

'You can sign it for me.'

'I want you to sign it, otherwise you will stay in this jail for a very long time before you are sent to a camp.'

I felt like punching hard at his face.

'If I sign it, does it mean that I accept the verdict?'

He said : 'You can sign that you do not accept the verdict, but that you acknowledge the sentence given.'

I had tried to gain time, but I could see that I was trapped. I had to give in, so I signed it by making a very obscene diagram as a signature. Fortunately he did not inspect it too closely. Back to the cells I went – tried, condemned and sentenced with all the due formalities of Soviet law. No wonder I laugh now when I read or hear about the justice of the system – like so many others, I have experienced communist justice for myself.

A Russian Joke

The vista stretched in front of me, seemingly endless at such a young age: five years of hard labour, five years of lost youth. But I knew myself and my abilities better now – though deep inside Russia, I would still escape. I regretted nothing!

3

First Encounter with Federovitch

I travelled with other prisoners on a special train on the long journey to Nibka 3 Kandalaksha, about one thousand and two hundred miles away, just inside the Arctic Circle in the north of Russia.

The intense cold of the Arctic winter meant that special clothing had to be provided for the men: special cotton quilted suits with an interlining which gave good insulation against the cold, winter hats with ear flaps, gloves and *valinki* boots, specially made for Arctic conditions.

At the end of January the temperatures were between -30°C and -40°C and most prisoners slept in their suits.

The labour force here was engaged in building one of the first MIG factories. While it was still dark at 7 a.m. every morning, the prisoners filed out through the gates to go to their work. On the gatepost a thermometer was attached. When the temperature went below -20°C no prisoner was officially permitted to go out to work, so the authorities, under the instructions of the Camp Commander, altered the thermometers when the temperatures went below the prescribed limit, and they still read -20°C when in fact it was much lower.

As the workers left the camp, rousing military marches and revolutionary songs were relayed over loudspeakers in the hope that they would be encouraged to work that much harder. Communist slogans were displayed on banners pinned to the walls.

The working day was ten hours and, as they shuffled out, I watched their swollen, grey, unshaven faces still creased as though asleep. Their place of work was about forty minutes' walk distant, along narrow roads. Though the snow made walking more difficult, they had to move as quickly as possible, four or five abreast, depending on the width of the road, egged on by guards carrying rifles topped with flashing bayonets and accompanied by Alsatian dogs. If a man fell he was either kicked by the guards or bitten by the dogs. So the lines of prisoners moved quickly, and their breathing became more and more laboured, the clouds formed by their breath rising in the cold air. At such low temperatures the whole face had to be covered, leaving only a narrow slit for the eyes.

When they got to the factory site they were given a shovel and a long steel pole with a sharp end, called a *lom*, with which they made holes in the frozen earth. At that time of year the top six inches of soil were so frozen that it was difficult for even the strongest man to crack the surface. As there were only a few hours of daylight each day, most of the work was done by the light of electric lamps. The steel poles alone weighed twelve pounds: the guards sometimes called them pencils.

The round-the-clock prison guards were the overseers of the work and the prisoners had their own brigadiers who allotted marks for work done. According to these marks the food tickets were handed out. Every prisoner had a ticket which stated which type of meal he should receive. The best, hardest workers were classed as *Stachanovitz* or *Rekordist* (record-breakers) and they received quite passable food: next were the *Obchoi* or moderate workers while the poorest physical specimens were called *Filon*. Before I was given my tickets I knew they would class me as a *Filon* as I had no intention of working for them. It is quite amazing to me now to recall all those scenes, and the life in the camp where I lived and so many died. Memory gets weaker, men grow old, but some scenes live on in the memory until you die.

The administrative services of the camp had many divisions: of these the most important was the NKGB whose head was Colonel Volkovitch. The Camp Commander was General Federovitch, a man in his late fifties or perhaps early sixties, a man of strong, domineering character. He had no pity for anyone; he had his orders from Moscow to complete this strategically vital factory at all costs: either he built the factory and kept his job, or he failed and lost his job and faced imprisonment into the bargain.

The internal affairs of the camp were largely run by the prisoners themselves, and the *nachalniks*, or bosses, therefore had enormous power which they exercised from their positions of authority. They could save you or destroy you. Every hut had its *nachalnik* aided by his assistants, and every group which went out to work had its head man, a brigadier and his assistants.

Ninety per cent therefore of the discipline in the camp was in the hands of the prisoners themselves; while the Soviet Camp Commander and his staff concentrated on carrying out orders from Moscow.

The *nachalnik* of my hut was called Fedeseyev. Now a prisoner himself, he had formerly been a NKVD officer, a man over six feet tall, a Cossack, aged about fifty – a very tough, strong fellow with a marvellous smile which showed his white teeth. His assistant read out all the names permitted to remain in the camp that day – they stood to one side. There were only two of us who had excused ourselves from work without permission, a man called Zimmerman, a Czech engineer, and myself. The same roll call was going on outside the other huts too. Fedeseyev approached Zimmerman, a small, skinny specimen who appeared to be dying on his feet. He grabbed his clothing and shouted : 'What! You again!'

He shook the unfortunate Zimmerman who fell to the ground, but the *nachalnik* dragged him to his feet again, saying : 'Get up!'

Zimmerman tried to stand but started to fall back again when the *nachalnik* struck him a blow on the back of the neck. He fell to the ground at my feet. As he lay there I felt as if I was the one on the ground. I said to Fedeseyev :

'Lift him up. He's dying!'

'Let him die!' he replied. 'He is of no use. He's a parasite and I want him dead.' As he turned to go I put my hand on his shoulder, twisted him round and punched him on the jaw. He fell to the ground. Quickly he stood up and started to laugh. Our eyes met. I bent down to pick up Zimmerman and he kicked me in the behind with his boot. I turned back quickly to fight him, but now he was surrounded by his assistants.

'Bring him to my office,' he said.

32

I had dared to confront him, and I could see from his expression that he respected me.

When I was brought into his office Fedeseyev was sitting in a big chair in front of his desk. His upper lip was swollen and bruised where I had punched him. He sent away the guards. 'No one has ever dared to lift a finger to me. You had the courage to do so, and I respect you for it. I shall make no report about this, but three guards saw what happened and you'll probably get yourself into trouble. Go back to the hut. I have nothing against you personally.'

I returned to the hut and after twenty minutes guards came to take me to General Federovitch. He was looking at the file which pursued me everywhere:

'I'm giving you thirty days' solitary confinement.'

I was led to a wooden building, unheated, with wooden slats for beds, nothing else, just the wooden floor, wooden ceilings and wooden walls. They locked the door behind me. I was left in the dark. The wind whistled outside, the cold was extreme. For three days and nights the door remained closed. The guards looked through a little hole to see if I was still alive. I exercised continuously to keep my circulation going.

It was difficult to know whether it was day or night. On the third day when the door was opened I saw it was daylight. I received my first food: a pint of hot soup, very thin and watery, and a hunk of bread.

There was no toilet but a small hole in the wall for urinating. It was so small that I often had trouble getting it through the hole. There was a bucket there for excrement. The guards used to shout, 'If you're hungry you can eat that!'

The shouts and screams of other prisoners who were being kicked and beaten occasionally interrupted the monotonous silence. There was no medical care here, although by law the prisoners were entitled to it. I completed the full stretch of thirty days there.

I had calculated that my release should be around 10 a.m. but the time of my release came at night.

When I came out the *nachalnik*, Fedeseyev, was waiting for me.

'You hit me, but I'm the first to greet you now.'

33

He brought me back to his office, sat me down, and looked at me for a long time. I must have presented a sorry picture in my unwashed, bearded state, and he took pity on me. He poured out a glass of *samogon*, a cheap variety of home-made vodka.

'Drink this, you'll feel better, young boy. Then go and rest because the day after tomorrow you will have to go to work. I only want you to know that the thirty days you did were none of my doing.'

That was how I spent my first month there without working. I had lost a lot of weight and my whole body ached. Hope and renewed energy returned when I said to myself:

'You will survive.'

So next morning, with Fedeseyev's permission I rested. During the afternoon I cut off my beard first with scissors as the hair was strong and bristly, then I shaved. I looked at my reflection in the mirror. My cheeks were hollow and sunken, my eyes seemed much bigger, the skin white. When I pulled down my eyelids I saw the signs of anaemia. Then I went outside and washed my body with snow, rubbing it in to promote circulation.

As I was shadow boxing I noticed Federovitch a short distance away wearing a black fur jacket and very high boots. He had wrapped the two long ear-flaps around his neck like a scarf. A uniformed guard stood on either side of him.

The three of them came nearer and, as I jumped up and down, the General turned to look at me and all three stopped. The ground sloped towards me, and as I looked at him the old man made a beckoning gesture in my direction. I looked around to see if he was signalling to someone else, keeping my exercises going at the same time. The guards waved to me. I, stripped to the waist as I was, went up to the three men who all wore fur coats. Federovitch asked my name and what I was doing. Was I a boxer? Did I work on the night shift?

He had caught me unprepared. As I rubbed my body, I said:

'No, I'm not well. The doctor has ordered me to stay in the camp.'

He asked me the number of my hut, then suddenly he lost his footing as though his leg had given way under him. He shouted out in pain. The two guards tried to straighten him but he clung to his foot.

I quickly tried to get his boot off to see if he had fractured his foot or ankle, but he refused to allow me to touch him and put his arms around the necks of the guards in an effort to take the weight off the foot.

'Perhaps you have a fracture, let me see,' I said.

'No, I have flat feet.'

The encounter had only lasted perhaps a minute. I had forgotten I was standing half-naked in a temperature well below zero.

'Go back to your hut,' he said.

I offered to help if he needed to be carried. At the time I was so thin that my ribs stood out. The idea must have struck him as comical:

'You want to carry me?' he laughed. 'Run back to your hut before you freeze to death!'

When I reached my hut I saw that Fedeseyev had observed the incident. I dressed and went out to walk around the camp which I discovered was as large as a small town. My thoughts were on my immediate future here: even if Fedeseyev had managed to free me from work it couldn't last. How many days would he give me? Had he tricked me? The daylight hours were very short during the winter months.

As I walked around looking at the huts I found one, surrounded by barbed wire, which housed women. I watched them through the windows – they looked quite nice. They were given mostly indoor work to do: sewing, washing, ironing, packing. Some of them came outside and started to chat to me through the wires. They were quite good-looking: Russians, Poles and other nationalities. With their thick, quilted suits, I could only see their faces. To one of them I said:

'You're a pretty girl. Why don't you take that suit off so I can see how your body looks?'

'Why don't you come over here and undress me?' she replied in Polish.

'How can I get over there?'

'There is a way through further down.'

The women's huts were separated from the main camp by a

35

double line of barbed wire, about five yards apart, and a look-out tower had been placed between them at one end, in which there was always a sniper on duty. There were large signs posted along the wires:

ENTRY PROHIBITED. TRESPASSERS WILL BE SHOT WITH-OUT WARNING. The main camp was also surrounded by lines of barbed wire and watch-towers placed at strategic points.

The 'way through further down' turned out to be a gate with a guard posted there. It was several months now since I had seen a woman, but I wasn't prepared to be shot because of my ardour.

I said to the girl: 'When I get stronger and find a proper way, I'll come and see you. What's your name?'

'Zosia,' she replied. She pouted, then pointed to the gate, 'Go on, have a try, they might let you in.'

I turned however and walked slowly, back to my hut. This was one of the few occasions when it was right to refuse a woman. It was nearly lunch-time. As I walked in, one of the men said:

'The *nachalnik* wants to see you, now, right away.'

When I went to him he said:

'Where have you been? I had you excused from work because I was sorry for you and partly because I respected you. But you have got me into trouble. Instead of staying quietly indoors you've been outside walking about all over the place. Now General Federovitch wants to see you immediately.'

Fedeseyev had a habit of thrusting his hands in his pockets, pacing up and down, grinding his teeth. He was worried now:

'You will tell the General that I let you stay in the camp if he should ask you. For the rest, the less you say the better for you. I have no idea why he has asked to see you.'

The General had a nice, warm room furnished with a desk and chairs. General Federovitch was wearing his uniform. At his side stood a colonel of the NKGB wearing a red and blue cap, and another officer on the other side. A woman, a lieutenant, was also in the room. I looked up at the portraits of Stalin around the walls.

Fedeseyev had marched me in. Now he stood smartly to attention, gave his name and hut number:

'Reporting with the prisoner Urban, sir.'

I was beginning to dislike the situation which was rapidly becoming like a courtroom. Federovitch stared back at him, and shouted :

'Leave him and get out. What's taken you so long ?'

Fedeseyev did not reply. Federovitch shouted again that he should leave the room.

'Come closer. Take off your shirt.'

I didn't know what to expect but quickly removed my shirt.

'Come round to this side of the desk,' he said. I came close to him. Then he took the flesh which covered my ribs between his fingers saying :

'This is the hero. The one who wanted to carry me. Come, try to find some flesh on him, because I can't.'

The woman officer stood still. He shouted at her :

'Try !'

She did as he said, then he told me to dress. As I did so, I looked at the file which lay on his desk with my name on the folder. He caught my glance and said :

'Sit down. Don't look at things which don't concern you. I have already looked through your file and don't intend to go through it again. You were sent here for counter-revolutionary activities, but you are also here for corrective purposes. It is our function to turn you into a real man. The judge who sentenced you recommended that you should be put on labour duties for six months and not be allowed to work in your profession because they consider you aggressive, impulsive and even dangerous. Your behaviour in this camp has proved the judge to be right. You picked one of the strongest men here to fight. You have been punished with one month's solitary confinement. Now you are so skinny that, if you persist with your aggressive ways, you will undoubtedly die here very quickly.'

I stood facing him without replying.

'There is no escape from here. Either live and work, or die.'

I was frightened at this, then an idea came to me :

'May I speak ?'

He asked me to sit down. As he removed the revolver from its case he was swearing in the most obscene language in spite of the presence of the woman. He started cleaning out his ears

37

with the barrel of the revolver, a long Russian one, loaded. He removed the wax from the gun and rolled it into balls. All the officers in the room seemed more nervous than I.

'The supreme authority here in this camp rests with me, the Camp Commander. This morning I could see that, although you are nothing but skin and bones, you are ready to fight to survive.'

He stopped to look up at the woman officer and the others. He wrote something on a paper and passed it to them all to read. The NKGB colonel nodded agreement; so did the woman.

'Do you know what I have written here?' asked the General.

'I think so,' I replied boldly. 'That you will allow me to work in my profession.'

'You're right. But only on special conditions. Colonel Volkovitch here and his wife, who is a nurse, will tell you about it.'

At that moment a doctor came into the room. The General said to me:

'Stay here and watch. Have you ever seen a decaying human or animal carcass?'

I said: 'Yes, I have.'

'Now you will smell live human flesh which stinks more than that.' Then turning to the doctor: 'Take off the bandages!'

Volkovitch left the room, but his wife stayed behind. With shaking hands the doctor eased off the General's boot. As he was about to give the final tug the General started to swear and curse at the unfortunate man. When the bandages were finally removed they revealed an open wound oozing pus from the knee down the shin bone to the arch of his right foot. As far as I could see from where I stood the wounds were similar to those caused by malnutrition. The stench was almost unbearable. As the doctor tried to dress the wound the General shouted and insulted him and, when it hurt most, even punched him.

The doctor was using a red-coloured disinfectant, a solution of potassium permanganate, to wash the wounds, then he dressed them with a white ointment spread on a piece of gauze. The doctor, still shaking, tried to replace the boot. Suddenly, I don't know why, I pushed him to one side, took the boot, handed it to the General and said:

'Put it on yourself.'

He looked up and smiled, revealing large twisted teeth like a donkey's.

'I can't put it on, I'm in too much pain.'

'You should only let someone else put your boots on if you have no hands.'

Very slowly, protesting, swearing, and shouting, he pulled the boot on to his leg. He sweated so much that the drops fell to the floor. When he felt the sharpest pain, and hesitated, I urged him on:

'Go on ... put it on.'

When it was done he opened the drawer of the desk, took out a bottle and poured himself a full glass of vodka. As he swallowed it he shook his head from side to side, making a gurgling noise. He shouted the name of the *nachalnik*:

'Fedeseyev, Fedeseyev!'

The guard told him that Fedeseyev had gone.

'Take the prisoner back. He is to return to solitary confinement for three days.'

I asked: 'For what reason?'

'For not going out to work.'

I looked at the woman, the doctor and then at this monster. Ten minutes later I was back in solitary confinement, the same hut as before, but in a different room. There I spent three days and three nights, with two meals a day: a hot drink in the morning with a large lump of black bread, and a thick soup in the afternoon. I paced the room thinking about what had happened and couldn't help laughing.

The *nachalnik* came to see me on the second day.

'What do you think will happen to you when you come out?'

'I shall work as a doctor.'

He laughed: 'You don't know Federovitch!'

In spite of this temporary set-back I had no doubt that my life would change. I understood the General. He was a sick man, bad-tempered and mean because of his pain, living under the most enormous pressures. I felt that he liked me, but then I asked myself: if he liked me, why would he put me in here for three days? Then I answered myself: it's his way of maintaining discipline. Let's wait and see. I had no intention of going out to work in those killing conditions, and, if necessary, I could find ways of producing a high temperature, to fool the doctors. As a last resort I would try escape and risk getting shot.

It was not only the terrible conditions which made me take this decision, not only the physical hardship, but even more the savage treatment of the prisoners by the guards. The workers would sometimes fall to the ground where they would be kicked by the brigadiers until they stood up, or fall down in the road and be dragged along by a guard in the snow. There were many other barbarities which I will not go into. I knew that I could never accept such tyranny, that sooner or later I would hit one of the guards and get myself shot, so the only way for me was to decide never to go out to work whatever happened so that they wouldn't have the chance to kill me. All my thoughts were concentrated on survival – I would survive, I would get out one day.

4

The Schtrafnaia and Death Brigades

On the day I was freed and told to go back to my hut the men were out at work. I was sitting on my bunk when the *nachal-nik's* assistant came to me and told me to follow him. He took me to Colonel Volkovitch's office. He had black eyes which made him appear kindly, even pleasant; if I had not known about his job, I would never have believed it. When he asked me to sit down he offered me a cigarette which I took eagerly. My head started to swim and I almost fainted as the smoke affected me.

He stood up and took my pulse, but I pulled myself together quickly:

'I'm sure you have no idea what to do,' I said. 'You aren't a doctor as well, are you?'

'Why be so sure?' he asked pleasantly.

'Well, aren't you supposed to be trained in eliminating people, not in helping them?'

His good-humour disappeared. 'Your tongue is too long. That's your trouble. Being a *politruk*, a party member, does not mean that we are all ... what you think we are. Do you realize that in your dossier there is a definite warning against your being employed as a doctor in any circumstances, in a hospital camp or anywhere else? In spite of that, the General has said that he is prepared to let you work as a doctor. You will probably be sent to another camp where the life is harder than this one. You know why, don't you? You have only been here a few weeks, and you have already given us all this trouble. What should I do with you? You seem to have forgotten that you are a prisoner. You will have to alter your ways, restrain your many impulses. Don't live with the dreams of the West. You will have to spend a minimum of five years in a camp – and stick to the rules – otherwise it means another ten or twelve years. There are thousands of prisoners here – every one of them has his own story. Some are Polish spies and traitors, some murderers, some exploiters of the working classes: most have accepted their situation here and are ready to live and work in our community.

'If you promise me that you will give us no more trouble, we will consider allowing you to work as a doctor but there is no definite decision yet. It will be under consideration.

'Go back to your hut. Go out to work with the others to-morrow. I warn you, don't stay in the camp!'

I thanked him for his frankness and left. My hut was only five hundred yards away, but it was uphill and it took me half an hour to reach it. I felt ill and started to vomit. When I reached the hut I sat on the doorstep and felt my pulse. I had a high temperature. Fedeseyev came out, looked at me in a strange way and walked past without speaking in the direction of the kitchens.

I struggled to my feet and just at that moment he turned to look at me. He walked back to me just as I started to vomit again.

'You are ill,' he said and, taking me by the arm, he led me to the infirmary.

The doctor examined me and said: 'You have a high temperature.'

He gave me leave to stay in the hut for twenty-four hours. I thought there was nothing much wrong. The nicotine had made me vomit, and I probably had a feverish cold. It didn't worry me, but my general situation did worry me. What would Volkovitch do now? I fell asleep.

When I woke I found orderlies helping me on to a stretcher. My temperature had risen and I had been delirious. They took me to a small isolation ward in the infirmary, since there had been no diagnosis yet. I was secretly very happy because it meant that I would have to remain there for at least a week.

On the Sunday morning, Volkovitch's wife, the nurse, came to see me and told me that her husband had given permission for me to be released for hospital work. She was very happy about it, she added.

It was amazing. I always find people who like me, but also

I find people who hate me. With women I have always been lucky, I have found that my personality and way of talking (although at times very crude) has appealed more to women than to men. I later discovered that in this instance the ones who had been instrumental in bringing about this change were General Federovitch and the *nachalnik*, Fedeseyev, since he was able under the rules of the camp to make very strong recommendations according to one's behaviour. In my case he would certainly have had to sign a report confirming my suitability.

That Sunday a new world opened before me. The joy at the miracle of my release was indescribable. I went to collect my few belongings: a metal plate, a wooden spoon, a metal cup and a few other things, and took them to the hut where the medical staff were housed. Outside it looked like all the others, but inside it was divided off into cubicles so that every doctor had his own bed and privacy. I received new clothing which was considerably better in quality and, an unexpected bonus, there were sheets on the bed. Life was worth living again. I would have my work.

With the agreement of General Federovitch, I was appointed doctor for the Schtrafnaia Brigade, a group of prisoners to which all the most dangerous criminals were sent: murderers, robbers and violent types, all of them Soviet citizens. They were housed in a separate block, away from the main camp, and they had their own working parties which did not mix with those from the rest of the camp. Should they take it into their heads not to work, there was no way of making them do so. For they were so violent and unpredictable that even the armed guards refused to go inside their block. There were about three hundred of them in all. Why had they picked me for such a dangerous job when they knew I was quick to take offence and would not permit myself to be manipulated?

After a few enquiries I discovered that no doctor was willing to take on this work. Until then, a rota had been worked out so that two different doctors would attend them, one in the morning and one in the evening, when they returned from work.

Most of the other doctors were Poles and were only too

pleased to know that I had been appointed as doctor for the Schtrafnaia Brigade.

Apart from this new appointment I was assigned to assist with the pathological research carried out in the morgue. I didn't mind the autopsy work because, apart from the extra pay, one could learn a great deal from it. The Soviet system of administration is very different from that in the West, as one man is afraid of the next, and always tries to back his actions or judgements with documents or signatures as a means of protecting himself. That was why, by involving others in the case of a patient who had died, not only was the medical report and cause of death required but also the opinion of the pathologist who performed the autopsy. Each one was a check on the other. So the doctors would give us copies of the medical reports they had made on the patients, naturally in the hope and expectation that our findings would not clash with theirs.

The morgue was an isolated building surrounded by a three-yard-high fence topped with barbed wire – not, I presume, to stop the dead from escaping, but to stop other prisoners from getting inside and then escaping, as it was near the main road. Guards in watch-towers were able to observe the morgue from all sides. It could hold around twelve bodies comfortably, but there would sometimes be as many as twenty bodies. There were concrete slabs arranged in shelves along opposite walls of the building to accommodate the bodies, and in the centre was a large cement-topped slab for performing autopsies, fitted with hot and cold water-taps and hoses and drains for sluicing the corpses down.

Now the bodies were often stacked one on top of the other. The man in charge was an ordinary caretaker who received the bodies and gave a signature for them. After the autopsy he would transfer the bodies and receive another signature when he handed them over. The names of the deceased were entered in a kind of ledger and there was another ledger in which were recorded the numbers of bodies released for burial.

The caretaker, Lebidoff, was a man in his sixties, slightly deaf, who would sometimes talk to himself. His sight was defective: he could see with one eye, but had lost the use of the other

through an untreated cataract in an advanced stage. He was a
skinny man with hollow cheeks, but he was wiry and strong
enough to move bodies around easily by himself. He would place
the bodies ready on the slab for the next autopsy. It was very
cold in the morgue, so I would put a white overall on top of
my overcoat before I started work. All the doctors who performed autopsies used the same assistant, Grisha Morozov, who
had plenty of experience. He had been sentenced to twenty
years in the camp and had spent three working in the morgue
with various doctors. He had to take down in writing the report
the doctor made as he dictated his findings. He would also make
the incision from throat to navel with a scalpel and open the
thorax with special scissors under the supervision of the doctor,
as the bodies became so hard and rigid that it would have taken
the doctors fifteen minutes to open one corpse. Morozov had had
so much practice that he could do it in five.

When I described the external appearance of the bodies I was
never permitted to mention malnutrition: I could say 'good' or
'satisfactory' but never 'malnutrition'.

One morning I arrived around 10.45 a.m. to find Lebidoff
searching in his ledgers: his lips moved in a chewing motion as
he tried to count on his fingers, then he would stop to scratch
his head or roll a Machorka cigarette. As I came in I told him
not to smoke and then asked him what he was looking for. He
took several seconds to untwist his lips and tell me he was short
of one female corpse. The bodies were all together, male and
female. He had made a mistake on the highest shelf and counted
five females instead of six. I had to calm him down as his pulse-
rate had gone very high.

I proceeded to work. It took the three of us, Morozov, Lebidoff
and I, three and a half hours to dispose of the work, and at the
end we all looked like butchers. Lebidoff wanted to speed up the
work because he knew that more corpses were waiting – liter-
ally waiting outside the door, on stretchers lying in the snow,
covered with sheets.

One day a male prisoner, Vishnevsky, a twenty-five-year-old,
presumed dead from broncho-pneumonia, was moved from the
hospital ward to the corridor outside on the orders of Dr Brodskaya who signed the death certificate. At around 9 a.m. he was

45

sent to the morgue. Lebidoff had placed him on the slab in the centre, to be the first for autopsy – but Vishnevsky was not dead. He had shown all the clinical signs of death : no pulse, no reaction in the pupils of the eyes, etc., etc. The nurse in the ward, overloaded with work, had placed the wooden tag on his ankle. Then they had proceeded as though he were dead. A rapid and sudden change in temperature in cases such as Vishnevsky's can be fatal but it can also have the opposite effect. In this case the change in temperature produced a crisis which brought him back to life.

He woke up in the morgue, on the slab, to find himself naked and surrounded by corpses. The sudden shock gave him a miraculous surge of strength and he jumped down on to his feet. He ran round the room like a lion in a cage, charged to the doors which he found bolted, dragged back the heavy bolts, opened the doors but, when he saw the deep snow, drew back inside, grabbed a blood-stained overall and put it on. Then he ran out on to the path and tried to scale the high fence where the snow had drifted into a bank at its base. The guard in the watch-tower saw what was happening, then started to fire in the air. When they asked him later what he had seen he was unable to utter a word for minutes. He had thought he was witnessing the resurrection of the dead. When I asked why he had fired and not telephoned the Commander's office he said he had challenged the man :

'Halt or I'll fire;' but Vishnevsky had just kept on, had scaled one fence like an acrobat and had run across and tried to scale the fence surrounding the camp.

'I intended to shoot him, how did I know what was going on ? It could have been a prisoner dressed like that trying to escape. I only missed by a miracle. He moved so fast dodging from one side to the other like a madman, and then he tried in the end to get back into the camp, so I fired no more.'

Vishnevsky had got over the fence, leaving strips of his bloodied overall hanging from the barbed wire, and run the 500 yards to the camp half naked. He went straight to the Camp Commander's office but found no one there. Most of the prisoners were out working. Then he ran to the block and found the bed where he usually slept. His things were still there. The

Commander had been advised of his death fifteen minutes after he was moved to the morgue.

Vishnevsky started to shout and insult everyone in the camp, especially the doctors. When the Camp Commander heard what was going on he went to Dr Brodskaya to find out exactly what had taken place. I was sitting there with her, a Dr Tichanoff, and Dr Reis at a meeting when the *nachalnik* burst in, trembling, to tell us what had happened. Lebidoff was called but he stood transfixed, his lips chewing away. Finally Vishnevsky ran in brandishing a long iron bar. He went for Dr Brodskaya:

'*Blath!* Whore! I'll kill you.'

They got him under control. It was Dr Tichanoff who overpowered him as the others were too frightened to go near him. They gave him a tranquillizing shot and put him to bed in a room in the hospital but, as he left the room, he was still protesting:

'Let me out of this place, let me out. You'll kill me again. I don't want to die, I want to live.'

He was allowed to leave the hospital the next day. He had no temperature. All he needed now was to rest and relax and eat well, in a special convalescent block.

It was a black day for all the medical staff in the camp. Vishnevsky quickly learnt to exploit their mistake. He put the wooden tag around his neck on a string and started to demand all kinds of privileges: he no longer waited in line for meals, he would push his way to the front. No one dared to object or do anything against him. He had been popular before, and now they looked on him as a god.

The prisoners, too, started to take advantage of the situation, saying they were too ill to work. If the doctor found that there was nothing wrong with them, they would swear and ask why healthy men were sent to the morgue. The medical staff were in reality being blackmailed, and often gave in. A lot of the prisoners refused to let the matter rest and made themselves wooden tags with Vishnevsky's name to wear around their necks. Over a quarter of the camp took several days off.

The authorities were furious. Brodskaya had to pay the price. She was sentenced to five years in a labour camp, a punishment which was not justified in my opinion, but the documentary evidence was there. Her post was taken over by Dr Tichanoff temporarily. The luckiest man was Vishnevsky: if he had remained unconscious for a couple of hours longer he would have been opened up by Morozov.

The Camp Commander tried to hush up the incident. Morozov and Lebidoff were so shaken they were unable to work properly; I must admit that some of the doctors, including myself, eyed all the bodies with great suspicion before we would commence autopsies.

I was also given another task. This was to stand at the gates every morning when the main body of prisoners left for work and make sure that they were suitably dressed, and be on the spot in case anyone should faint or collapse on the way out. I had to decide on the spot whether the ailing prisoner was fit for work that day or not.

So as a prison doctor I had considerable power. But, powerful or not, during my first week of medical care for the Schtrafnaia Brigade I was always accompanied by two guards armed with revolvers and other guards would be posted outside the hut with machine-guns.

Furthermore, the general security precautions for the Brigade were of course much stricter than those in the rest of the camp: there were more numerous look-out towers and guards on duty, and the movement of the prisoners was much more restricted. They were not allowed to walk around the camp at will like the others. Their doors remained locked except when food was served or when they went out to work.

The medical examinations took place in a room near the main door for an hour in the morning and two hours every evening. On the first day the guards advised me to stand outside the door and tell the men who I was, as it was too dangerous to go inside.

I had dressed in a white medical overall over my warmest clothes and on the top I wore an overcoat and a warm hat. As the door was opened for me I could see a long hut with two tiers of beds on both sides: the room was smoky, overcrowded and stinking. Many of the men wore no coat or jacket over their shirts. Some were playing cards.

Before we opened the door it had been very noisy, but now

48

when they saw me everyone was quiet. I could see that the tougher types occupied the top bunks.

'Who is boss here?' I asked.

A short, thickset man, wearing only trousers, stood up. His torso was covered with tattoos, and there were many scars on his body which looked like old knife-wounds. I beckoned to him to come nearer the door. He in turn made the same gesture to me; he wanted me to go to him. I told him to come to me, otherwise all the prisoners would remain without medical attention for a whole week.

The tension broke as he laughed and walked over to me.

'I am the new doctor in charge of this block.'

As I stretched out my hand to him, he smiled and hesitated, unsure whether to take it.

'I am a prisoner too, you know. Shake hands.'

He took my hand and shook it.

'My name is Sacha Stogoff,' he announced.

'Sacha, I want to see all your men. I want to see every one of them at close quarters, to look at their faces. I have heard all the stories about what you do to the doctors here. I will stay here inside the building with you if you will be responsible for my safety.'

The others had quickly formed a circle around him. He said nothing. I signalled to the guards to close the door behind me, and although they were reluctant to do so I insisted on it. When the door was closed I stood with my back against it, hemmed in completely by the men who stood only a foot away.

I told them to stand back so that I could get a good look at the living conditions and, if necessary, help to improve them. They didn't move, so I started to push them back to make a way through. I walked the complete length of the hut and studied every face closely as I walked past. There were many who looked at the point of death, and most were suffering from malnutrition. I lifted their eyelids and inspected their gums; they had the symptoms of the deficiency diseases: anaemia, pellagra and others. I was still some distance from the door when I found myself surrounded again by a circle of them. One said:

'Undress. Let me try on your clothes.'

Another in a loud voice shouted:
'Yes, let's undress him. He's our doctor.'
They started to manhandle me. I could see there was no escape. I shouted loud:
'Stogoff!'
But the first man had already got my coat unbuttoned. I punched him and he fell to the ground. He was the tallest of them, and I later discovered that he was Stogoff's rival for the leadership.

The guards had heard the shouts and a squad of them, armed with truncheons, burst in. I don't think the prisoners would have harmed me physically in any case, although I was relieved to see the guards. As they bundled me out I shouted to Stogoff:
'Tomorrow no one will go to work. I want to examine every one of you to see who is fit and who is not.'
All heads turned to me, and they suddenly became quiet again. Stogoff said:
'You heard that, *bratse*, you heard that, brothers – we shall all be in tomorrow. We can go after the girls!'
They probably took my order as a joke. They couldn't believe that they might all be allowed to stay indoors the next day. As the door was locked behind me, one of the guards said:
'If you allow all of them to stay in camp tomorrow, Federovitch will put you in there to join them. It could cost you your job and even some extra years in here.'
'They will stay here and I shall examine every one of them. I have to disinfect their living quarters, make the place hygienic, and get rid of the stench. If I have to join them, then I'll join them.'
Next day, checking the list of prisoners in the hut, I discovered that there were only two hundred and forty-nine. In the medical book I made the entry:

'249 prisoners, all remaining in camp for 48 hours.
Reason: suspicion of epidemic disease.'

The day before I had sent one man to the isolation ward although he had no temperature. I had to cover myself in case Federovitch should take measures against me.
The head of the medical staff, and, in certain cases, his assis-

tants, were free men, but more often they were ex-prisoners who had served their sentences, then remained to work in the camp. I was directly under the orders of my immediate superior in the medical department, and it would have been far wiser to consult him before taking such a drastic measure, which was unprecedented and bound to be opposed. I had acted in a way I had considered right but it had been on impulse. All my life I have always gone ahead with my own course of action without seeking the advice of anyone, believing that when I act I am doing so for the best.

It was not long before General Federovitch learned that all my Brigade were still in the camp on my instructions, and the reason I had given. The first step he took was to ask to see the medical report of the prisoner Krilenko, the man I had put in the isolation ward the day before.

In the report I had written a tentative diagnosis: 'suspected intestinal typhoid' – since the patient had been suffering from dysentery and was under-nourished.

Halfway through the morning I went to the Schtrafnaia Brigade hut, went inside, had a table placed near the door, had all the men undress completely, and file up to my desk, their clothes over their arms, turn slowly round, and then proceed. Any cases which looked suspicious I stopped and examined closely in the mouth and eyes. The whole process went quickly and in an orderly fashion. An assistant at my side would note down the names of the men who looked most sick. We had seen about two thirds of the men when the door burst open and a group of guards came in. One of them told me to go at once to the *nachalnik*'s office. I told him to tell the *nachalnik* that I would come when I had finished my work, not before. The guard was not satisfied with this and ordered me to stop working and go with him.

'I will not come until my job is finished,' I repeated.

I had not noticed that Stogoff and his men had gathered near, surrounding us and cutting off the exit. I would not have been able to leave even if I had wanted. One of the guards, unarmed, had been cut off with me. Stogoff took him by the throat, held a long kitchen knife under his chin, and shouted to me:

'Carry on – examine every man!'

The other guard had been pushed out and the door closed behind him. It was not easy to carry on in those circumstances. Some men had dressed, some were naked, and others undressing. Some shouted to Stogoff:

'Kill him! Slit his throat! Kill him!'

I had to try to defuse the situation. I went up to Stogoff and tried to take the knife from him.

'Just keep away, or I'll cut your throat too!'

Through the window I could see that guards were surrounding the hut. They had dogs with them. They locked the door from the outside. Suddenly I heard a shout of pain and saw that one of the prisoners had cut another across the neck with a knife. He was naked, and bleeding profusely. I didn't know why he had done it: perhaps he had taken advantage of the tense situation and used it to settle an old score. Guards were breaking the windows with the butts of their rifles, pushing them through the iron grilles which protected them.

My concern at that moment was how I could get the guard released, and attend to the bleeding man, and get the men back under control. There was so much noise and shouting that I had no chance of being heard. All I could try was to shout:

'Stogoff! Stogoff! Stogoff!'

As I shouted at the top of my voice the confusion started to abate.

'I came here to help you men. Is this how you show your gratitude?'

Stogoff released the guard, turned to me, folded the skin of his abdomen between his fingers and sliced at it three times.

The door opened, and the armed guards pushed everyone back against the wall. Medical orderlies took away the two injured men, and guards pushed me out. I was taken directly to General Federovitch's office. He was there with Dr Morozova, the head of the medical department, Colonel Volkovitch and two NKVD guards. The General's face was white with rage. He took his revolver from its holster, walked up to me, and pointed it straight at my head. I remained calm and indifferent. Then he said:

'Shall I put it through your brain or your mouth? No, I shall not shoot you. I shall ask you a few questions, then send you back to join the prisoners.'

Dr Morozova interrupted him, turning to address me:

'I think you were right to isolate the prisoner Krilenko and to stop the others from working,' she said. 'I examined Krilenko: he has bleeding dysentery with certain symptoms of abdominal typhoid.'

I listened to her justification of my professional conduct with great relief and quickly went on to add my own explanation:

'I examined over half the prisoners. The majority are not fit to work. Their living conditions are filthy and sooner or later will become a source of epidemic. We must take immediate steps: they must be divided into groups and a general disinfection of the hut and all their belongings carried out. In the meantime they should be kept together, in quarantine, until a definite diagnosis has been confirmed on Krilenko. Then, General, I will show that these men will be your best workers. If you give me permission to take these measures I will give you all my co-operation. There is no need for you to try to frighten me with that gun. If I do not have your full support in every way you may remove me from my job.'

There was silence.

Federovitch paced around his desk like an animal. I had my hand on the edge of his desk. Suddenly he smashed his fist down on my hand. He almost missed, catching only the tips of my fingers. I think the jolt gave him much more pain in his leg than he had caused me. He screamed:

'Take him away. Put him in solitary confinement for twenty-four hours, then bring him back to me.'

On my way to the solitary confinement block I could hear shouts and the reports of rifle shots coming from the direction of the Schtrafnaia Brigade. Whether they were warning shots or serious disturbances I couldn't tell.

The guard in charge of the solitary confinement block greeted me:

'What, you again? You're becoming a permanent guest!'

As he was searching me, a guard came in quickly and told him that I was to be sent back immediately to the General's office. I couldn't understand what was going on, but I found myself back in the office in less than ten minutes.

'I have altered my decision. There is a full-scale rebellion going on in the Schtrafnaia Block, they are threatening to cut a different prisoner with a knife every fifteen minutes if you don't go back. They want the medical examinations to be completed on every man. Go. Go ahead with your sabotage. I hope they kill you. Get out and never come back.'

I ran quickly to the hut wearing my white medical overall stained with blood. The scenes I saw before me I shall never forget until I die. Only now as I write this can I recall everything as it was: the faces, expressions, groans of pain – oh God I wish I had never started this – but I never go back if I start something. . . .

I learnt that the practice of cutting the skin on the thorax was frequently used by hardened criminals, such as these men were, as a form of protest.

It would have been difficult to find a group of men who had been turned more dangerous by the treatment inflicted on them. From my own experience of life I have found that there are always reasonable men, even among criminals: many have been victims of their own social environments, or of blind justice. Isolation in a prison has not yet been proved to be the most effective way of rehabilitation to a normal decent life. On the contrary most men forced to live in such a prison quickly become criminals themselves.

As these men were mostly thin and undernourished the skin tended to be loose on their bodies, especially if they had lost weight. They would hold the skin away from the vital organs and make cuts in it, but on occasions they would make a mistake and penetrate too far.

When I entered the hut, I found men screaming, blood everywhere. I called for help to take the most serious cases to the infirmary. My colleagues later told me that most of them required only minor surgery involving the insertion of stitches.

After a week or so I had established that nearly sixty per cent of the men were unfit for hard physical work, and the rest were undernourished and underweight. The latter I divided into three categories and arranged that all of them should receive decent food rations until they were in a condition to work. They promised to keep their side of the bargain and go out to work willingly. Forty of the men I sent to the infirmary. With the help of Mrs Volkovitchova the building was disinfected and cleaned up.

After two months ninety per cent of them were going out to work. On any one day I gave leave for ten per cent of them to stay inside providing they had worked hard and done sufficient. It is hard to believe that it was the worst criminals in the camp, those who had been isolated from all the others, who had responded so well after I had shown a willingness to take an interest in them, to provide better conditions for them, and to treat them as workers not criminals. They had become fond of me, but perhaps, because of this, I found that I had made several enemies among the medical staff.

At this stage, however, I applied for a transfer to the infirmary to do the hospital work which I really favoured, for I felt that, now I had broken the ground, someone else could take over my job with the Schtrafnaia Brigade. The request was granted and I was given work in the hospital, but General Federovitch insisted that I should continue to visit the Schtrafnaia Brigade twice a day. I could understand his reasons: he couldn't afford to lose two hundred of his best workers every day.

On my first day at my new job in the infirmary, when I had finished the morning consultations, Dr Morozova called me to her office and informed me that General Federovitch wanted me to dress and bandage his foot. He had got tired of the other doctors. She advised me not to get into conversation with him about what had taken place in the past. I should remove the bandages with the greatest care, very slowly. Finally she wished me luck. When I asked about the dressings and treatment she told me that everything I would require would be in the General's office.

As I went into the office the General was sitting at his desk looking at some documents. He seemed to be in a genial mood:

'Sit down, doctor,' he said in a kindly way.

He took two more telephone calls, looked at more papers, gave me a cigarette and finally told his secretary not to take any

more calls for him until the doctor had finished. He asked me:
'How are you getting on? You probably hate me. I suppose
you realize you are in my debt?'

I replied:
'The only debt I have to settle is with the Soviet State, not
you.'

'You are still on my list as not having completed the twenty-
four hours' solitary confinement I ordered. Sooner or later you
will have to do it. However, I have taken into consideration the
excellent job you did on those criminals, so I have told Dr
Morozova that you should be given your own room in the
hospital. It will be looked after and cleaned. You did a good
job.'

He too was a heavy smoker, Russian cigarettes with long
filters which the General used to clean out his ears. Then he
broke off the end, threw it away, and smoked the rest.

'Here,' he said abruptly, 'help me to get this boot off, I can't
do it alone.'

He seemed to have forgotten his previous lesson. Or had he?
'No,' I said, 'you must do it yourself.'

He ground his teeth, placed his boot on a special stand and
started to ease it off. After half a minute of effort he was running
with sweat. I stopped him and helped him across to a divan
which was against the side wall of the office. Quickly I removed
the boot. He tried to sit up but I pushed him back and dragged
off the other boot. I had the medical box there at my side and
undid the bandages with great care. The stench was not as
overpowering as before. After dressing the wounds I bandaged
the foot. When he cried out in pain I told him to be quiet. When
all was ready I told him to replace the boots. As I was tidying
up he walked to his chair, opening the collar of his tunic:

'You did it better than anyone else so far. You're a rude,
aggressive young man, but you certainly know how to master
your patients.'

I told him I would be changing his treatment from that
day. After a month my patient Federovitch had improved
enormously.

It was not my intention to influence him in any way, or to

take advantage of my position of new-found favour with him. For my part, what I had done was done spontaneously, without ulterior motives. Human nature remains very constant: cities, towns, buildings, technology alter, but men are guided by basic feelings. This domineering, rough tyrant, Federovitch, who could be pitiless and cruel – he was said to have killed men at point-blank range with his revolver – could also fall under the influence of another human being.

He was probably impressed by my energetic response to every kind of emergency, and that was my good luck.

One day, General Federovitch asked me if I would speak personally to three religious agitators. I had to examine them and confirm that they were not ill, as they were to be executed in twenty-four hours by firing squad. A report on each man's physical state was required. I was given their files and saw that another doctor had examined them two days earlier.

'Why do I have to examine them again?' I asked Federovitch. 'They were only examined two days ago.'

'The rules require it,' he said, a sad expression on his face. He put his hand on my shoulder:

'Go, Garri Semionovitch, please go.'

It was the first time he had called me by my patronym, a very good sign, a sign almost of friendship on equal terms among the Russians.

I found them in the bath-house of the quarantine block. Everything appeared to be as normal except for the few armed guards sitting outside. I walked in wearing my white medical overall. The bath-house was full of steam and I had a job to find them. I saw the three of them standing naked in a corner, in a circle, ashamed for their nakedness. They all held rosaries. Their heads had not been shaved yet. Their bodies were emaciated from pelagra and malnutrition. They were bald but wore short beards. The rest of their bodies had been shaved. I went up to them, told them who I was, and asked if they needed my help. None of them replied, perhaps they were too deeply engaged in their prayers which they continued to recite with closed eyes. I tried to be especially kind and gentle to them. Their faith moved me. I tried to explain that I was not a Russian, I was from the other side, and if they were ill they should tell me, I could postpone their execution. Not one of them looked up or spoke one word to me although I tried to communicate with them and gain their confidence for a long time. I tried to comfort them, and told them that I suffered if they wouldn't answer me, that I was myself a prisoner, but all to no avail. Suddenly they all opened their eyes simultaneously – either by instinct or because they had come to the end of their prayers. They said nothing but I thought I could read an expression of gratitude on their faces. I told them one thing which perhaps they believed. I told them I had helped many people before in the face of death, but I had never in all truth actually seen the Soviets execute anybody. I touched each one of them as I left and said :

'Goodbye. God help you.' I am not religious myself, but I think perhaps my demonstration of sympathy had given the three Jesuits some kind of consolation.

As I left the bath-house I felt very ill. Not only was I deeply affected by what I had seen, but also hurt that they had shown no sign of acknowledgement when I had spoken what was in my heart. They had not answered a word, but I understood.

I went directly to the office of Colonel Volkovitch to hand in the certificate of health pertaining to the three priests. I wrote the report as a true observation of what I had seen : they were suffering from malnutrition. The *nachalnik* of the NKVD looked up from the reports :

'Why write all this nonsense? . . . Weak? . . . Undernourished? The other report says they are quite healthy. Must you write this?'

'Yes, I must.'

'Why?'

'Because it's the truth for one thing and, for another, I shall be the one who has to write the autopsies.'

He made no further comment.

'Leave the reports here. You may go.'

In the Nibka 3 camp I never witnessed an execution by firing squad, but I saw bulletins posted on notice boards that an execution had taken place, and the reason. The following morning a bulletin was posted confirming the execution of three Jesuit agitators for counter-revolutionary activities.

Gradually General Federovitch became more and more confident in me and my work.

According to the camp rules, every prisoner had the right to a certain number of calories per day, the amount being in direct proportion to the quality of work he did. Federovitch wanted to keep this rule but it was an impossibility for him to check on every department of the camp, so a complete network of black marketeering and outright robbery had grown up, with the connivance and participation of the staff and the *nachalniks*. They worked together to ensure the smooth running of the operations and, if anyone refused to co-operate, they saw to it that he was removed from his job or dealt with in other ways.

One day the General called me to his office where I found him most agitated, pacing up and down. With him was the head of the catering department. They were both carrying revolvers.

As I closed the door behind me, Federovitch took out his gun and waved it at the Captain who was head of the catering department:

'You deserve a bullet through your mouth,' he yelled, 'but I have to take my orders from the government and the party, and your life is not as important as my job here.'

My position was an awkward one: I was only a prisoner and I was witnessing a fight between two high-ranking officers. I didn't know what to say or why I had been called in. The Captain remained silent. Finally Federovitch turned to me:

'You are here in this camp because of a war. I know that many of you prisoners are good men who have committed no crimes, but it is up to you to prove to the Soviet authorities what you are. There is a full-scale racket going on in this camp: the *nachalniks* are robbing food right, left and centre thanks to men like the Captain here. An entire trolley of food disappeared from the kitchens last night.'

Then he read out a list of food which had been on the trolley: sides of pork, beef, rice, salt, sugar and oil.

'You, Captain, are directly responsible. You are a weak man and you like to sleep. That gives them the chance to rob you.'

Having dealt with the Captain, he turned to me and barked out:

'I am taking you off your hospital appointment. You will be Inspector of Health, working with Mrs Volkovitchova. It will be your responsibility to see to it that the prisoners receive the food they deserve, both quantity and quality. If they get good rations they'll work harder!'

As he talked he was walking round the room. When he finished he sat down at his desk, unbuttoned the collar of his tunic, took out his gun and engaged in his favourite pastime of cleaning out his ears with it. I relaxed. When he started to do that, it was a sign that he was calming down.

Exactly what would be involved in my work as 'Inspector' I didn't know, but next day I discovered that Dr Morozova and Colonel Volkovitch were my superiors: I was Morozova's second-in-command. I had to move from the good room I had at the medical block to a room in another hut occupied by prison staff. It was situated near the kitchens, main gates, food stores, and General Federovitch's office.

Every day I visited the food stores, looked at the menus, watched the food being cooked, but still the men were hungry. I was powerless to alter things; I would sometimes go round the kitchens at night and find some of the prisoners outside, scratching among the discarded scraps. They would even eat food which was rotten.

One day I saw the Czech, Zimmerman, the skinny one who had such a hungry face and enormous eyes, as he stood waiting outside the kitchens, holding his tin can. I went outside to him. He recognized me straight away. I asked:

'Why aren't you working?'

'How can I work? I'm so ill, hungry and broken.'

I called him inside, took him to the cook, handed him the tin can and told him to fill it; that day there was a good thick barley soup with pieces of meat and potatoes in it. I told him to eat it where he was in the kitchen. He grabbed at his can and started to eat ravenously, but the soup was still boiling and he burnt himself. I asked why he didn't use a spoon. He told me he didn't have one. Spoons, even the wooden ones with which they were issued on arrival, were very scarce, and the prisoners would hide them in their socks, tuck them in their trousers, or up their sleeves. He told me he had sold his. We found him a spoon.

That night I went to bed at about 2 a.m. I was tired, but not very satisfied with my new job. I didn't know it at the time, but what I had done for Zimmerman was enough to get me into serious trouble. I acted without thought for the possible consequences. I would have to be more careful and calculating even in ordinary everyday decisions. Where there were questions of life and death I was always very careful.

In the morning I was woken by the shouts and noise of a motor. I looked out of the front door to the main gates: a heavy truck with double wheels was surrounded by a group of people. I dressed quickly and ran outside.

Beneath the wheels of the truck lay Zimmerman. His head had been half-crushed by the wheels. I took his pulse – he was still alive. The truck had moved forward so I could lift him and hold him in my arms. He looked into my eyes, trying to speak, but it was only a mumble.

As the realization of the injustice and futility of it came over me, I broke down. The orderlies prized my arms open to take him and place him on a stretcher. Such a great sadness had overcome me: I had asked him why he wasn't working and he had probably decided to die content, with a full stomach. I was told later that the poor man had been in perpetual trouble, most of the time in solitary confinement, because he had refused to work. He died on the way to the infirmary. With a friend I went to the morgue to look at his body: he was in the second stage of pellagra, his corpse a mere skeleton.

Later that morning I was called to General Federovitch's office. He was in a relaxed, quiet mood, most unusual.

'Your friend left you a note,' he said.

Colonel Volkovitch came into the room. Federovitch handed me a piece of paper on which there was writing in German which said:

Doctor, after such a long time my dream has come true. I have eaten a good meal, probably my last. I am a Jew and we are approaching the High Holydays and Yom Kippur. I have no calendar but I think they must be about three weeks away. By then I shall be dead and frozen. I don't know if you know what Kaddish is, but ask some of the Jews to say Kaddish for me on Yom Kippur.

Of course the General must have had the letter translated for him before he showed it to me, but when he had handed it to me he had said:
'Read it and translate it into Russian.'
I told him exactly what it said. He started to laugh:
'You killed him. You'll have it on your conscience always. You cannot do what you did! You encourage them to steal!'
Volkovitch stepped in saying that charges would be brought against me. I cut in:
'Alright then. I resign my job as Inspector of Health. I never liked the job anyway. I wish to return to the hospital.'
They were both silent for a moment, then Federovitch said:
'You must be mad to give it up, I would take such a job myself with pleasure.'
After my resignation I was sent back to Fedeseyev's block again, to be sent out to work. This was a surprise move for me: usually when a man was removed from a responsible job he wasn't sent back to the company of the ordinary prisoners as they often had accounts to settle and took revenge in their own ways on those who had lately had authority over them.
I had got used to a good bed and good food, and the injustice of my plight weighed upon me as I knew I had done nothing wrong. Later I discovered it was not only my uncompromising attitude to the pilferers which had brought about my dismissal, but also alarm because of the growing confidence which Federovitch had placed in me. I decided I would have to escape. I would go out to work with the prisoners next day to study how it could be done.
But I had worked only one day when, on my return in the evening, I learnt that I had been given a new appointment: the medical care of the Death Brigade.

Apart from the main camp with huts for the ordinary prisoners, there were two which were quite separate: one was the Schtrafnaia Brigade which I have already described, and the other was the Death Brigade. The hut of the Death Brigade was high above the rest of the camp about half a mile away.

Here were sent the most incorrigible prisoners who had been given up by the authorities: nothing would persuade them to go out to work regularly so, instead of shooting them, they were sent here to die from natural causes, or to change their minds about going out to work. The men were housed in a tent about fifty yards wide and about a hundred yards long. A single tier of wood ran all round on which the men slept. The only heating was from tin stoves which were extinguished at 11 p.m.

No routine medical checks were made. If someone got a high fever a nurse or a doctor would come over from the camp to visit them. The conditions were nothing short of slow torture. Occasionally prisoners volunteered to go out to work for, if they didn't go out, they got no food at all. The ones who were too ill to drag themselves to work died of malnutrition at the rate of two or three a week. Their world was one of complete and utter despair. Once I myself saw one of the prisoners leave the line of marchers. He ran off the track which they were supposed to follow, shouting:

'Goodbye, *bratse*! Goodbye, brothers!'

The guard shouted: 'Stop.'

Then without warning he fired at the man's head. As he fell he still managed to say:

'Goodbye brothers!' once more.

No one was allowed to stop and pick him up. The guards had their dogs at the front, back and middle of the column. I had decided to come with them to see exactly what work they were doing, and I was walking near the back.

The guard let me go to the dying man. The skin at the back of his neck had been split open to form a spreading wound, the result of a dum-dum bullet. He was dead. I asked the guard if we could take back his body, but he wouldn't let us and told us to carry on walking. Many chose this way out. At that time I had no idea what was done with the bodies, or who removed them.

The camp authorities presented me with a death certificate

which they asked me to sign. The cause of death was: 'Shot while attempting to escape.' I refused to sign.

Another method of suicide they often chose, and which happened three or four times a week, was to wait until the fires went out at night, then get off the bunk and lie down on the ground where the snow seeped in under the tent edge, where it was −20–40°C. They would die in their sleep. Yet another was to slit the vein at the wrist, then lie down in the snow, which quickly became stained with the red of the warm blood and melted.

I never learnt exactly how many men were supposed to be in that tent. Life there, for the aptly named Death Brigade, was indescribably savage. The tension between the prisoners was aggravated by their conditions. They did not know how to live, nor how to die.

Sometimes, when the tin stove became red hot, one prisoner would drag another up to it by the hair and press his face on to the glowing metal, twisting it until the skin stuck to the tin. The poor wretch would scream for help which never came, and the others watched him die in agony. The few who survived lived without hope. Food was almost non-existent and the guards had *carte blanche* to employ any barbaric methods they chose on those men. My daily duties were short – ten minutes in the morning and another ten minutes in the evening.

I would not co-operate with the authorities in signing death certificates which stated that the men had died through natural causes or during an attempt to escape. My application to be transferred was placed in the hands of Colonel Volkovitch. I told him I could not stand by and watch such terrible suffering, that the guards had prevented me from helping the men, that they were asking me to be a party to murder.

I decided that my attempt to escape must be made soon.

5

Exit from Nibka 3

The exact location of Nibka 3 was kept as secret as possible from the inmates but, after making many discreet enquiries, especially from Volkovitch's wife, I found out that we were only about a hundred and fifty miles from Finland. There were several camps scattered around this area between Kandalaksha and Murmansk chosen partly I suppose for its remoteness from the main centres of population in Russia, and partly for the harsh climatic conditions, both of which discouraged escape attempts.

No one was allowed to travel anywhere in the area at that time without a special travel permit called a *komandierovka*. The only persons allowed to travel to and from the camp were the staff who came in from outside, and they all knew each other. I wouldn't be able to mingle with them or ask for a lift from them.

The only way would be to make a break across the snow steppes from the camp boundaries which were dotted with watch-towers manned by snipers, and patrolled by heavily-armed guards who wore white suits and when necessary moved on skis. They had been specially selected for their prowess at cross-country skiing and were given orders to shoot any stray prisoners on sight.

After I had been out with the working parties a few times, I realized I had no chance unless I could get help from someone else. I would have to bide my time until I could find someone able and willing to help me.

One day I was walking about the camp and found myself passing Colonel Volkovitch's office. The door was open but I couldn't see him anywhere. I walked inside; in the little room leading from the main office, where he sometimes relaxed, I

65

noticed a uniform tunic hanging from the hook on the wall together with a peaked cap. There was a cupboard which I opened: hanging inside was another uniform and two pistol holsters, one empty and one containing a pistol. Hearing footsteps, I quickly returned to the main office. Volkovitch's wife came in holding her hand which was bleeding. She looked shaken and afraid:

'Where's my husband?' she asked.

I told her that I didn't know, that I was waiting for him. She allowed me to give her first-aid for the cut which she said had been caused by an accident with some glass. Close contact with her made me realize what a pretty woman she was, on the short side and rather plump, but with a nice full bosom. She was wearing her uniform jacket. Everything happened so quickly. I was caressing her breasts, had pulled her close and was starting to kiss her when we heard footsteps approaching. Five or ten minutes later would have found us in a much more compromising situation. I had to release my hold.

When Volkovitch walked in I was still attending to the cut on his wife's finger.

'Uri, where have you been?' she asked him.

We all three of us looked at one another. He asked:

'What happened to you? What is he doing here?'

'I came here to speak to you, but when I arrived your wife was in need of medical care,' I explained.

She rolled down her sleeve saying:

'Thank you, doctor; I would invite you for a glass of tea but I'm afraid the regulations do not permit it.' She left the room.

Volkovitch asked me:

'What is your problem?'

I told him that I wanted to work in the hospital again, or in the infirmary in the daily examination of prisoners, that I had done nothing to warrant taking me away from my work, and asked him to help me. He replied:

'Your case is no longer in my hands. You are being transferred from here very soon. Please go now.'

Next day General Federovitch summoned me. He told me about the transfer:

'I want you to know that I have always been the one who

has defended you. I got you transferred to another camp where my friend is the Commander. I told him that you are a good doctor and that I suggest that you be allowed to work as such. Please try to conform, keep your impulses under control. I have no idea when the transfer papers will arrive, but in the meantime Dr Morozova has agreed that you will take the morning consultations at the infirmary. . . . Goodbye. . . .'

Tears came to my eyes as he spoke to me. I didn't know what to say. I don't think I said anything. He had not said where I would be sent, but he had confirmed my belief that he had felt friendship toward me and had done his best for me. Even a tyrant has very human sentiments on occasions.

I returned to the old routine, examining twenty to thirty prisoners in the morning: the usual crop who didn't want to go to work.

One day I found a tiny little man standing in front of me, thin as a skeleton with a short, cropped beard. He looked deep into my eyes. He gave his name as Spund. This was the same man who had been tyrannized by the Polish officer in the prison at Stanislav, the editor of the Jewish newspaper *Chwila* in Lvov before the war. I signalled to him that he should not show any sign of recognition. I let him off work that day, giving my diagnosis as 'Cold with temperature. A feverish state'. I noted which hut he lived in and, when all the men had left the camp, I went to him to find out what he could tell me of the others we had known.

He told me that next week would be the fast of Yom Kippur. He knew the exact date, which was not an easy piece of information to discover in that remote place. He said that he and some of the others wished to pray Kol Nidre (which was recited on the eve of Yom Kippur) and they needed a minimum gathering of ten Jews to pray.

'It will be up to you to see to it that we can stay away from work and pray on that evening, which is the most sacred in the Jewish calendar. You will have to tell one or two of the other doctors.'

I promised I would try to help, as usual without considering the possible consequences.

A few days later he gave me a list of twenty men who wished to join the prayers which would be held in the sewing rooms where the prison uniforms were made. Of the sixty tailors who worked there, eleven were Jews, most of them included on the list Spund had given me.

I was still thinking hard about my plans to escape. How could I get hold of the spare uniform I had seen in Volkovitch's office? It was my size, I knew, because Volkovitch was more or less of my stature. The problem was how to get through the main gates without being recognized and then to get as far as Murmansk. The only person I felt might help me was Volkovitch's wife.

I was not able to comply with Spund's request entirely: some of the men on his list were strong and healthy, but I managed to give permission for the sickly ones to be free of work on the day of Yom Kippur. The evening preceding it was the time arranged for the Kol Nidre service. It could not be at the sunset hour which custom demanded, but would have to be later when more of the prisoners would be able to take part.

That evening, after supper, I spoke to Spund before the service. I asked him if the prayers would be valid at such a late hour. He answered:

'In the circumstances it will be in order.'

I asked him not to forget the name of Zimmerman in their prayer for the dead, the Kaddish. He promised he would remember it.

While they were praying I received a message that General Federovitch wished to see me in his office. He told me that he wanted me to accompany him on an unexpected visit to the kitchens, and that he did not want to take a guard with him. He said that someone was stealing part of the deliveries of pork and other foods and we might catch the culprit. He stood up, put on a white overcoat and we both left his office, taking the direction of the kitchens.

Our path would take us near the uniform sewing workshops. I took his arm and tried to guide him to another path to avoid going near the illicit meeting, but he objected saying that the other way was quicker.

As we came nearer the workshop voices could be heard

distinctly, chanting in unison in a language that wasn't Russian.

'Can you hear something?' he asked me.

As I started to hesitate, he pointed towards the workshops:

'It's coming from in there. Come with me.'

Suddenly his ailing legs turned to steel. He pushed me to one side, ran to the door and threw it open. I ran up behind him.

A few candles burned in the darkness, the faces all turned towards us, the tears streaming down them. Spund stood in the centre. The General took out his revolver shouting:

'What goes on here? Why are you all crying. Why these candles?' His voice rose in anger as he questioned them. Their faces swam before my eyes. I walked up to him, placed both hands on his shoulders, and looked into his eyes.

'They are praying. Today is their most sacred day.'

Replacing his revolver, he shouted:

'Put out all those candles! And get out of here, all of you who shouldn't be here!'

I shall never know how I pulled him away. We walked toward the kitchen. He turned to me:

'Was this your doing?'

'Yes.'

'Then this time you have put a chain around your own neck. This will not be tolerated: it is outright sabotage, counter-revolutionary, and you will be shot for it.'

'I didn't do the organizing and after all they are not harming anyone by praying.'

We toured the kitchens in silence. The snow was hard and glassy. I took his arm to help him to the office. I was wondering what would be my punishment for my latest 'offence', and I thought it better not to start trying to make excuses for myself. I would wait and see what happened.

On our way back past the tailors' workshops he stopped.

'Go in and see if all those parasites have gone.'

I went to the door and opened it. The electric lights were switched on, and normal shift work was in progress. There was absolutely no trace of the tears and sighs of a few minutes before. Tragic memories had united those few Jews in the light of candles, with thoughts of their dead and distant families. They had disappeared, leaving no sign of their holy meeting.

I turned to go back to the General, but he was standing at my shoulder. We trudged back to his office. He asked me to tell him exactly what had happened, the whole story. I told him the truth.

'This will be an excellent case for Volkovitch, and certainly another twenty years for you in one of these camps. You're young and stupid. When will you learn how to survive?'

With a heavy heart I went back to bed to sleep. At about four in the morning I was wakened by a guard who told me to dress and come outside. There he and another guard told me to get on to a sledge that was waiting. I had no idea where they would take me or what would be done to me, but their faces seemed to confirm my worst fears. It was a bitterly cold night, the stars brightly lighting the whole camp. We were going in a direction which was off the normal pathways, then I recognized the hut of the Schtrafnaia Brigade. The guard on the door said that I had been sent there on the General's orders and would be there for four days.

This was a new trick, but I had known that I would have to undergo some kind of punishment, and it was even possible that it would be no punishment at all.

Inside it was freezing cold, unheated. The men were beginning to get up to go to work and I recognized a lot of them from the time I had been working there. The ones who recognized me were surprised to see me. The only two mattresses in the hut were taken by the two bosses. One of them said:

'Doctor, you can have this mattress. We will work hard enough for you not to go out. You will be our own doctor. We need one. We have heard about you from our brothers in the main camp and we know you are a good man.'

After their meagre breakfast they left for work, leaving two of their number in the hut to clean and sweep.

I sat down to consider my latest position. To find myself here with these notorious men was depressing, but my optimistic nature would not allow me to be sad for long.

That afternoon, before the men returned from work, I looked from the window and saw in the distance two men on horses coming towards the hut. They had a riderless horse with them. As they came nearer I could see that one of them was a lieutenant and the other a guard. They called my name and told the guard in charge that they had orders to accompany me back to the main camp. The officer told me to mount the spare horse and ride between them at the same speed. I liked riding and enjoyed the brisk ride back to the camp in that crisp cold atmosphere. We went straight to General Federovitch's office.

'How does it feel to come back from hell?' he asked without waiting for my answer.

'We have a special commission arriving here tomorrow from Moscow. I want you to be in charge of the Death Brigade and the solitary confinement block. Dr Morozova will tell you everything you need to know. . . . I'm counting on you, Garri Semionovitch.' So I was back in favour again with the capricious monster. I wondered why.

I went directly to see Dr Morozova who tried to explain why the Death Brigade had received such poor medical attention.

'We have done our best to provide them with medical care, but there have been no doctors who were willing to spend time there except you. We could do no more. From today regular medical checks must be made among those prisoners. I bear the burden of responsibility for the health of the entire camp, but so much happens here over which I have no control that my job is extremely difficult . . . you, I am sure, understand what I mean. So when the commission arrives the General and I expect you to co-operate with us.'

I looked her straight in the eye:

'You want me to carry the can for all the men who have died, in whatever way, through suicide, by getting shot for some reason, or through near starvation?'

'Don't worry about it. They might never ask to see the records.'

I could do nothing, I was powerless. I was told I would find my belongings back at the medical staff quarters.

Why had I been chosen as the scapegoat? Perhaps they

71

reasoned that, since I was a prisoner myself, the only punishment I could be given was a few more years in the camp.

It was quite clear to me that the forthcoming inspection had been prompted by grave doubts in Moscow about the efficiency and correct running of the camp. The ice had cracked. Now there would be enquiries and probes, and someone would have to pay.

I had heard that the prisoners in the Death Brigade had tried to send a message to Stalin, and I had met a prisoner myself who had cut off a piece of skin from his chest the size of a large coin and sent it to Stalin with a message. I had listened to him at the time not really believing he had done it because I couldn't see how he could get a message out of the camp.

A few days later, when I was about to leave on my rounds of some of the huts, a convoy of cars with chains on the wheels moved in through the main gates. Then a number of officers, men and women, got out. They wore uniforms and greatcoats; one, in particular, I thought must have been a general since he wore a leather coat and a fur hat. I later found out that I was right. This was General Kretchmar, the head of the Commission of Enquiry.

The morning after the Commission had arrived I was called to General Federovitch's office. He looked pale and frightened, his eyes red from lack of sleep. He introduced me to the members of the Commission individually and explained that I was in charge of the medical care of huts Numbers 1, 2, and 3. General Kretchmar asked me my name and went on to enquire about the general living conditions of the prisoners, and my estimate of their physical state.

I told him that he would be able to see this for himself. I would not have lied about it, even to back up Federovitch, but I could see that they already knew the score themselves.

It was the first time that I had been interviewed by so many high-ranking officers in one room: apart from General Kretchmar there were colonels and majors, one of them a good-looking woman. They were speaking to me not as a prisoner, but as a citizen with equal rights. There were no veiled threats. Suddenly Kretchmar said:

'Let's go and see the "Sanatorium".'

For a moment I didn't know what he meant, then Federovitch hastily interjected: 'Detention Block Number 3'.

One unrehearsed incident en route amused us all a lot: there were in the camp a few hundred Russian delinquents aged about sixteen years upwards who were treated with considerable leniency and given less harsh conditions than the other prisoners. They were in the camp because no one had been able to reform them; they stole whatever they could lay their hands on, spoke the dirtiest language in the camp, and were the biggest trouble-makers there.

As we filed out of the office to get into the cars there was a group of these young delinquents standing there watching. The woman major went up to one of them and said in a very kind way:

'You're a nice-looking boy. What have you done to be here? You ought to be in school.'

The boy jumped back from her, and started to make fun of her, repeating her exact words in a mocking tone, then added:

'You're a bitch! You ask me what I'm doing here? You don't ask how we live, how we eat, or how they treat us? Is that what you came here for? Well, I'll tell you why I'm standing here! I came to give you a welcome . . . with this . . .' and he undid his trousers and took out his penis.

'Come on, kiss here, you bitch!'

The guards closed in around him and hustled him quickly away. Kretchmar turned to Federovitch:

'I can see that your re-education of the boys is also not going according to plan!'

Some of the officers got into the cars to ride to Block 3 which was at some distance from the main camp. I walked with the others. Federovitch had called it Block Number 3 but this was the block I have referred to as the Death Brigade.

The members of the Commission did not spend a lot of time there. General Kretchmar had already heard about the reputation of the block: the barbaric conditions, the sadistic guards and the suffering. He asked very few questions. He didn't need to, he himself had been in command of various Soviet camps. He ordered a few of the men to remove their shirts; everything was clear to him. In my presence he ordered Dr Morozova to have all the prisoners in the block moved to the hospital. When she tried to explain that there was not room for them all he cut her short:

'If there is nowhere else, put them in your bed.'

He quickly gave orders for a warm block to be prepared to house the prisoners from Blocks Numbers 2 and 3. Then he looked at me:

'Has anyone died here in the last twenty-four hours?' he asked. I remained silent, then he asked Dr Morozova who said: 'No.'

Suddenly one of the prisoners shouted:

'If you want to know how many, come and have a look under here!'

He pointed under the wooden tier where they slept. He then jumped down and started to pull away the wooden floor slats. Beneath the slats, frozen, as in sleep, were three bodies. About twenty-five of the prisoners were in the hut at the time. At the sight of the bodies they started to shout:

'Save us! Save us from death!'

Some broke down, the tears streaming down their faces. Others took off their shirts and started to cut their flesh with glass. Blood spurted on to the floor. The woman major was crying quietly. Kretchmar pushed me towards the men to try to stop them from harming themselves. From outside came the noise of the dogs barking, alarmed by the commotion. The situation was quickly brought under control and the injured men sent to hospital.

On Kretchmar's orders the guards brought in cans of petrol and within minutes the infamous Block Number 3, which was only a tent, was reduced to smouldering ruin by fire.

As we stood clear of the fire, the heat of the flames warmed our cheeks and my heart.

Federovitch stood alone, his face like a mask, stripped of all authority in the presence of the prisoners.

As we left the site I saw one of the officers whisper in Kretchmar's ear. Then he nodded and said:

'You're right. We shall see no more blocks today. Take all the men out of Block 1 as well as those from Block 2 and 3, have them transferred to other quarters to await medical examination. In twenty-four hours I want a list of every prisoner here and his state of health.'

He gave these orders to Dr Morozova. It was plain to see that Federovitch's head was at stake. My job was to move the Schtrafnaia Brigade prisoners to a hut near the hospital which was sometimes used as an annex to it.

That night, just before supper, a commotion broke out in the annex where the Schtrafnaia Brigade had been moved. I rushed outside to find guards carrying arms at the ready running in the direction of the annex.

I burst in to find Sacha Stogoff wearing only trousers and two of his friends wearing trousers and vests, all three of them brandishing steel choppers which glinted and shone as though they had been polished. They were all very drunk. Stogoff was shouting:

'Vanya, come out of your hiding place. We know you're there!' His friends were pulling out the benches and moving tables, searching frantically.

A loudspeaker had been set up outside and a sergeant ordered all the prisoners to come out. He called on Stogoff to surrender. As the men moved towards the door, Stogoff got there first and blocked their way.

'The first man to go out will walk out without his head!'

I knew Stogoff had some respect for me and I tried to catch his eye. He was too excited to notice. The disorder turned to panic as the three with choppers swung wildly at the wooden tiers where the mattresses were. The splintered wood crashed to the ground. They were still shouting:

'Come on out! Whore! Traitor!'

The report of rifle shots could be heard outside; I suppose they were trying to frighten the maddened prisoners inside. Suddenly one of the three shouted:

'Here he is, I've got him, brothers!'

The unfortunate Vanya was huddling on the top bunk between some of the other prisoners. Stogoff opened the door to let everyone except Vanya leave the room. His two comrades were holding Vanya pressed to the wall, his arms raised high. Stogoff approached slowly:

'Leave him! He's mine!'

I shouted loud:

'Stogoff, don't kill him. Leave him!'

He must have heard me because he hesitated for a moment, turned his head in my direction, looked at me, then carried on moving toward Vanya. With his left hand he lifted Vanya's hair then, with a tremendous blow, chopped off the man's right hand.

'You won't write with that hand any more!'

Then with a second blow he cut off Vanya's left hand.

'And you won't be able to sign with that one either!'

Stogoff's friend shouted:

'What about his tongue? Cut off his tongue, so he can't talk!' While Stogoff was still holding the hair, the other, with a great swing, severed the head from the body in one blow.

The truncated body fell to the ground. He had screamed to the last moment. The three of them fell upon the body and hacked him to pieces. The guards burst through the door, firing at the three madmen. One was shot dead instantly, another wounded in the arm.

From where I had flung myself on the floor I could see parts of the body still twitching. Stogoff threw the head at the guards shouting:

'So dies a traitor. Ask him something! See if he can talk now!'

He threw down the bloody chopper. I staggered out. I don't know how I dragged myself from the scene of such butchery, but I went straight to the hospital and drank two glasses of surgical spirit.

Next day I discovered the reason for this slaughter. Stogoff had been making love to one of the women in the camp. Vanya had discovered it, informed the authorities, and then made love to the woman himself. Later, afraid that Stogoff would discover what he had done, Vanya signed a statement affirming that Stogoff was seeing the woman regularly and that they had been arranging for other women to come to the men's huts to make love. One of the guards in the look-out towers had been bribed in some way and knew what was going on. He had been removed and placed under arrest. Stogoff and his two friends had decided to mete out their own kind of justice.

Such stories are not uncommon in camps where male and female prisoners are held in close proximity. Whatever precautions are taken, sexual desire will overcome every barrier, even at the risk of getting shot.

I came across many other instances of violence while in the camp. When I held my morning consultation period I always had a guard with me in the room since some prisoners were so dangerous. One morning a prisoner came up to my desk, speaking in a broken voice:

'Oh doctor, I'm so ill. I can't even undress myself. Please help me.'

He was doubled over in pain. Slowly he unbuttoned his shirt, his back turned to the guard, and showed me the head of a chopper he had thrust into his trousers. The tone of his voice changed from a plea to an urgent threat:

'Please help me. I would like to stay indoors for a few days. I'm very weak.'

The expression on his face frightened me more than the chopper.

Another case I remember was that of Yasha Kogan who came into my room with a guard. He came forward to place himself between the guard and myself, took out a matchbox, and said:

'I'm coughing blood, doctor.'

Then he opened the matchbox to show me a human ear which was still bleeding. There were many more cases, all of them moving.

However, I never allowed any of them to feel that they had intimidated me. I might say:

'Of course you can stay in the hut today, I'll come and see you later,' but before the others went out to work I would go to the hut and say to them:

'You will go out to work today, and next time I will let you off if you promise never to come to me again with blackmail threats.' I did this in the case of the man with the chopper. He looked at me and laughed:

'It's a deal!' he answered.

To the one with the ear in the box, I sent a message through another prisoner that he had to go out to work.

If I had allowed them to blackmail me, they would have finished me as a doctor and I would have been at their mercy. Sometimes, when I thought it would help, I would tell some of the prisoners about these two cases, without mentioning names, and would remark that their tricks would not work on me.

I think I gained their respect because I was firm with them, and secondly because I would go to endless trouble on their behalf to try and get their conditions improved in every way.

Within a few hours of General Kretchmar's arrival there were considerable improvements in the lot of the ordinary prisoner in the camp. Better, warmer clothing was distributed, including boots, shoes and gloves; spoons which had been in such short supply were also issued as well as drinking mugs. The food improved too. All this did not alter the fact that they lived under a regime based on fear.

I knew who would have to pay the ultimate price for whatever was found to be wrong in the camp. Nevertheless, I also knew that I might be a victim too if heads began to roll. For the time being all the charges against me, including the occasion when I had allowed the men to pray and miss work, and the threats of transfer to another camp, had been shelved. But I resolved that if I saw my chance to escape I would take it.

Many of the officers in the Commission wore the same uniform as Volkovitch, that of the NKGB, and they were circulating in all areas of the camp at all hours of the day and night. I noted that at the main gates and checkpoints the guards would come smartly to attention whenever these officers passed, and that, most important of all, they went through unchallenged.

My plans for escape began to crystallize, but I had to consider the many stumbling blocks involved. Even if I succeeded in getting safely away from the camp I would come to the principal checkpoint outside the city of Kandalaksha, about fifteen miles from the camp. Along the road to the city there were a few scattered houses, mostly occupied by camp staff. I would have to be well clear of the main gates, at least three miles along the road, before I could try to stop a car to get a lift.

What would happen if I was caught? They would probably give me twenty or thirty days' solitary confinement and perhaps another ten to fifteen years added to my sentence. I didn't think they would shoot me unless they actually saw me trying to escape: so it had to be a clean getaway.

The plan was simple: I would change into Volkovitch's uniform and try walking through the main gates at a time when I could mingle with the Commission officers. Sometimes all their cars left the camp together, at other times they left singly or in pairs. Not all of the guards knew my face: I would just have to hope that if any of those I knew were on duty the uniform would make me look different. One aspect of the plan bothered me: I was too young to have a rank as high as Volkovitch. The same basic uniform was used by all officers, from lieutenant up to general, the only difference being the inisignia on the shoulder tabs. I would have to remove some of the bars. Doubts about unforeseen snags preyed on my mind. Would Volkovitch's wife be willing to help me? Our relationship had by now developed into a very close one, and I felt she would. I disclosed the whole plan to her.

At first she was speechless, then she turned to me and said:

'And if they catch you?'

'Don't worry. If they catch me, I'll never sell you out.'

Next day I had an opportunity to try on the tunic, hat and boots. They all fitted perfectly except the boots which were slightly large, but that didn't matter. When she saw me Katya Volkovitch said:

'You look so handsome in uniform. You should stay at the camp and finish your time, then you could become a real officer. I'm sure you could quickly become a captain or even a major. Why don't you become a Soviet citizen?'

What she was saying reminded me that she was a NKGB officer's wife – an expert in flattery and possibly, a worrying thought, in treachery too.

I quickly took off the uniform.

'I'm going to try the escape tomorrow, if the chance arises. I'll take the uniform with me now in this sack.'

She argued:

'If you walk out of here now with a sack in your hand the guards will certainly stop you. I'll bring it to you tonight before I leave the camp.'

As I left I saw that her eyes were brimming with tears. Was she afraid of the possible consequences of her part in my escape, or was she sorry that I would be leaving?

It was to my advantage that this was a period of readjustment and transition in the camp: many of the free officers and administrative staff, *nachalniks* too, had been replaced by others, so there were many new faces.

The circumstances in the camp would never be better for my escape. I spoke fluent Russian, I had the guts, I would go on. So far I had managed to keep away from the visiting Commission officers as much as possible, so that they would not recognize me later. Next day around three o'clock in the afternoon I looked through my window and saw Katya, my beautiful nurse Volkovitchova, coming towards my room carrying a brown paper parcel. When she came in I saw she was wearing two uniforms and a coat over them. She quickly removed one of them saying:

'I have to go back for the other half – I couldn't carry too much in one go.'

The boots were in the parcel. She went away and returned with everything I would need: gloves, a scarf, hat, leather holster and belt (no gun). I asked:

'Why will I need a holster if I'm wearing an overcoat?'

'If you are on a train and have to take off the greatcoat it would be noticed if you didn't wear a belt and holster: it's part of the uniform. It can get quite hot in a heated train. Try to sit so that the holster is against the window.'

She had left only one bar on the shoulder tabs which would reduce my rank from colonel to lieutenant. She had even obtained a pass as far as Leningrad stating that I was on a special mission for the NKGB – this was my chance. It was a very tense moment. I asked her why she had taken such risks for me. She answered:

'Because you asked me. I want you to know that this is not

my husband's uniform, none of it. If you get caught, you have my fate in your hands.'

And to think I had suspected her of treachery! Now it was my conscience that started to bother me: why should I accept help from this generous woman and put her freedom at risk as well as my own? But my longing to get away was so great that I was unable to judge whether I was doing right or wrong. One thing I knew, I would never give her away – I was prepared to die rather than that. The uniform I would be wearing was that of the highest Soviet security organization, and I would be tortured to death to find out where I had obtained it if I were caught. I would resolve the problem by getting some poison from the hospital pharmacy.

We stood facing each other. She was overcome with sorrow at my leaving, and I was full of excitement and trepidation. She spent the next hour with me. Before she left she said:

'There is some money in the pocket – enough for a couple of weeks.'

Then she gave me the telephone number of her parents in Kharkov, and made me repeat it several times.

'If you need help, go to them and tell them the truth.'

She had fallen in love with me. Most Russian women are very sentimental; once they love you they are woman, wife, friend, mother to a man. Her actions had proved her feelings.

'If you were free now you would probably leave your husband for me, wouldn't you?'

For the first time she said:

'I shall probably leave my husband in any case, very soon.' She was crying as we kissed for the last time.

I was now at a fever pitch of excitement. My pulse raced. I hid the uniform and hoped that there would be no unexpected searches as sometimes happened. I trusted Katya completely and I felt in command of my body. I was not at the point of panic, but I felt tuned to a very fine pitch. This was not like the mental preparation involved when digging an escape tunnel or filing through iron bars. It would be one swift plunge.

I went to the hospital, looked at the people I had come to like, and said 'goodbye' in my heart, then went to the dispensary and took what I needed in case I got caught, together with a few other medicines I might need.

As I walked back from the hospital I thought to myself that I would like to see Federovitch, see how he was. I had thought about him a lot. He had two personalities: one was a warm attractive one, and the other ruthless and cruel. I decided that he had become cruel because of the tremendous strain he was under from the party to complete the plan and finish the construction of the MIG factory. In the Soviet Union, if one of their plans, industrial or agricultural, is not completed on time, the highest official or minister can fall into disfavour and disgrace, even face imprisonment and execution. This mental pressure can turn any man from a human being into a beast, slowly squeezing out all humanity in the fear and anxiety to save his own skin. Basically Federovitch was good: he had shown me that he cared about getting the men good food and good clothes. It was his job to see that everyone worked in order to finish the factory. As I got near his office I thought:

'What shall I say? I can't go in there without some pretext.'

As I looked around me, each corner of the camp held its own memories: I looked towards the annex where Stogoff had chopped Vanya to pieces, I remembered the scenes as we opened the door on the Jews praying Kol Nidre, their white faces in the candlelight.

I continued in the direction of Federovitch's office. The head of stores was standing outside speaking to him. I went up, though I had no idea what I would say to him. I looked him in the eye and for the first time no words came. He took control of the situation and said:

'How is everything? I suppose you were happy to see that block burnt down.'

I said:

'Yes, I was happy. A prisoner is a prisoner – we are all prisoners here, without trial, without justice. You cannot expect to get work out of a weak and dying man at the point of a bayonet. The majority of the men here are not fit for such heavy work. Take your own case: if you were a prisoner, what work would you be able to do? It would just be physically impossible for you. By the way, how is your foot?'

'Well enough,' he replied. The quartermaster at his side had not uttered a word. Federovitch turned the gaze of his strong blue eyes on me:

'So what was it you wanted to tell me?'

'I only came to see how you are.'

'Thank you, I'm alright.'

Those were the last, very ordinary phrases that we exchanged – almost as two friends, two civilians, might have done. I felt no animosity towards him now. I turned from him and walked back along the path, reflecting that he must have been able to sense my concern and sympathy. I could see many of the Commission officers standing near the main gates. This was my chance, I couldn't ask for a better one – it was nearly dusk, that time of day when the light could play tricks. I hurried to my room and changed into the uniform. The only thing I had prepared to take with me was a bottle of spirit, I had no guns or knives of any kind. I swallowed a tumbler of spirit which made my whole body tingle and my pulse race. Dressed in the complete uniform I looked into the tiny mirror I had, unable to see the total effect. My eyes stared back, the pupils enlarged by drink.

Five minutes later I walked from the room directly toward the main gates. It was almost dark now. I hoped the uniform was all correct. My old clothes I had tucked out of sight in the room. When I was close to the gate I saw to my dismay that there were no officers or Commission cars in sight – there was not even one person there to distract the attention of the guards from my presence. But if I turned back someone could easily spot me and recognize me; I had to go forward. The offices where the guards reported had large windows overlooking the gates. There were four or five guards talking inside, usually there were fewer.

My heart pounding, I walked straight past the window and through the gates, expecting at any second to hear a raised voice shouting after me. I quickened my pace. I must have been walking for about three minutes when I saw the lights of a car approaching from behind. I turned to look back, silhouetted in the headlamps of the oncoming car, and raised my hand to shield my eyes from the strong light. It stopped. I couldn't see who was inside but walked to the driver's door. I looked in. In front was an army driver and in the back seat the woman major who had been so insulted by the juvenile offenders in the camp, seated next to another officer.

'Can you give me a lift to Kandalaksha?' I asked.

'Of course, get in.' It was the woman who answered.

I introduced myself as Garri Semionovitch Urbanoff, I was trying to get to Kandalaksha as quickly as I could because my wife was expecting to give birth at any moment, and I had to get to Leningrad where she was. The other officer said:

'We'll drop you at the station. There's a train at eight o'clock which you should catch.'

They dropped me at the station. There were three trains due to leave; one to Moscow, one to Leningrad, and a local train. I intended to go on the Moscow train.

PART TWO

Vodka and Women

6

Leningrad: Tatiana

Everything had gone so smoothly, it was difficult to believe.

While we were travelling in the car they asked me no more questions. The only comment the woman made when they dropped me near the station was:

'I wish you a son,' since I had told them how much I would like to have one.

As I walked to the station and looked at the people in the streets they appeared to me to be no better dressed than those in the camp. Only an hour and a half before I had been in that camp, where my whole life was planned, timetabled and programmed for me. Here I was on an unknown railway station, completely by myself, wearing a uniform I hated, but which I could not discard until I reached a large city.

At this time of the year most of the officers wore heavyweight greatcoats, but mine was of only medium weight, adequate enough for a city like Leningrad, but not for these Arctic conditions. This slight variation in my appearance from the usual caused me some anxiety. I considered the best course of action. Dr Morozova might wonder why I had not turned up at the annex, but she would not have started any enquiries that same evening. My absence, then, would not be discovered until the following morning or during the course of the next day, so that I had a whole night's start on them.

The first train due was for Leningrad, not Moscow, and I decided to board it. The train had some accommodation in couchettes as well as ordinary seating, but the couchettes were all reserved. It had come from Murmansk, and would stop at Belomorsk before arriving in Leningrad. Specially trained military police made very strict checks on all passengers on all Soviet trains, passing through the carriages examining travel permits and asking questions: their suspicions could be aroused very easily and anything out of the ordinary would give cause for more searching examination.

I went along the platform passing the carriages, each of which was numbered. I chose to get into one that had a woman conductor with a wide Asiatic face like the people of Kazakstan. As I stepped into the carriage she said:

'Are you the passenger for Number 26?'

'Yes, you're quite right,' I answered.

As we stood in the corridor she asked me for my ticket. I had been too nervous of discovery to buy a ticket on the station: if questions had been asked later, someone might have remembered seeing me. Searching through my pockets I said with regret:

'I must have lost my ticket, I can't find it.' – the old chestnut.

'And haven't you any luggage with you?'

Perhaps her suspicions were aroused.

'I had no time to pack anything I came away so quickly. My wife is in a clinic in Leningrad . . . she's expecting a baby and I had word that they had taken her to hospital . . . there was no time for packing a suitcase.'

She appeared to accept my excuse and told me she would put me in a compartment as far as Leningrad with two other passengers. All I wanted was to get as far away from the camp as quickly as I could, and this train would take me the longest distance in the shortest time. She showed me to my place, and told me that she would have my ticket prepared for me in the morning – I could pay her then.

I stopped her from moving on at once by chatting to her and flirting with her; I wanted to find out what would be the best time to go to sleep as I knew there would be at least one strict check on passengers during the night. She said that no one would bother me if I went to sleep there and then: the whole carriage was occupied, mostly by officers, and one check had been made already between Murmansk and Kandalaksha.

'Alright,' I said, 'I'll leave my papers with you and get some sleep.'

That was a mistake. She smiled saying:

'You should know better than anyone that you shouldn't

allow your documents out of your possession. If there is a check they will certainly want to speak to every passenger personally.'

'Well, I was just seeing if you knew your job,' I laughed rather shakily. Half an hour later I was asleep on the top tier without having seen, or spoken to, the other passengers.

I woke early next morning before we arrived in Leningrad. It was already daylight when I walked into the corridor. I engaged my woman conductor in friendly conversation. She gave me coffee and bread. I gave her fifty roubles and we forgot about the train ticket. She showed no qualms about taking the money, and in fact appeared to be accustomed to receiving such payments; even in Soviet Russia bribery was an accepted practice.

I had no idea in which direction to set off once I had arrived at the station. On each platform there were special railway police who watched the passengers closely; those of lower rank saluted me, and I saluted those of higher rank.

Outside the station I took a tram. The ticket collector asked me where I wanted to go. I replied :

'All the way.'

He gave me a curious look but handed me the ticket. After a few stops I saw a crowded street market and decided to get off. I would need clothes. I bought warm trousers and jacket, two shirts and a few other things which were put into a large brown paper bag. I didn't try anything on for size except a warm hat. The most pressing necessity was to find somewhere to change out of uniform into civilian clothes. If I went to an hotel, I would be asked for my papers. It looked like being more difficult than the actual escape! I was afraid to trust anyone, and even if I could find someone to trust, would they trust me? After all, I was wearing an NKGB uniform, which was the most hated of any Soviet uniform, especially in that market place. While in the camp I had heard that market places were dangerous – there were always police close at hand or patrolling, or even surrounding them. I would have to get away from the market area.

I thought of going to a restaurant, then using the toilet to change my clothes; this was the most practical idea so far, providing no one recognized me, as I was leaving, as being the same person who had been dressed as an officer on coming in. I went into a couple of *stolovaya*, or tea rooms, looking for a good place to change. In one of them I had a cup of tea and chatted with a man who came to my table looking for someone to talk to.

This of course prevented me from changing but it did give me time to reflect. Although I gave no sign of nervousness, I felt all eyes upon me. I needed to buy a holdall since my ultimate destination was Moscow, or even further south, Kiev. When travelling by train the absence of a *chemadan* or bag would prove conspicuous, and my difficulties would be increased as a civilian since I had no document of any kind, whereas up to now I had used the travel permit.

My experience in the camp had shown that there was no efficient method of keeping records of the names of inmates, so I decided I would not alter my name, since the real one would not be a handicap. But I must obtain real identity papers.

My first need however was much simpler – an urge for tobacco! The Russian Machorka cigarettes didn't suit me and good cigarettes were very expensive, if they could be found. I came out of the *stolovaya* and made my way back to the market, passing two military police who looked at me and saluted. In addition to market stalls, there were many traders standing around who showed goods from their pockets. Items normally unobtainable could be bought at a price. My attention fell upon a short fat woman who covered her stall quickly with a cloth as I came near. When I lifted the cloth I saw she had boxes of Belomorcanal cigarettes which contained a light tobacco which I liked. She became nervous, explaining that she had a sick husband and had to make a living here in the market. When I asked for five packets of cigarettes she let me have them very cheaply, the first bargain I had found in the market. Then, pursuing my plan, I purchased a small suitcase. Next would come the papers – for which I would need professional assistance. Fortunately the criminals in the Schtrafnaia Brigade had taught me a great deal about the ways and mentality of the underworld and I was not now without possible contacts.

As I moved away from the cigarette stall I noticed that the special military police, wearing red arm-bands, were quietly surrounding the market. I would have to move quickly. Strictly speaking these police had no right to ask me for my papers, concerned as they were mostly with simple soldiers, but they often worked closely with the security police who were entitled to question even the most high-ranking officers. I walked straight towards the police where they were standing awaiting orders. When I had passed them and was about to cross the street a voice said:

'*Tovarisch*, Lieutenant!'

I stopped. A knife seemed to be stuck in my chest. I turned slowly and saw to my immense relief that one of the men about ten feet away had been calling out to one of his own officers, a lieutenant.

As I was about to cross the road, and I saw a beautiful woman, quite well dressed, wearing a thick winter coat, a scarf tied under her chin. She looked me straight in the eyes.

'Hello Tanya, how are you?' I asked.

'You're not far out,' she answered. 'But my name is Tatiana, not Tanya.'

'Good. Then, Tatiana, we'll eat something together.'

She accepted with a smile and suggested a place some distance away. As we walked along I felt much better. Carrying my case in one hand, I took her arm with the other, although at first she didn't seem to like it.

My troubles seemed to diminish now that I found myself once again in the company of a lovely woman. The restaurant she took me to was quite different from the tea rooms in the market area; there was a different clientele. As we sat at a table by ourselves I noticed that the waiters already knew Tatiana. It was warm. I took her coat to hang it up. She was wearing a high-necked sweater which was stretched tight over her breasts. As I sat opposite her and we talked, my whole body was aware of her presence. I looked round the room for another table where I could sit next to her, but there were none vacant. This would be the first meal I would eat in Russia as a free man, and I was in the company of such a good-looking woman. After talking for several minutes she said:

'You're not Russian by birth, are you?'

This surprised me since I spoke perfect Russian without any accent.

'Why do you say that?' I asked.

'Our men are not so refined.'

I couldn't help looking at her breasts which were paralysing me. I learnt that she was not a native of Leningrad, but came from the Ukraine, from the city of Kharkov, where I had been in a transit prison, and she would be going back to see her parents there next week. In Leningrad she was living by herself. Her brother was a colonel of the NKVD in the district of Kharkov. I asked:

'Is that why you smiled at me, because you have a brother who wears the same uniform?'

'Not at all,' she answered, 'you wanted to talk to me, and I felt like talking to you.'

'I intend to go to Kharkov myself next week,' I said. 'Which day will you be travelling?'

She told me she had her studies at the police academy to consider – she was studying to become a policewoman. I felt frozen to my chair. She must have sensed it:

'I'm a waitress' – she laughed and put her hand over mine – 'here in this restaurant. I've had other jobs too.'

'Why did you tell me you were studying to become a police-woman?'

'Well, I wanted you to feel at home,' she answered gaily.

She had two days off work. When we had finished the meal, at about three o'clock, we went to her room which she shared with another waitress called Maruja.

Over the meal I told Tatiana that I had only just arrived in Leningrad and would stay there a few days before continuing to Kiev. She said she could get me a room in the same building. Before her friend Maruja arrived we became very friendly. She ran water for me to have a bath. As I was enjoying this extra-ordinary luxury, she came into the bathroom and asked me if she could fetch anything from my suitcase. I jumped out quickly to stop her opening the case, took her hand and invited her to have a bath with me. I love having a bath with a woman, and Tatiana was a real woman in every sense: she soaped and washed me and we started all over again. It is not difficult to imagine how I felt after being in a camp to find this woman who slithered her body over mine like a serpent, with her tongue flickering out to ensnare her victims. I was a willing victim.

92

Then she towelled me down – we were drinking vodka the whole time. Dry outside but not in, I danced like a ballet dancer in front of her, and as I danced I told her to take my ballet costume from my suitcase as I wanted to dress the part for her. She opened the case, pulled out the paper bag and handed me the clothes. The trousers were a good fit, and warm. The jacket, the shirts, and the new hat all fitted me. I continued to dance around the room. She was still naked. I lifted her high in the air. Then suddenly the reaction to all the excitement and tension set in. We fell asleep until Maruja came in and woke us. I had put all the uniform clothes in the suitcase. The room was divided by a curtain so that Maruja could get to the bathroom without disturbing Tatiana. My case was outside Tatiana's cubicle. I asked her to bring it inside.

In the morning I said to Tatiana :

'I'm going to tell you something now, and I want you to say immediately if you don't want to get involved in my trouble.'

Against my better judgement I had decided to tell her the whole story. I knew very well that a man in such danger should talk as little as possible, especially to a woman, but I went ahead. When I had finished she was shaking and pale, almost fainting. She placed her hand on my arm and started to kiss me, saying :

'You see, *Garinka*, I told you that you were not Russian. I knew it. A lot of people know about the way a lot of Eastern Europeans have been sent to labour camps for no good reason.'

She had pulled herself together. She was marvellous. The first thing she did was to burn the uniform when Maruja left for work.

'You will stay here with me until we can both go to Kharkov together,' she said. 'You will stay indoors, you could be stopped and questioned.'

My money was running out. My fate was in the hands of this woman.

I was now worried about having bared the whole truth to Tatiana, but my delight at my new-found freedom brimmed over and obscured my vulnerability. She had been so good to me that I became very sentimental, especially when we both drank vodka. But my misgivings kept coming back and I would seek reassurance from her. Why would she help me if she was the sister of an NKVD man? Why should she take such serious risks for me? Before she left each morning for work I would ply her with questions, and it would always end with our kissing and making love again. She must have been late for work every morning as a result.

Waiting for her to come back in the afternoon was particularly difficult. I would say to myself: 'Dress, get out while you can!' But then I would consider the proofs of love: how she showed her love, how she had burnt the uniform. Then I would say: 'No, stay and wait for her.'

When she got back the first day she had brought food to make a Ukrainian lunch. I watched her crack egg after egg into a frying pan – there must have been two dozen at least, together with tomatoes and onions.

'Are you expecting someone for lunch?' I asked.

With a kiss she replied:

'It's not lunch. It's breakfast for the two of us.'

Later I discovered that such quantities of eggs were normal for breakfast: six for a small breakfast and twelve for a large one. Tatiana seemed to know everyone of importance in the black market, and must have had quite a considerable sum of money set aside. She was quite a woman: warm and sweet, but she could also be very firm – good to look at, with plenty of sex-appeal. We made love day and night, and over the five days we spent together in her room I don't know how many bottles of vodka we drank. We just couldn't stop. She would say:

'Come on and fuck me again.'

After two nights poor Maruja moved out to stay with friends so that she could get some sleep. I could understand her. Tatiana bought me shirts, a couple of suits, some gloves, everything I would need. Like every woman she tried to find out if I was married or engaged, and I told her that I enjoyed life too much to settle down with one woman, and would only marry when I felt that I could be good to one woman and stay with her. She laughed:

'At least you're sincere.'

It was not going to be easy to obtain two reservations for such a long journey, but she was sure she would manage it.

Identity papers would have to be procured for me, and photos would be required too. She asked me what name I would like on the papers. I remained silent for a moment watching her expression, doubt in my mind.

'I'll travel under my own name,' I said.

She said that would be dangerous because a list of escaped prisoners would have been circulated throughout the country. I explained how disorganized the authorities were with their records: they might search for me by circulating my description, but they would never expect me to use my real name. In any case, I told her, photos were only required for passports at that time. Other documents, including the important *komandierovka*, or travel permit, had no photograph. Nevertheless, when we were out together she insisted on having photographs taken of me.

A few days later she brought me a Soviet passport, bearing my photograph made out in the name of Grigori Makarov. Makarov was her surname. I poured myself a large tumbler of vodka:

'Long live Makarov!' I shouted, raising my glass. I swallowed half. She took the drink from me, drank the rest and said:

'Come on, make love to me now while you have the chance. After Thursday we are supposed to be brother and sister.'

Well, we made love yet again. Every corner of that room had been used for some act of love. I never asked where she got the passport from or what price she paid for it. My situation forced me to accept something which was against my nature – help from a woman.

It was a Thursday evening when we finally boarded the train for Kharkov. We had reservations in a carriage with couchettes. No pillows or blankets were supplied: men and women slept fully dressed. I was given a middle-tier couchette with Tatiana sleeping above me. As the train moved forward through the night she started to talk to me, saying how happy she was, how in love, but how she had a bad feeling about something. She was trying to force me to enter into a serious discussion with her about our future but I would not be drawn. She had spoken in a low voice so that the other passengers could not hear. We were sitting very near the entrance of the carriage when an

95

official who wore no uniform, probably from the NKVD, started checking all papers. Tatiana handed hers over first. When I took mine from an inside pocket and was about to hand them over to the second of the plain-clothes inspectors, the first official leant over and took the papers, looking at me in a very strange way. After returning Tatiana's papers to her, he started to examine mine very closely. He looked first at Tatiana then at me:

'Are you husband and wife?' he asked.

'No, brother and sister,' she answered.

He asked to see her passport again, while still fingering through mine.

'Considering you are brother and sister, you have very different educational backgrounds and professions. This is a new passport, isn't it?' he asked me. 'What have you done with the old one?'

'It was stolen, so I applied for a new one.'

As he handed back my papers, he eyed me suspiciously. He went to speak to two uniformed guards who were waiting for him at the end of the carriage, then all three of them came back to us, asked for both passports again, and went off with them to a small office they had on the train, assuring us they would bring them back very soon. I tried to remain calm. Obviously they were not satisfied but they had given me no reason to think that they had any idea of who I really was. The suspense was unbearable; even the passengers sitting around us watched us and muttered to each other. Tatiana, usually so talkative and vivacious, had lost her voice. I thought, if I get up and walk around that will not look good: either I must make an excuse and go to the toilet, or else sit still and wait.

If I had not been supposed to have been her brother, I could have started to kiss her and comfort her, giving her the reassurance she so badly needed at that moment. As it was we could only wait. I wondered what it was that had given rise to a suspicion – perhaps there was some imperfection in the forgery. I would have welcomed a large glass of vodka at that moment but I knew it would be fatal to show any sign of apprehension or nerves.

They came back.

'This passport has not been countersigned by the authorities,' the plain-clothes policeman pointed out.

'That's not my fault,' I said. 'I didn't even notice that.'

'Well, make sure you get it countersigned or renewed when you are in Kharkov,' he said, handing me both passports.

Tatiana's eyes changed colour as she relaxed again. Our route was a direct one, travelling overnight, but there were many stops and much shunting of carriages. It was nearly midday when we arrived at Kharkov.

At the station there was a routine check for all passengers as we got off the train. Tatiana had better luck here: when she smiled at the guards they waved her forward without examining our passports. I felt relaxed at having managed to get so far from the labour camp where I still had so many years to serve. We stayed with friends of Tatiana's, a couple with one child. They gave us a room to ourselves.

But soon the atmosphere changed. Tatiana became worried and edgy about me, saying she knew I would leave her soon. When I asked her why she felt that, she said:

'You've changed. You aren't so happy as you were in Leningrad. You're thinking about something all the time.'

'I can't deny it,' I said, relieved that she herself had broached the subject. 'You're right. You have been my salvation. No one could have done more to help me. I cannot find words to express my gratitude to you. I shall be obliged to you all my life.'

I had been planning how I could get across the frontier to Roumania – it would have to be back to Lvov first, or even through Nazi-occupied territory, I hadn't made up my mind.

'Let's enjoy our last few days together,' I tried to console her. 'Another thing which bothers me is money. I can't go on accepting your help. I shall return the money you have spent on me, every penny.'

She started to cry like a baby and put her arms around my neck. She held me close, sobbing:

'Oh no, no, you can't go. You owe me nothing – don't worry about that but I beg you, don't leave me, promise to stay with me, at least until the spring, until all the flowers come out, then it will be easier for me to face the loneliness.'

My face was wet from her tears. I could not give her an

97

answer. I kissed her all over her face. Already I knew that I could not stay more than a day or two. I felt only love and gratitude towards her; if times were different I would have been happy to stay with her, not only because of what she had done for me, but because she was a lovely person to be with. She couldn't stop crying. I tried to make her laugh, and her friends invited us for a meal. After my experiences I knew what a luxury it was to be able to sleep in a good bed.

Next morning I announced that I would be going to the Ministry of Health to see if I could arrange for papers which would enable me to apply for a job. She reacted strongly:

'No, you can't do that. It would be far too dangerous for you. They will know why you want the papers. I will get you the papers. My brother will help me.'

I could see that she would go to any lengths to keep me at her side. And it is true that if a Russian woman really loves you there is no length to which she will not go for you. She will sacrifice her life to make her man happy. When we kissed now I felt guilty; when we embraced I could feel her heartbeat throbbing on my chest. I stroked her face and wiped away her tears.

But, quite apart from my goal – escape from Russia – I knew that if I remained this dream would turn into a nightmare. Perhaps the risks we ran heightened our awareness and intensified that period of passionate love-making. She had drained me physically: we made love so often, day and night. We both had impulsive natures, quickly inflamed, and loath to stop. She took everything a passionate woman can take, and I had reached the stage where it was physically impossible for me to carry on for the simple reason that my weapon had become sore and painful through over-use. We had both become crazy with each other. She had her troubles too, but she never complained.

Every time I looked at her and our eyes met I felt great love and gratitude towards her, but I knew in my heart I must go. And as quickly as possible.

Next morning, I paid a visit to the local offices of the Ministry of Health. The government official who screened applicants for medical posts became quite friendly and gave me useful advice. He advised me to get to his home town of Dniepropetrovsk where I would find it easier to get a job in one of the rural areas under the jurisdiction of the city. Rural doctors were in short supply. He also gave me the name of relatives who lived in Dniepropetrovsk, a woman called Edkina Sosnow who lived in a large house where I would probably be able to stay. I should give her his regards. I asked if he could issue me with a travel warrant to Dniepropetrovsk. He laughed:

'Travel warrants are for people who are working but, since you are looking for work and need the help, I will issue you with a one-way warrant valid for three days, and a *naprablenya*, or recommendation, addressed to the health authorities of the city.'

So in the space of a short interview I obtained a newly-issued identity document stating my own name and my profession, and the purpose of my journey to Dniepropetrovsk, to apply for a post as rural doctor, all duly signed and stamped.

Next day, abruptly, secretly, my heart breaking, I set out for Dniepropetrovsk.

7

Dniepropetrovsk: Luba

The architecture of the city of Dniepropetrovsk made a very favourable and pleasant impression on me as I walked from the station. Leningrad, so famous for its historical buildings, I had hardly been able to see, but Dniepropetrovsk had been re-designed and enriched at the instigation of Catherine the Great, a woman after my own heart, and had originally been named Ekaterinaslav after her. A pity she was no longer around; but I felt at home.

The house I was looking for was in a side street off a wide avenue called Prospect Karl Marx. It was easy to find, a pleasant house, standing in its own garden.

A middle-aged woman, quite fat, with a lovely, kind face opened the door, and looked at me enquiringly with her expressive black eyes. Before she spoke I told her the name of the person who had sent me. She said:

'*Zacha ditye*, come in.'

She asked me to sit down and took my case from me. She spoke beautiful Russian, although from her name I thought she might be Polish. I explained my reason for coming to the city and asked if she knew of a place where I could get a room at a reasonable price. She smiled before she spoke:

'There are quite a few places that have rooms to let with their own bathrooms. Personally, I don't know of one, but my daughter who is a student of medicine would be able to enquire. She'll be home soon. In the meantime you must have something to eat. Leave your case here, go to the health department to make your enquiries, then by the time you come back Luba will be here.'

She turned to a table, took a photograph from it and held it out to me:

'That's Luba, my daughter.'

A good-looking girl. I complimented her on having such a nice daughter.

'My husband is dead, you know. He came back after a trip to the United States a few years ago and died. I live here alone now with my daughter.'

She seemed to have more than a passing interest in me from the way she looked at me. I thanked her and said I would be going to the Health Institute.

'Oh no,' she said, 'from my home no one, especially a hungry young man like you, can leave without eating.'

It would have been ungracious of me to refuse. I ate first. The health department was only about fifteen minutes' walk from the Sosnow house. I was directed to the second floor where I handed my papers to the person in charge who told me to return next day at 10 a.m.

When I left the building I strolled around the city looking at the most important buildings and landmarks. Everything was going smoothly. My thoughts returned to Tatiana. I was afraid she was still suffering about me and I couldn't help feeling guilty. Ought I to have stayed with her a few days more? I had warned her that I would have to leave when she least expected it, without saying goodbye. I could still see how her face turned to stone. But what good would it have done to have stayed with her, as she had pleaded, till the springtime?

It was early afternoon when I stood before the front door of the Sosnow house again. When I knocked I heard hurried footsteps in the hall, then Luba opened the door. She stood still in the doorway while we looked at each other for several seconds:

'*Pazalosti sachaditie.* Please come in.'

An appetizing smell of cooking was drifting from the kitchen. Luba asked me to take off my coat and sit down; she shouted to her mother:

'Mama, he's here. Come!'

Her mother came in smiling but said nothing. There seemed to be some conspiracy between them. At last the girl could stand it no longer:

'Tell him,' she said.

'We have decided to offer you a room here until you get settled. You can live with us.'

Luba looked at her mother thankfully. To me she said:

'My mother and I have been arguing. Mother thinks it wouldn't be proper for you to stay in the house with the two of us on your own. I think that's old-fashioned. The youth of the Soviet Union is not bound by old traditions. You are a doctor. Soon I shall be a colleague of yours, next year in fact. How can we let you go to live in some strange house? This is such a big comfortable house. We have two bathrooms, and you can have one of them.'

From my point of view it would be a very convenient arrangement. I was not thinking about the proprieties either: my concern was to find a place I could live in safety, to work and make some money, send money back to Tatiana, and only then make plans for the future. In spite of this something warned me not to stay in that house. I thanked them both for their kindness and told them that I already had an address where I intended to stay. The two of them immediately started trying to persuade me. Luba was at that time exceptionally beautiful, in her early twenties, with her mother's big eyes, but hers were green with black lashes and black hair, her skin a lovely golden colour. They managed to convince me that it would be the best solution for me. After all I had nothing to lose – or so I thought.

I shall never forget that day. On that day I committed one of the biggest mistakes of my life, one that I would regret for fifteen years.

My first evening at the Sosnow house was not a pleasant one. Luba's mother was watching her, praising her, saying how beautiful she was, that she was still only a child, that her whole life was devoted to the happiness of her only child.

'Are Jewish mothers where you come from as crazy as we Russian Jews are about their children?' she asked.

That night I went to bed early to escape from the boring conversation. I was sad too because I had lost my own mother as a boy of fourteen, and all my memories of her were good ones: how she loved me and looked after me. I carried her image in my soul and will do so until I die.

I lit a cigarette, pacing the room, wishing I had some vodka, when there was a soft knock on the door. It was Luba.

'I could hear you walking up and down and striking matches,' she said – the Russian matches certainly did make a loud noise when struck. Without an invitation she walked into the room:

'You know that's my bed and this is my room?'

'Why did you give me your bed then?' I asked.

'Well you said you were looking for a room with a bathroom, and you have one right here.'

'It's too early for me to sleep, can't we go out and you can show me the city?'

'There's nowhere to go. Only on Saturday or Sunday. There's more going on then.'

I asked her if her mother was asleep. She said that she wasn't and that she probably wouldn't sleep until she was sure that we were both sleeping.

She was giving the distinct impression that she had come here to flirt with me and that this conversation was only a pretext. She had fastened her green eyes on me, which I couldn't avoid, when suddenly she came up to me and kissed me directly on the lips – nothing erotic, a sisterly kiss, but it was enough for me. I took her in my arms and kissed her properly, the way an attractive woman should be kissed, and kept on until she was drunk with my kisses. I could tell she was not very sexually experienced. She was at the point where she would willingly have made love. I am never so carried away that I am unable to calculate. I knew her mother wasn't asleep, and I would have to get her out of my room. I pushed her away, with excuses about her mother hearing us. I knew from past experience that if you make love to a girl in her own house there is no way to stop her mother from hearing what's going on. My desire was aroused but I would just have to sleep.

Next morning, when I was eating the excellent breakfast Luba's mother had prepared, I could see she was looking at me in a strange way. Luba kept walking round the table in a freshly ironed white blouse, which contrasted with her golden skin, green eyes and black hair. When I had finished eating she asked if I would like to go to the University with her on the tram, and we could talk on the way. I declined, with the explanation that

I had been asked to return to the health department at ten that morning.

At the office they received me cordially. When I showed my papers I was told that no appointment could be made without an interview with the head of the health department for the whole municipality and with the head of the rural department of health. Furthermore, I would have to go to Moscow before they could issue a work permit. It was decided that I should travel to Moscow the following week and, since I had no money, they gave me a travel warrant for the return journey plus an advance of four hundred roubles. My application for a rural post was duly registered.

My luck had certainly held ever since I left the camp. I had expected many awkward questions, but it had all been remarkably easy and at the Kharkov health offices I think they were happy to receive applications for posts. They told me to come back at three in the afternoon to pick up the travel warrant and the money. When I returned in the afternoon they had also prepared a letter of introduction for me addressed to the head of the department of rural health in Moscow. The man who had worked on my application was a big, talkative chap:

'You're in luck. You'll be in Moscow in a few days,' he said. Usually I'm a big talker, but on this occasion I was pleased that I couldn't get a word in edgeways with him. He gave me two addresses of lodgings in Moscow.

That night, Luba's mother prepared me an especially good meal. When I showed them the documents I had been given and they saw I would soon be leaving, Luba turned quiet and sighed. Her mother looked at her.

'What's the matter?' I asked. She became embarrassed and tried to pass it off.

'And when do you expect to leave?' she asked me.

'It depends on you,' I replied. 'If you would like me to go now I can, but if it's alright with you I would like to stay for a few days more and get to know the city.'

Luba couldn't conceal her satisfaction at this:

'Oh that's good. We have a social evening at the Institute of Medicine on Saturday. You can come with me, and I'll introduce you to my friends – they all want to meet you.'

That evening there was vodka and a sort of home-made wine at dinner. In the more relaxed atmosphere we drank and I told jokes, which I enjoy doing, although sometimes I tend to go over the limits of decency, especially seeing that Luba's mother was there. The stories were rather obscene; I told joke after joke, some of them Jewish jokes. They both laughed so much that Luba's mother had to go and fetch a handkerchief to mop the tears from her eyes. She even told me one Jewish joke herself. It was an entertaining evening and quite late when we went to bed.

I must have been sleeping soundly when I woke to the touch of lips on my mouth. Luba was kneeling at my bedside. The room was in darkness, and when I put out my hand to switch on the light she put her hand on my arm:

'No, you'll wake her up. She's fast asleep now. I came to thank you for making her so happy this evening. I've never seen her laugh like that since father died.'

In general I don't like making love in the dark, but even in the dark one can find the right places. She got into my bed. Her nightdress was a long one, of thick material, difficult to hoist up, so I got her out of bed and tore it open down the front. The nightdress was so wide I wrapped it round my body as well. All she asked me was to be quiet so as not to wake her mother. It was difficult for me to curb my feelings while making love but we managed and she told me later how much she enjoyed it. We slept together until dawn.

The next day I felt very guilty and avoided Luba's mother. At first I thought she must be aware of what was going on, then, when she said nothing, I thought perhaps I was mistaken. When I asked Luba whether she thought her mother knew, she said:

'Don't worry.'

I told her not to come to my room any more, it was too risky. It didn't make any difference. I was woken again the next night; she was already next to me in the bed, naked and starting to kiss me.

'Why aren't you wearing anything, it's so cold?'

'To tell you the truth I didn't want to ruin another nightdress.'

'What did you do with the other one then?' I asked.

'I took it out of the house today and threw it away, but I

can't keep doing that, mother knows how many nightdresses I've got.' We finished up making love again, although I couldn't give myself wholeheartedly to the matter in hand because we were always afraid her mother would hear and come into the room.

Next night I locked the door with the key. The day after that was to be my last at Luba's house. As we sat at the dining table, when her mother's back was turned, Luba held up the key to my room to show me I wouldn't be able to do the same on the last night. So that last night was another love-making night, although I think she enjoyed it more than I did. By then I had been in the house a week.

When I left for the station next morning Luba came with me and made me give her my word that I would return to her house as soon as I got back to the city. But fate intervened. I didn't come back to Dniepropetrovsk until 1945, almost five years later. The only contact I made was to write to her mother thanking her for her kindness to me and telling her about my new life, but deliberately not giving my address.

A few months after leaving Dniepropetrovsk I sent a letter to Tatiana in which I sent her the money she had spent on me, and received a notification from the post office that the letter had been delivered.

8

Moscow: Gala and Co.

Winter in Moscow. It was the beginning of December 1940. I stood in front of the Kremlin watching the crowds crossing the square. Everybody was poorly dressed and, if one looked closely at their faces, there were signs of poor nutrition too, but they seemed quite cheerful and content as I discovered when I got into conversation with them. I have always hated being shabbily dressed myself and managed to find clothes from Western Europe on the black market. At that time a lot of consumer goods had been brought back by soldiers of the Soviet Union from Poland, especially clothing: shoes, shirts, coats, ties, anything they could lay their hands on. The Russian army of occupation had printed its own banknotes for use in occupied territories, and goods were paid for in this currency.

I registered at the Ministry of Health and was issued with a *carnet* signed by the Minister to the effect that I was a doctor of medicine awaiting an appointment as an Inspector of Health. I was given an advance of six hundred roubles a month until I should receive a salaried post. In the meantime I would be examined by a special commission which had the task of screening all the persons who arrived from Europe and applied for medical posts. After passing these tests I would be issued with a document which would entitle me to work in any part of the Soviet Union, always of course on appointment by the Minister of Health in Moscow. It seemed a lengthy and unnecessary procedure to me but I later discovered that it was a routine they observed with non-Soviet citizens about whom the Soviet authorities still retained some reservations.

So I stayed in Moscow, living in a comfortable room in a private house, and quickly got to know all the livelier elements. In this period of peace, in the winter of 1940–41, the most famous hotels in Moscow were the National and the Astoria: that is where the action was. They were frequented by foreign diplomats and visitors and the atmosphere was the closest one could get in Russia to the city life of pre-war Warsaw or Lvov. In Warsaw I had frequented the numerous *té dansant* where I could find the most elegant women whose husbands were busy in their offices. I had always been attracted by married women as a young man, and the attraction was mutual.

The women of Moscow could not compete with the elegance of Warsaw and practically all the attractive women I saw at the National or Astoria were the well-dressed mistresses of foreign diplomats who supplied them with European clothes and per-fumes. These women, the most sophisticated in Russia, were often double agents, and the parties they – and I – went to were riddled with NKGB men and informers. But even the most resolute woman agent who worked for the NKGB could, and often did, fall helplessly in love with her victim. So she had to play both sides for as long as she could get away with it. I was not involved in any of this. I just enjoyed life, and enjoyed it all the more because of the women of Moscow. To these women the men from Europe were enormously attractive: we behaved differently from the Russian men, we treated them differently. The Poles would gallantly kiss the hand of a Russian woman when introduced, usually on the back, but I (though secretly I despised the habit) would sometimes turn over the hand and kiss the palm, or open a door, or place a coat around a pair of shoulders: all attentions which women appreciate, and which the Russian men never paid.

This behaviour made the foreigners irresistible to the women and the Russians naturally resented it. However I did not care what the men thought so long as I never had difficulty in finding female company. Another attraction for the Soviet woman was the way the non-Russian men would kiss them on every part of their body. I was never indiscriminate in this practice, but, often, in the heat of passion and drunk with vodka, I would kiss them all over.

One of these women, Gala Bacharova, was the mistress of the First Secretary of the French Embassy, a tall willowy blonde with blue eyes, a wide Slav mouth and an irresistible smile which showed off her even white teeth. Her close friend, the deep-eyed Nokka Kapranova, was involved with the French Military Attaché.

I met Gala in the bar of the National Hotel. After a few days we became intimate friends. She told me it was not good for me to be seen hanging around hotels because most of the guests, Soviet or foreign, were under surveillance. When I asked why, she called me a stupid *durak*. She was right. Even in those days it was expensive. So far I had managed on my salary and the free hospitality I enjoyed at parties, but to go to the hotels three or four times a week would arouse suspicion. I had been able to augment my official salary with gifts pressed on me by friends and their families to whom I had given my professional services. But I loved the hotels and the parties, the food, the violins, the music, the women, the whole atmosphere. One invitation led to another: I met film producers, actors, opera singers, artists, many of them Polish Jews who had taken refuge in Moscow. They were living in high bohemian style; theirs was a privileged existence which they were given, or had snatched at, in recognition of their artistic merits. And these privileges the Soviet system tolerated and even encouraged – partly for genuine ideological reasons but partly of course as the most successful way of trapping those First Secretaries and Military Attachés.

On New Year's Eve, the last day of 1940, another friend of Gala's, Kira, gave a really splendid party. All the guests were either influential or beautiful: diplomats, artists, entertainers, military officers, high-ranking NKGB men in plain clothes, women with or without their husbands or lovers, some counter-espionage agents and informers. By this time I knew a lot of them, and was well known to the others there, especially the police who always remembered anyone seen frequently in the company of good-looking and well-dressed women.

I was at a table with a well-known actor and director of the Jewish National Theatre, Shlomo Lev Michelis. He was wearing decorations given to him by Stalin, who later had him liquidated. He was quite a character, with a bulldog expression. He was interested to hear my story, especially about how Jews lived outside Russia. When I told him that anti-semitism existed all over the world, not only in Nazi Germany, he whispered quietly to me in Yiddish :

'You're right, even here.'

I tried to keep off political subjects and got into conversation with Peter Kireczek, a Russian opera singer, a baritone. His wife, Tanya, had an exquisite face – even people who didn't know her would come near to look at her. We were sitting at a large circular table. There must have been eighty to a hundred guests in all, half of them beautiful women, but she was the one who really stood out. Her husband Peter wore a constant expression of jealousy; I took an instant dislike to him with his crocodile-like teeth.

Tanya excited me, and I could see that she was interested in me too. We ate large quantities of caviar, with pickled cucumbers and tomatoes washed down by vodka. I had managed to sit next to Tanya. There were plenty of other girls there but most of them seemed to have their escorts with them. Under the table I took off Tanya's shoe with my foot. At first she showed annoyance, but perhaps she was afraid to make a fuss because of her husband. Anyway she said nothing and by the time the toasts were being drunk I was tickling her instep with my toes. She started to laugh and even blushed. When an accordionist, a singer and guitarist came to our table she, her husband and I exchanged looks. I don't know why husbands never trusted me but I suppose they were right. By now I was stroking Tanya's leg under the table.

The toasts were followed by dancing. I danced with some of the other women first, then with Tanya.

'You have caused me the worst harm possible,' she murmured, 'I shall never forgive you!'

'What harm have I done?' I asked.

'You tore my silk stockings!'

In those wartime years a woman would rather tear a leg than a silk stocking. I squeezed her close. She didn't have the ideal figure for my taste, but I whispered in her ear that she needn't worry – I would get her another pair if I had to travel to Warsaw for them. I felt a gentle touch on my back. It was Peter. He wanted to dance with his wife; I relinquished her.

Kira, the hostess, had a charming little girl of five who had been woken by the noise and stood at the top of the stairs shouting:

'Mama, Mama!'

I ran up to her and talked to her to amuse her. I love talking to children between four and ten years old, and can capture their interest. I told her a story and made a bet with her for ten roubles that she didn't know where her mother kept her silk stockings.

She turned and walked to her mother's room, took a pile of stockings from a drawer, some new, some used.

'Here's the ten roubles,' I said as I paid the bet. I took her back to her bedroom then crept back to take a pair of silk stockings for Tanya.

On my way downstairs I could hear laughter coming from one of the rooms; when I pushed the door open I could see it was Gala making love with someone I didn't recognize:

'*Garinka*, you should close the door, he might catch cold.'

I went back to the party knowing it was time for a chat with one of the Russian men. The ones who worked with the secret police were very careful never to ask direct questions at a first meeting. They probably knew a lot about you before they spoke, and then they would allow you to do most of the talking to make it easier for them. When drinking is going on, the pattern can alter.

A Colonel Konyev of the special branch of police got into conversation with me in a very smooth way:

'You're a *vratch*, a doctor, aren't you? How did you get to know such lovely girls, when you've only been in Moscow such a short time? And to speak such good Russian so quickly – how did you manage that? Did you speak Russian before? You know, you could be very helpful to us. Why don't you come and see me? Here's my name and telephone number. Give me a ring, and we'll have lunch together.'

'Of course' – I looked at him – 'when I have time, I'll get in touch with you. What makes you think a man of my profession doesn't have the right to be in the company of such nice people? How would I have had the pleasure of meeting you if the door had been closed to me?'

'You're too clever,' he laughed. 'Here, let me give you a kiss,' and he kissed me on the cheek. 'Of course you are right. I like you. I hope I haven't offended you. Mostly people offend me but I never give offence to anyone.'

He was drunk, and I got rid of him. It was now the early hours of the morning, and many of the guests had left the party. Long after midnight Peter Kireczek had told his wife he was tired, but she told him she was still enjoying herself and if he wanted to go home he could – but by himself.

The floor was littered with debris and broken glasses. People were swaying, holding each other up and shouting '*Snovom Godom*, Happy New Year'. Peter didn't want to leave his wife. I could feel the packet which contained the stockings in my pocket. I must give them to Tanya, but her husband was stuck close to her side. I went over to Kira:

'You must get Peter away from Tanya, just for five minutes.' She was happy to help me and went up to Peter:

'Come on, Peter, you haven't danced with me yet,' she said. He tried to refuse, but she took his hand and pulled him on to the dance floor.

I quickly went to Tanya and danced with her. We danced very close: it's the only way to dance if you're a real man and she's a beautiful woman. Moving to the music in unison makes you feel that every part of your body lives; if you can get your knee between her thighs and she accepts it you're a new-born man, and if she doesn't accept it you have to make her. I tucked the stockings into the bodice of her dress. The stiff paper made one of her breasts look bigger than the other. She was slightly drunk and asked me where I had been.

'I went to Warsaw,' I whispered in her ear. Peter had gone back to the table and was watching us closely.

, Kira had seen what happened with the stockings and rushed Tanya off to the toilet. I stood by a potted plant near the door and talked with another girl with whom I intended to spend the next few hours. When they came out Tanya's dress had been rearranged and, though Tanya was laughing, Kira was serious: but she had got her stockings back. You could buy anything in those days with a pair of silk stockings or fine underwear or perfume.

The later it got the worse the room looked. Gala came down

the stairs bleeding from the face, with a black eye. When I asked what had happened to her she said it was her own fault.

'What do you mean?' I asked.

'*Garinka,* the Russian men are still not so expert in making love in the French manner. When I tried it, he beat me up and called me a swine!'

I left the party with Katya, the girl with whom I had spent the later part of the evening. When we left the place was devastated, as if the New Year, 1941, had been ushered in with an earthquake. The Russians are heavy drinkers and can be quite dangerous when they get out of hand.

Katya and I didn't recover until 2 January, but I hadn't forgotten Tanya.

On 3 January I went back to continue training at the outpatients' clinic in the suburbs of Moscow. My work was to be in epidemiology and food conservation and hygiene. I was not anxious to become a state health inspector and would have preferred general medical practice and abdominal surgery; but I had no choice, I would have to do the job I was given. I never lost sight of my goal, which was to get out of Russia. But, till the situation changed dramatically, my best chance would be to work well at my profession wherever I was most needed.

So I worked energetically for long hours and, outside work, I took everything I could get from life.

About three weeks after the party I discovered that Colonel Konyev had been taking a lot of interest in me and had made enquiries about me in the Ministry of Health, I learnt from one of the high-ranking administrators in the Ministry. It worried me to think what he might uncover. My escape was still very recent. Ought I to go into hiding or should I stay put and let what would happen happen?

I didn't have long to wait. I received a written invitation to present myself at the NKGB headquarters.

It was Colonel Konyev who wanted to see me. These NKGB secret policemen usually had two methods of treating people, a two-faced system: on the one hand they would try to impress anyone they were interested in that they were his friends, but of course they would only waste time and energy this way if they thought you could be useful to them in some way; on the other hand they would give you to understand some of the many ways they could make life difficult or even unbearable.

Colonel Konyev was looking at a small dossier when I was shown into his office. He looked up:

'I regret that it was I who had to invite you to come to see me,' he began. 'I would much have preferred it if you had come of your own accord.'

I laughed and asked him:

'What about me? How do you think I feel? You are the representative of a famous organization, and you must know that most of your compatriots are afraid of you. What shall I tell my colleagues when they ask me why I was called here?'

He laughed himself, a jolly, hearty laugh:

'The problem may not arise, you know. Some of our visitors don't go back to see their colleagues at work at all. They spend a few years here with us.'

Having let this sink in, he leant back in his chair and offered me a cigar.

'You know, you have a privileged position in a way. I would really like to become your friend and it's not for political reasons, it's because I would like to get to know, personally, all those girls you go around with.' He sighed. 'It's very hard for me; I mix with them and drink with them, but they know I'm closely involved in the surveillance of the diplomatic corps here in Moscow, and of course that makes it difficult for them to relax.' He sighed again.

'You hardly expect me to take you very seriously,' I said.

'Why not?'

'Seeing that it's common knowledge that nine girls out of ten work for your organization and are probably on the most intimate terms with you in private. . . .'

Angrily Konyev stubbed out his cigar; he seemed on the point of an outburst, but then regained control of himself.

'I hope you will take this seriously,' he said. He thumbed through the dossier in front of him. 'We have had our eyes on you ever since you became involved with all these Muscovite tarts here. I know that what you've said has always been extremely favourable to the Soviet government. But you have retained your Polish citizenship and so have a means of entry into the circles of the Polish government-in-exile here. We know however that you are very proud of being a Jew, a nationalist Jew. You are extremely able and courageous and can render the nation an exceptional service. As a citizen's duty we would like you to become one of our Soviet agents; we would train you for the job, and eventually send you into German-occupied territory to work for our Soviet people.'

I laughed :

'You really see the right qualities for a good agent in me?'

'Yes, unique and exceptional qualities. You speak several languages fluently, you are physically strong, a good drinker and a good entertainer. As a qualified doctor you can make yourself at home anywhere.'

He sat back, very satisfied, and re-lit his cigar. I stared at him in silence, thinking that he was nothing more than a policeman after all. He raised his voice :

'Why are you looking at me like that?'

'Why do you shave your eyebrows?' I asked.

'Why do you ask that question?'

'In the West only pederasts shave their eyebrows.'

'Well here in Russia every other man does it; and what is more there are hardly any pederasts here in Russia.'

I had thrown him off balance. He stood up :

'We have talked enough. It's lunchtime. You will not mention this conversation to any person under any circumstances. Come back to me in one week with your answer.'

I stood up in my turn :

'There's no need for me to come back in a week's time. I can give you my decision here and now. Firstly, I will never in my life became an informer or co-operate with an institution like yours. The government is paying you a lot of money to put innocent souls in prison. I think you should do the hard work, get the information you need for yourselves and not depend on informers to get your decorations and medals for you. To become a spy against the Nazis is another matter; but I don't think I could do even that – I don't want to do it anyway. But I am perfectly prepared to serve the Soviet people, whom I much admire, as a doctor.'

He ran up to me, grabbed my lapels, thrust his face into mine:

'Do you know, do you know what we have offered you? Millions would be only too pleased to help me. But here you are, a parasite, leading the life of Rasputin in Moscow, fucking all the most beautiful women of the so-called high society. But we don't intend to interfere with your life if you accept our proposal.'

'And if I don't?'

'You seem to have a lot of sympathy with – what did you call them – innocent souls in prison. Dead souls, I would say. You may soon share their fate.' He sat down and thumbed through the dossier:

'It says here that you have an exceptional, almost an electronic memory. We'll remember that!' That brought a little smile to my face: Konyev could not imagine how much sympathy I had and why. I looked at him disdainfully:

'I must congratulate you on having the audacity to propose that I help you with your dirty police work! But if that's the way you want to get people to risk their lives for the Soviet Union, by threats and blackmail, you will have to look for someone else. I wish to go immediately.'

In a dispirited voice he said:

'Go home. I had hoped you were more patriotic and would be pleased to help us in the fight for socialism. Come back in a week with an answer.'

I never did, of course, for he already had my answer. But I often wondered if what I said then in the heat of the moment – before this, as Konyev said, I had always been very careful to speak favourably of the Soviet system – started off a train of investigations.

The long cold Moscow winter dragged on. I knew they would not let me remain in Moscow to work once my training was completed, and that I would have to go to one of the outer Republics. After I had made enquiries I had three possibilities to consider: Tbilisi, or Tiflis in Georgia, between the Black Sea and the Caspian, or the city of Tashkent, or Samarkand, even further distant in the province of Uzbekistan, in the heartland of Asia.

I spoke to as many people as possible who could describe conditions in these places.

Another pressing reason for my interest in getting away from Moscow in the spring of 1941 was what I considered to be the imminent threat of war between the Soviet Union and Nazi Germany. Although very little news was given officially, I was able to listen to foreign radio stations, and rumours filtered through from the diplomatic contacts I had made. Much of the confidential information I acquired was through a friend called Nusbaum who was a relative of Madame Litvinoff, wife of the ex-Foreign Minister, and directly from Madame Litvinoff herself. Born in England as Ivy Low she had married Max Litvinoff in London in 1917 and moved to Moscow after the Russian Revolution.

By April, the Moscow winter seemed interminable. It was not till two months later however that my friends were proved right.

On 22 June 1941 the Germans swarmed over the Russian border. The volcano of the Second World War erupted with all its force, and the destruction and fighting which we still continue to witness in every part of the world is the result of this major upheaval in the history of our poor divided planet.

9

Tashkent

By May I had tired of the hectic life in Moscow. My training was complete, and I made up my mind to ask the health department to send me to Kazakstan or Uzbekistan. It was not difficult to obtain a *komandierovka* (travel permit) from the health authorities, together with a letter of introduction to their department in Tashkent in which it was suggested that I should be placed wherever they considered most necessary. I travelled to Samarkand, about a thousand eight hundred miles to the south-east of Moscow, at the foot of the northern slopes of the Himalayas.

In addition to the local populace, mostly Moslem, many families from Moscow, Leningrad and other more northerly cities used to come south to Samarkand in order to escape the intense cold of the Russian winter; but by now there was a much more pressing reason: the imminent threat of war with Germany. So, even though the 'fashionable' winter season was over, an influx of the well-connected, the families and mistresses of the higher ranks of government and party, was pouring down from the north.

Before going on to Samarkand, I stopped for a while in the city of Tashkent to visit the father of Nokka Kapranova, an engineer who had been in charge of the construction of the railways of Uzbekistan, a workers' hero, by birth a Muscovite, in his late fifties at the time. He received me very kindly in his *dacha* outside the city, introduced me to his second wife, Zoya, and asked me if I needed any help. He was a very outspoken anti-Stalinist, though I tried to avoid talk of politics with him. I got him on to what I thought – wrongly – was a safer subject: his family.

'My daughters in Moscow have written to tell me that they

want to come here for the summer.' He looked at me over the top of his half-spectacles. He had a little grey beard.

'What can the *vragi*, the enemy, be up to if my children want to come here at this time of year? They will probably bring their mother here too. How do you like that! I am a bad father, divorced twenty years ago from my first wife, but they always want to come here! I suppose they love the big peaches in the garden, or the honey. They always used to hate the climate here in summer, so why do they want to come here now?'

We walked together around the garden. He took me into a little shed which he used as a workshop. He started to file on some metal and suddenly looked up:

'Well, you have only just arrived from Moscow. What's going on there? Do you know all four of my daughters?'

'Only two of them,' I answered.

'Which ones do you know? The one who is married to the army officer or the one with a Jewish husband?'

'What is that, a Jew?'

He removed his glasses and scratched his beard, ignoring my question.

'Come on back to the house. I'll introduce you to Zoya. I should think she'll faint when I tell her my ex-wife will be coming with the four girls.' He continued along the path in front of me:

'Like it or not, they are all my children. My first cow gave me four daughters. With Zoya I have no children, but she gives me a quiet, peaceful life.'

Back at the house he presented me to Zoya, a pleasant woman at least twenty years younger than Kapranov. We all sat down for a drink.

Zoya said:

'It will be your four daughters, and all their children too, to say nothing of their mother. My God, where will we fit them all in? If we hadn't rented the cottage to Koch and his family we would be able to manage.'

Her husband looked at her:

'Don't you worry. There's no need for you to worry.'

Then he suddenly put me a question:

'So you don't know what a Jew is?'

'No.'

He grunted and said nothing. I wouldn't let the matter drop:
'What is a Jew, Mr Kapranov?'

'Jews are the people who have all the highest government jobs, starting with Kaganovitch and finishing with Beria.'

'But Beria isn't a Jew,' I corrected him.

He laughed and said:

'But you must be.'

'If you say so, you're probably right,' I answered.

I left soon after. It was nothing new for me to find Russians who did not like the Jews, and when it suited them they would name as Jews people who were not.

I spent a few weeks in Samarkand, and visited Bukhara, Ashkabad and many cities of Uzbekistan and Turkmeniya and the surrounding countryside which was very beautiful – intensely cultivated steppe, producing rice, wheat and cotton interspersed with plentiful fruit trees, especially peach trees, bearing enormous red and yellow fruit, as well as apple, plum and pear trees. There were a variety of melons, tomatoes and mushrooms too, as well as vineyards. At sunset flocks of sheep wound along tracks shepherded home by men and dogs. All flourished in the benign climate.

The peasant homes were constructed of mud caked on to timber frames, then painted white; the few brick-built houses belonged to the wealthy, but the peasant dwellings looked well in the beautiful surroundings.

I had saved a little money from my work in Moscow and registered with the health authorities to await a post in Tashkent, the largest city of the region, which had become a centre for non-Russians exiled by the war. I even found there people I had known before the war.

At Tashkent life was easy and pleasant. The Soviet authorities were obliged to close their eyes to the capitalist style of life which the people enjoyed, and which extended as far as Georgia and Armenia. Even to this day the three most prosperous Soviet Republics are Uzbekistan, Georgia and Armenia.

In Tashkent we didn't get the news of the German invasion until two days after it had begun. Although the city was so far

away from the frontier there was an awareness of the serious-
ness of the new development, and soon more tangible evidence
of the misery of war was brought to everyone by the daily
influx of refugees from the Ukraine, Russia and Byelorussia.
The young men were conscripted for military service. At the
railway station distraught parents embraced their sons while the
refugees continued to pour in on the trains. Every fit young man
and every specialist who could be of use in the war was called
up. The *blitzkrieg* launched by the Germans was catastrophic
for Russia at first. They lost city after city, powerless to stem
the German advance. The news we got was the news which the
government wanted us to know, censorship was strict, but the
incoming flux of refugees told their stories of what they had
seen, and from these accounts and other contacts something of
the truth became known.

I had been told that all the Kapranov daughters had now
arrived at their father's home, and I took the earliest opportunity to go to the house, for my friends had told me that
Nokka, the second daughter who had been the French Military
Attaché's mistress in Moscow, had been trying to get in touch
with me through some of my Polish friends; she was anxious to
see me because her sister Tanya's child was very ill. It was a
pleasure to see Nokka again and to treat her niece.

Meanwhile, Tashkent was changing by the hour.

As the refugees poured into the city in wave after wave, day
and night, the black market, which had already existed before
the influx, started to boom. Then the local Moslem population,
confronted by this invasion, started to exploit the needy. Food
became currency. The homeless gave away their most valuable
possessions, whatever they had been able to carry with them:
clothes, cutlery, gold coins, gold teeth, watches and jewellery,
in exchange for food.

I personally witnessed these deals myself on many occasions.
Once while travelling on an open tram I saw a local Moslem
holding a sack of rice between his legs. Wrapped around his
body he wore a rolled-up scarf containing notes. He was busy
bargaining with two Russians and dipping his measure into the
sack to serve them. His two customers kept complaining that
he was giving them short measure while, during the argument,

another Russian slit open the money bag from behind, gradually extracting notes and passing them forward to his friends. They paid for the rice with the same money! Suddenly another Moslem saw what was happening and gave a shout. The sack fell to the floor of the tram and split open. The Russians got well away. The other passengers laughed heartily. But by no means all the local populace were so avaricious – nor all the newcomers so crafty.

Those refugees who were lucky enough to have friends or relations in Tashkent, or Uzbekistan or Kazakstan, or the outer Republics were accommodated somehow, but for the hundreds of thousands, perhaps millions, who did not, it was a terrible experience. They even slept in the open fields.

Meeting places were set up at the railway stations and families who had got separated went there in search of each other or to hear news. This influx and confusion continued day after day. Outside the railway station at Tashkent there were public gardens which had been taken over by rows and rows of refugees who lay on the ground in despair: not only Russians, but Poles, Byelorussians, Ukrainians, Jews and other nationals from all of the countries occupied by the Nazis.

Heartbreaking scenes were enacted there, some of which I myself witnessed: a mother who found a lost child, one brother finding another brother, a husband reunited with his wife.

The resources of the local authorities faced with such a mass of people were soon exhausted. I became fearful of the outbreak of epidemics which would inevitably result: typhoid, dysentery and other intestinal infections.

I went to the station every day in the hope that I might find one of my brothers or sisters or their children, for, of course, Russian-occupied Poland was the first land to be overrun by the Nazis. We had been a family of forty-three, and of them all I loved my little brother Mischa the most because my mother had died very young, my sisters had married, my father remarried twice, but Mischa had been still a child and needed love. He had been living more or less dependent on his older sisters, who had their own husbands, and on his stepmothers. That is why I always looked for him. When I had last seen him he had been a small boy of twelve or so, with bright blue eyes and big ears (I think the fact that my father used to lift him by the ears made them even larger, and he would sometimes twist them as a punishment; he hadn't been able to do that to me).

The daily procession of tragedies I witnessed at the station made me think of ways of helping these victims of war. I reported to the local health authority and offered my services, free if necessary, to help ease the lot of the refugees. They accepted me immediately on a temporary basis, and I was appointed Health Inspector in charge of the refugees. Apart from my medical training, my ability to speak many languages fluently and my administrative experience all helped, and I was paid a salary.

We saw one face of the tragedy by day, but at night there were other dangers. Often we would hear a despairing scream as a sleeping refugee awoke to find that he had been robbed of the last coins and valuables he had managed to keep. Such robbery was easier at night. One old man I saw chasing a thief, shouting 'Robber!' at him, dropped dead as he ran, struck down by a heart attack.

The town officials seemed impotent before the weight of the problem. What more could I do to help? Days, weeks went by. Sometimes I managed to scrounge a supply of food: meat, oil, salt, flour, rice and even sugar, but the need was always greater than the amount I could find. Friends distributed the food in accordance with my instructions; I knew which were the really destitute, and which were the ones who had money and who even took part in the local black market. They preyed upon their fellow refugees, buying their last valuables for next to nothing and selling them at high profits.

My ways of supplying food were unorthodox and often illegal. Food supplies had to be provided by *kolhozs*, or local farm co-operatives, which were headed by the secretary of the *raispolkom*, or local council. They in their turn were under the administration of the *oblastnoipolkom*, or rural district and the local Party Secretary. I knew some *kolhozs* had plentiful supplies of food in storage, and the municipal authorities could order any *kolhoz* to hand over food stores for any special emergency.

At a party I had got to know a Lieutenant Cepuik of the NKGB who was working at the time with a high-ranking officer in Tashkent. He had asked me to see one of his children who was ill because Nokka Kapranova had told him how I had helped her niece. His two-year-old daughter had entero-colitis, and I treated her when he gave me to understand that he had more confidence in foreign doctors.

I decided to take him to the station to show him the plight of the refugees there. He was a good-hearted man and was stunned by the misery. That same evening we had dinner at the National Hotel and got quite drunk. I asked if he could help me to help those people. Drunk as he was, he grabbed my lapels, brought my face close to his, and whispered:

'I can, and I will, do a lot for them. Remember what I say, I'm not drunk . . . you will see.'

A few days later I was at his home to see my little patient who was not yet fully recovered. As I was drinking tea he came in, obviously pleased to see me. He called me into his bedroom, closed the door and took some official orders from his pocket. They were orders addressed to different *kolhozs* to hand over to the bearer the provisions listed. They were all signed by the secretary of the *oblastnoipolkom*.

He spoke quietly:

'I have obtained these orders under false pretences, and we could both be imprisoned or even shot.' He went on: 'If you undertake this, and something goes wrong, you won't give me away – you asked me for help, and the only way I can help those poor devils is to get the food. Don't ask me any questions. I trust you. I can get you orders like this once a month. Tomorrow the Colonel's driver, Yuri Zoyev, will be coming here. You will meet him and he will arrange for the transport of the supplies.'

I quickly switched from tea to vodka, thanked him for his help and the confidence he had placed in me. I assured him I would never sell him out if anything went wrong but asked why he was taking such a risk.

He looked straight at me (he was quite good-looking except that he had plucked eyebrows):

'Feelings for humanity,' he said, 'and because you saved my child.'

There was no need for me to talk more, or to get drunk with him. I left with the orders in my pocket. That night before I slept I took out the orders and re-read them: they were all that I needed.

Next day I went to see Nokka Kapranova and her sister; I was now a regular visitor to the *dacha* outside Tashkent, well received by all the family except Tanya whom I didn't like. She was a widow who tried to be something of a snob, a cold fish as far as I was concerned.

In view of the increase in the size of his family the old man had notified the Jewish family, Koch, who lived in the adjoining cottage, that they would have to leave. It would not be an easy matter to oust them as they had a signed lease which did not expire until a few months later.

Old Kapranov would rant:

'My house is full of enemies, *vragi*. My family I have to accept, but I'll get rid of that fat Jew in twenty-four hours! He showed me an identity card which says he is a special agent for the NKGB. He told me not to try any monkey business. He told me he won't go. How do you like that? And in my own house!'

Nokka tried to calm him:

'*Papachka*, be patient, don't upset yourself. We shall manage until the time comes for him to leave.'

I could see that the old boy had had a few drinks, something he did not do normally. He kept nodding his head; then, looking over his half-spectacles at me, he addressed himself to Nokka:

'Why did you all have to come here? And why did you bring that old cow with you? Since you arrived I've been unable to sleep. I've lost my peace of mind. Why should I stand for having my house full of enemies?' His voice grew louder and louder: 'I told you once, a long time ago, that you would all come begging for my help one day, and now you're all here, ugh ugh. . . .' He shook his head from side to side.

She was embarrassed and tried to quieten him. I already knew him well and how to handle him. I took his arm:

'Come with me. I want to speak to you alone.'

Talking gently, I led him from the room out into the back garden down the steps. He took a watch from his pocket and shook me off:

'In a few minutes you will see something you will remember all your life.'

I tried to walk him round the garden, but he hurried into his workshed where he had a good view of the front gates and the cottage. He stumped out of the gates on to the road:

'They're late.'

I enquired whom he was expecting.

'Two friends of mine in their lorry. They are going to move that Koch out of the cottage.'

'Have you an order to authorize you to do that?' I asked.

'Of course,' he replied.

I wondered how he intended to carry out his threats. Something told me it would be unpleasant. He took out his keys and locked the front door of the house, then went round the back and locked the other door too.

It was late in the afternoon when a large open lorry pulled up at the gates. There were three men inside in addition to the driver. Kapranov opened the gates and directed them to stop in front of his house. Then he closed the gates. He looked at me:

'If you like you can watch and see how I get rid of Jews.'

This sort of remark was a red rag to me. In other circumstances I would have resorted to physical force, but Kapranov was an old man and, after all, he had always been very kind to me personally. So I kept my temper under control.

He hurried to his workshop and returned with some papers, then went up to the door of the cottage and shouted to Mrs Koch:

'In the presence of these witnesses I will read to you an order which has been signed and stamped by the local authorities which directly concerns you!' Then he started to read from the document:

'Alexei Kapranov, Hero of the Soviet *Trud* (an award for exceptionally hard work), orders that you should leave these premises within one hour. Your belongings are to be loaded on to this waiting truck and will be transferred to another cottage, also the property of Alexei Kapranov, where you may remain as long as you wish. This cottage will be occupied by his own family from today. Signed: Kapranov, proprietor of this *dacha*.'

The woman started to laugh, but soon stopped when the men pushed past her and started to move out the furniture. She started to shout and ran to the telephone to call the police, but the wires had been cut. She screamed and cried, but Kapranov took no notice and shouted:

'Pack, pack, you have to get all this shit out within the hour!'

It was terrible. The desperate, lonely woman, powerless to oppose him, started to cry and plead for help.

The commotion had been heard in the main house. Nokka opened the window:

'Papa! What are you doing?'

I said: 'Be reasonable, wait at least for her husband to get here.'

He pushed past me, ran into the workshop and emerged with a loaded rifle. He fired into the air, shouting:

'If any of you lot come out of the house, I'll shoot you.'

Then he turned his attention to the men who were moving out the furniture and loading it on to the lorry in a disorderly fashion with clothes spilling from the drawers.

I tried to console the woman as she watched their belongings from the two bedrooms, living-room, bathroom and kitchen being bundled out. The old man stood by with his loaded rifle. I knew he had been drinking and was afraid of what he might do next. I thought of ways to get the gun from him.

At that moment, when the loading was almost complete, Mr Koch and his son arrived at the gates. Finding them locked, he called to his wife. The son too shouted;

'Mama.'

She cried all the more, and shouted back to them. Her son tried to climb over the high gates, but Kapranov let fly with his rifle and he dropped back. Their distress was too much for me, and I ran to the old man and dragged the rifle from him. I pushed him into his workshop in spite of his loud protests and opened the gates.

The son had not been hit. When father and son rushed in I

locked the gates behind them. Then I removed the bullets from the rifle, and let Kapranov out.

The removal men were still busy, but the cottage was now almost empty. Kapranov, Koch and I all looked at each other, speechless. Koch went towards the telephone but his wife told him that the wires had been cut. We were all outside the cottage and Kapranov went to the door and locked it. The lorry moved out. Suddenly the old man took out a loaded pistol from his pocket, pointed it at Koch, and burst out:

'You may be an NKGB agent. You may even work for Beria himself, but this is my house. I let you in here out of pity, not for the money, and now I have all my family here. . . .' He kept shaking the pistol in Koch's direction. I edged away.

'Your things have been taken to another house. It's a good place and you can stay there. Don't try to make any trouble. I will shoot you or have you arrested if you do.'

Koch, a tall fat man, stood quite still. His son had his arm around his mother who was still sobbing. Kapranov continued:

'My other telephone is still working, and unless you go now I will have you charged with black marketeering. You bought gold coins from me at a black market price, and you've been in other shady deals too.'

He was getting more and more wild in his accusations and so enraged that he was hardly aware that I had edged up to him and quietly prised the pistol from his hands. No blood had been spilt.

All Kapranov's family, his two wives and his daughters, were watching from the windows of the house.

Koch's only words were:

'If I go to prison, you will come with me.'

The old man, who by now had lost all control, replied:

'I'd rather be in jail in peace than have all these enemies in my house.'

I told him to go into the house and remain with his family. Koch I advised to go to the other house quietly. It had been a terrible experience for him and his family but, in spite of the danger to life and limb, Kapranov's measures had proved effective. Before he left Koch thanked me for what I had done.

From that day onwards I had to respect Kapranov: firstly

because he had had the determination, organizing ability, and courage to plan the whole move, and to tell no one until the last minute; secondly, because I realized that his action had nothing to do with Koch being a Jew. He had wanted more comfort for his family and himself; and, although he shouted and swore at them, he loved his family.

Later we were all sitting in the first Mrs Kapranov's room, where she lived with Tanya and another of Nokka's sisters, when the old man came in with a bottle of vodka and a hunk of fat bacon. It was the only occasion on which I saw him speak to his first wife:

'Can't you see, you cow, that I had to make space for your children?'

He asked me to come to Nokka's room where we had a drink to celebrate his victory. I thought of the old woman, pale and silent.

'Why don't you ask her in, just for a drink?' I asked.

He waved my remark aside:

'That old cow! She's never had a drink in her life!'

Then he worked out who should move where.

'The cottage will be for Tanya and her two children. You, Nokka, will have your own room for yourself, and your mother will be alright with Claudia.'

Nokka went to him and kissed his forehead:

'*Papinka*,' she asked, 'weren't you afraid to do such a thing?'

'There was no other way.'

She persisted:

'What will happen if he comes back with the police?'

'Don't you worry about that. I'm too old to be sent to prison and, if he goes to the police, he's the one who will end up in jail.'

From Kapranov's *dacha* I went to keep my appointment with Yuri Zoyev who proved to be a strong, squarely-built, Slav type. He wore plain clothes although he was in the service of the NKGB, and I got into the limousine. He drove. We went somewhere near the railway station for a drink. He already knew everything and took the four orders from me.

'We shall put the supplies from all four of these orders into one official military truck. I shall drive it and you will sit next to me. Come to my home next Monday evening, and we shall leave early Tuesday morning at 6 o'clock. It's an hour and a half's drive from Tashkent, so it will be quite early when we get there. Two of the *kolhozs* are near to each other and the other two are en route. If all goes well, we should be back in Tashkent by lunchtime.'

I had little to say, and agreed to everything without asking questions. I took down his address. I must admit I was uneasy; I had no idea what risks might be involved, what checks might be expected, and worst of all I had to rely on someone else's ability and intelligence. But the hunger and misery of those wretched refugees I saw every day at the little park at Tashkent made me overcome my doubts and sharpened my resolve.

A few days before our expedition I was at the station at Tashkent when a man called Rubin, a compatriot, a refugee from Kolomyya, told me that a Polish girl had arrived in Tashkent and was somewhere in the garden outside the railway station in a miserable condition. She had been told I was in Tashkent and had come specially to see me.

'Who is it?' I asked, baffled.

'Cristina.'

Cristina! The lovely singer with whom I had spent my last night in Poland before I tried to cross the Roumanian border, who had been so good to me and visited me in jail – almost a member of my family, one might say!

The news had an indescribable effect upon me. I rushed out to the gardens running from one side to another like a lunatic, looking into every face. Many of the refugees were still sleeping, their faces covered against the morning sun. I lifted the coverings to look at the faces. I knew where to go because I always knew where the most recently arrived had been sent. Several times I thought I had found her. I went round and round in circles:

'Oh God, I must find her and help her.'

As I stood before a bunch of people; men, women and children, I suddenly saw her, sitting on top of a bundle, in a grey coat with a grey fur collar. She had her back to me, but I recognized her. I came up to her, placed one hand on her shoulder and, with the other, cupped her chin:

'*Kshisha, kohana,* darling.'

She stood up slowly, tears rolling down her pale cheeks. A scarf was tied under her chin. I started to kiss her eyes, cheeks, lips, but it only embarrassed her, she returned my kiss like a stranger. She had completely altered. The people around started to stare; they had seen me several times. I took her by the arm:

'Come with me.'

She wanted to lift up her bundle.

'Leave it there,' I said.

'No, I must take it,' she said.

I took her to Nokka's home. On the way there, twenty minutes by car, she told me she wanted nothing from me, that she had heard that I was always to be seen in the company of beautiful women, that she would make no claims on me, only that she was glad to see me.

She had been told that I was well and working in Tashkent. Her first reaction had been to try to get away, to avoid meeting me, because she was so ashamed of her appearance, but then she decided to wait for me.

'Why did you cry so much when I found you?' I asked.

'I saw you coming from a long way off, I saw you searching for me. I don't know why I cried so, whether it was happiness or shame.'

Before we arrived at Nokka's house she told me what had happened after she left me in the prison in Stanislav. The examining magistrate with whom she had formed an intimate friendship in order to help me had himself been arrested and placed in prison. She had been imprisoned at the same time. They had released her after a few months and she had been sent to a town called Zitomir near Kiev.

We arrived at the *dacha*. We were lucky to find Nokka at home. She showed us into her room. We left Cristina there for a moment while I explained outside and told Nokka how she had risked everything for me. I had not yet become Nokka's lover, my girl friend then was Gala, so she was not jealous. In any case, Nokka was very kind and good-hearted. She looked deep into my eyes:

'Of course, *dorogoy*, my dear, of course I shall help her. I'll find some clothes and let her rest and recover. Leave her with me.'

So I left Cristina with Nokka.

Next day I took a bitter decision. When she had rested and was dressed in decent clothes I gave her some money and sent her on to some friends in Samarkand who had been entertainers. I gave her a letter to take, in which I asked them to help her find work. She had a lovely voice and if those people outside the station could have seen her again they wouldn't have recognized her. It was at the same station that I put her on a train and said goodbye. She leaned through the window as the train pulled out. We kissed, both of us in tears. I never saw her again. She never wrote. She understood that she had no place in my life any more.

Circumstances sometimes force us to act against our feelings. As soon as she had heard I was in prison, this woman had risked her liberty and perhaps her life by coming to visit me there and, furthermore, had brought me a revolver in the mistaken belief that it would help me. She knew how aggressive I was and had certainly thought I would use it to escape. Frequently I had reflected on what might have happened if I had taken the gun and used it. I would surely have been dead.

The last occasion, when I had met her in the prison, now seemed like a dream. Most people say dreams are fleeting, but this was a dream which would not leave me. I had thought of her so often: in prison, in the camp, in Moscow. She paid a price to get into the prison to see me: she had paid with her body. Did my thoughts return to her because I loved her?

Over the past eighteen months our lives had not been so very different; but she was morally broken after her release from prison, and had existed since then in poverty with no hopes for the future, whereas I had managed to make the best of a difficult situation. Do we not shape our own destiny? Here she was, a year and a half later, in wretched circumstances.

When I had kissed her in the little park, while the others all stared at her, did I feel love for her – or was it merely pity? Why had I not let her stay with me longer?

If I had let her stay with me, to try and repay her for her

goodness to me, she would have altered my life. But I no longer belonged to myself. I had dedicated all my efforts to obtaining food for the refugees, although I had often asked myself:

'Why are you doing this? Why risk so much for them?'

The reason was simple: there were wretches of all ages and kinds there, young and old, and no one had raised a finger to help them when they most needed it. I had to carry on.

Cristina and I looked deep into each other's eyes for a long, long time. She cried. I cried because I had not been fair to her. Goodbye, *Kshisha*. I stood watching the train draw away into the far distance.

10

Nokka: Nokka Alone

That Saturday night Gala, my beautiful blonde Gala, was throwing another party, which I remember as the party not this time of the silk stockings but rather more dramatically of the silk pants. It happened this way.

Gala and many of the old Moscow crowd, I should explain, had come south to Tashkent at the same time as Nokka Kapranova. She had enough influence and protection to travel wherever she pleased. The usual people were there mingling with many new faces; about forty or fifty altogether. Lovely girls and delicious snacks were thick on the ground. Tanya Kireczek was there with her husband, Peter the baritone, plus Nokka, Kira, and some of my Polish friends, among them Karl Gudman (who now lives in Amsterdam).

Jazz was all the rage. It was a calm, cool night, the stars shining brightly. There were two large rooms, one of them divided into compartments by screens behind which there were beds. There was plenty of music, drinking, singing and eating.

It was getting quite late when Kireczek was called to the telephone to be informed that his mother was very ill, and that he should go to her immediately.

Tanya prepared to leave with him, but he said :

'No, there's no need for you to come. My mother doesn't even speak to you, so she will want to see you even less now. I shall go to her alone. You can go home now, or else I can come back here and fetch you.'

I winked at Kira who persuaded Peter to leave Tanya with us. He concurred.

Gala was a highly-sexed, jealous girl. However much I made love to her and satisfied her, she was always ready to start again.

She used to say I would know when she had had enough when she lost consciousness. She was strong, but I could manage her. Sometimes she was so exhausted from our love-making that she fainted. Once revived and with a vodka inside her, her desire would flare up again. She flirted with all men.

The only person she really feared might be a rival was Nokka. In Moscow I had not found Nokka particularly attractive. She was good-looking, with an exceptionally lovely figure, but I had no chance to get close to her or involve her in conversation because Gala was a very jealous woman. She watched over me like a cat. But even in Moscow she could not prevent the exchange of looks between us. Nokka's deep blue-green eyes were not as dramatically beautiful as Gala's, but she always had a fine, clear look about her.

I suppose that, since I made a point of visiting her father as soon as I reached Tashkent, she must have made a considerable impression on me. Sometimes we already love.people before we come to recognize the fact. Or did I seek out Nokka's father simply to have some contact in my new place of work? Whichever it was, Nokka was to play an important role in my life, as Gala had instinctively realized. For a woman often has a feeling about these things: even if she says nothing, she knows what's happening.

Until now I had never made advances to Nokka, but I had enjoyed dancing with her because she had very curvy hips, and I would hold her there as we danced. She was more refined than Gala, who was more of a show-girl type. But no one could challenge Gala's unrivalled beauty.

When Gala spotted me dancing closely with Nokka, she came up to us and started to rub noses with me – it seemed to turn her on. When the dance ended she forced me into her bedroom, which she had to herself, and asked me to make love to her. It was no hardship! Although she was the only occupant of the room, there was a screen around her bed.

She unbuttoned my trousers for me and guided me on to target. It all took some time, as she was a woman not quickly or easily satisfied.

People noticed we were missing and suddenly Tanya Kireczek

walked in. Gala was ready to leave, straightening her dress. Someone in the other room shouted to her:

'Gala, come on out!' and she left the room.

I grabbed Tanya and led her to the bed. She started to protest, saying: 'No, no.' I stopped her mouth with kisses and undressed her at the same time. She began to lose control and I quickly took off her pants, which were of very fine silk, and stuffed them into my pocket. As we made love, I felt she had surrendered herself completely to me. Eventually she wanted to go back to the other room but, when we tried the door, we found it locked. Gala had done it, and had removed the key. She let us out in the end but it must have been nearly one o'clock by which time Peter had returned to collect his wife. He looked at me suspiciously. I didn't feel guilty, elated rather, because when I get it into my head to make love to a woman, I must do it, whatever the risk involved, and even if I have to travel thousands of miles.

The party broke up. As Nokka left, she kissed me on the cheek:

'Good night, *Garinka*.'

As I prepared to leave, Gala said:

'Oh no. You'll have to stay here tonight,' and she came up to me rubbing her nose against mine, with a glass of vodka in her hand:

'Drink!'

She handed me the glass and poured out a tumblerful of vodka for herself. We both drained our glasses. There we were again, back in bed, naked. As she sat on me and leaned down:

'Well, you *yobar*, you fucker, you Rasputin, who fucks better, Tanya or me?'

As we were trying to test the point, we were interrupted by bangs on the window. It was Peter.

'Come on, open the door!' he shouted.

There was nothing for it, we had to stop, he was making such a racket. Some of the girls in the other room went to the door. We were the last to come out of the bedroom. He had a gun in one hand, and Tanya's hand in the other.

'Now then, bitch, tell me where you lost your pants! Come on, who was it?'

Tanya was crying and looked as though she had been beaten. We tried to quieten him and reassure him, but he started to search under the beds and everywhere to see if he could find the pants. I then remembered that they were in my pocket.

'While I was visiting my sick and dying mother this bitch was here making love to someone! She never even had time to put her pants on.'

'But it's not true,' she protested.

He hit her.

A man called Sasha, a pilot, grabbed Peter, and started laying about him, but we managed to pull him off. It was not till near dawn that Peter left with Tanya. We who remained were unable to sleep and we sat around talking and drinking until daylight.

I have often wondered why I put the pants in my pocket. In the heat of making love one certainly doesn't analyse these things. Perhaps I was not used to seeing such fine underwear in Russia (probably the same would be true even now!). The others told me that Peter had always been terribly jealous of his wife who for many years had been faithful to him. She must have finally tired of his brutality and possessiveness. Peter even knew how many items of underwear she possessed. I gave the pants to Gala who took them to Tanya the next day. Tanya had told him that she had had no underwear on that evening, and eventually, if a woman persists enough, she will succeed in convincing the most suspicious husband – or so I have always found.

On Monday evening I went to Zoyev's house, as arranged. It was a small wooden house near the railway line, overlooking the main street. Dinner was nearly ready. His wife was a very talkative, solid woman.

We drank with our meal, which we ate the three of us together without the children.

We went to bed early and, as we went to our rooms, Zoyev said:

'There's a military truck ready at the back of the house. You will wear civilian clothes. There will be another driver in soldier's uniform, but you don't have to explain anything or talk to him at all. I will do all the talking that's necessary. You will hand me the orders and check the goods, then sign for them. Remember – say nothing at all.'

It was a surprise for me to learn that we would have someone else with us. I had been under the impression that we would be alone and that I would have to wear a uniform. However, I was in his hands. We left Tashkent at four in the morning and arrived at our destination before six.

The administrative staff at the *kolhoz* were up and about, and after we handed over the order they had everything ready in twenty minutes. The person in charge of the stores had already received a copy of the order we held: four sheep's carcasses, three dozen chickens, four sacks of rice, onions, cooking oil, flour, potatoes. The whole order must have weighed about 600 pounds.

By eleven that morning we had been to all four *kolhozs*. The loaded truck was covered with a green tarpaulin, and we arrived back in Tashkent early in the afternoon. Zoyev told me I should come back to him that evening to plan the distribution of the supplies. I had to find a place to store everything but he would be able to transport it to me. My only remaining problem would be its distribution.

When I came back to Zoyev's house late that evening the arrangements had been altered. The supplies had been transferred to a limousine which was used by his commanding officer. I was to receive only a part of the total amount, and the meat had been cut and prepared, the rice transferred to two-pound bags, and everything fitted into the boot and back seat of the car.

'Oh, that's very good of you to prepare the stuff for me like that,' I said. 'I'll be back for the rest later.'

'Don't be stupid,' Zoyev replied, 'we have to pay off our people too. That's all you get on this load. That's how it is.'

Within two days I had distributed all I had received to the most needy. Gala and Nokka took it round, and Tanya too. I could see now what had happened. Cepuik didn't even know that Zoyev was taking the lion's share of the supplies. A few days later I asked Zoyev what had been done with the remainder. He told me it had been sold: half the proceeds went to the *kolhoz*, a quarter to him and the driver, and a quarter to me. I resolved never to collect supplies with him again.

As winter drew on, my personal life took a turn for the better. I had many good friends – but, above all, I had become involved with Nokka.

One night, four of us were dining at Gala's house: Gala, Karl Gudman, Nokka and myself.

During the dinner I could see that Gala had set her sights on Karl Gudman. She even offered to take four litres of paraffin for heating to his sister's home, and a couple of bottles of good vegetable oil. She had a generous nature.

To give her a chance to remain alone with Karl I offered to take Nokka home, but he left with us. I laughed and joked with him:

'Is that payment for services rendered?'

He laughed too but said nothing.

It was a cool fresh night. At the door of Nokka's house I kissed her goodnight on the cheek and hand. Then she offered her lips and we kissed long and deep. I held the curves of her body against the hard wall, and we made love there, standing, dressed. Even today, when we live in a different world, it would still be unusually erotic. She was highly-sexed and, in addition to her natural aptitude, her former French lover had certainly given her some excellent lessons in lovemaking and in how to please a man. She, for her part, loved making love.

We had moved inside to her bedroom where we both thrashed about and made so much noise that her old mother must have heard everything. I slept there that night and, when we woke in the morning, we found pieces of clothing all over the room. We made love again, but now she was less abandoned:

'Please, quietly, my mother must be awake now, she'll hear everything.'

My heart opened to her. I fell in love. She was distinguished, refined and a hell of a woman. She told me that she had loved me from the first day we met, but she had not wanted to take me from Gala because Gala had always accused her of stealing her boyfriends but begged her not to do so with me. However, Gala had told her that she had made love a couple of times earlier that evening with Karl Gudman; so there and then she had decided to make love to me. The sexual excitement never went out of our relationship up to the time we were forced apart.

By January 1942 the character of the Asian Republics had been altered considerably by the influx of refugees. The over-crowded insanitary conditions were creating problems for the health authorities. The centres of chemical industries which supplied medicines had been overrun by the Nazis, although the heavy censorship which had been imposed left us all in doubt as to exactly how far the Germans had penetrated. The sheer numbers of the refugees confirmed that the situation was grave though now in the depths of winter there were no more exhausted figures of sleeping bodies in the park by the railway station or in the public square.

I had heard that Lieutenant Cepuik had been transferred elsewhere. One day I met Zoyev by accident in the street, and he told me that he would be driving out towards the town of Arys in the country. He asked if I would like to go, it would be a lovely drive, and we would be able to buy honey and other products from the countryside. We could leave in the morning and be back by evening.

I agreed reluctantly and he picked me up from Nokka's home at 6 o'clock next morning. An hour's drive out from Tashkent, crossing the steppes, we ran into heavy falls of snow and, although we had chains on the wheels, they were ineffective. We managed to get the car to a little village, a typical Moslem hamlet that would at least provide us with shelter for the night. Next morning when the snow would be firm and crispy we would be able to move the car, we were told. We had no choice. It was usually best to take the advice of local inhabitants on these occasions, though Zoyev was anxious because he had to be back at work next afternoon.

Night fell, and we ate a meal of shish-kebab with rice pilaff, tea, and the local bread, *lipiochka*, in the village *chaihana* or tearoom. There were no alcoholic drinks there, but Zoyev always had vodka with him.

We took a look outside after the meal, but conditions were

even worse; we had come in along a very wide road, but now there was no visible sign of it at all. I wondered what we would do even in daylight.

'Don't worry,' Zoyev reassured her, 'even the largest military trucks get through here. There'll be other cars' tracks for us to follow in the morning, and anyway the local people are obliged to keep the roads passable.'

We were both slightly drunk, dressed in sheepskin coats, with *valinkis* (felt boots) and we started to wrestle in the snow. I think he was really testing my strength and was surprised that such a thin man as I was could roll him over and over in the snow.

We went back to the *chaihana*, which had a room for wayfarers attached to it, glad to be inside the warm, our faces red with the cold. The landlord offered to dry our wet outer clothing and advised us to get some sleep. We removed our *valinkis* and our jackets. The sleeping room was long and narrow, with a small pilot light in the corner. There were rows of sleeping bodies down both sides. We were shown our places. I had to squeeze between two others. The light was too dim to see their faces. As I was settling down to sleep I suddenly felt someone opening my trousers. My first reaction was to jump up, but then a hand guided mine to a woman's breast. I was relieved to feel it was a woman as there were plenty of homosexuals in this Moslem area. I couldn't see her face, but she opened her jacket and trousers and turned her back to me. It was only natural that I should plug in within seconds and bring matters to their inevitable conclusion.

There were no curtains at the windows so the light in the room was very strong early in the morning, the white reflection of the snow outside making it even lighter. I stole a glance at my neighbour; it was a woman of between fifty-five and sixty, without teeth, a monster. She looked at me with gratitude. Such a thing had never happened to me before – or since, I might add!

I got up quickly and went to find Zoyev. We went to the door and looked out. He was right : heavy trucks and cars had already passed along the road, and we could follow their tracks.

We left in the limousine with chains on the wheels to start

our drive back to Tashkent. Progress was slow, a maximum of twenty miles an hour. Suddenly Zoyev noticed a lot of pigs running about on the steppe near the road. He stopped the car and took out his revolver:

'Come on,' he shouted at me.

Striding over to the largest animal, he shot it at short range five or six times.

'Come on, give me a hand,' he urged, as I stood stunned. The pig was screaming so hard that the echoes reverberated over the steppe in every direction across the fine crisp snows.

'For God's sake,' he bawled, 'don't just stand there like a big *huyey*, a big prick. Give me a hand!'

I ran forward and took one of its legs, but it was still screaming. He had to fire another shot, then we started to drag the carcass towards the car. Its weight was enormous, more like a horse or a cow. We tried to turn it on its back but the snow banked up on one side. As we dragged it painfully toward the car I looked back to see a trail of red blood soaking into the snow. The next problem was to lift the carcass into the boot of the car. Its eyes were still open. We were both sweating profusely when we finally banged down the lid of the boot, only to turn and see a car coming along the road towards us. Our white sheepskin coats were red with blood. As the car moved nearer, Zoyev shouted:

'Get in quick, let's go.'

'No, they've probably seen the whole thing,' I said. 'It's better to wait here and let them pass.'

'No. They'll take the number of this car, it's an official number plate.'

'Alright then, but take off those clothes and put them under the seat.' We both tore our jackets off quickly and stowed them away. He started the car, and we moved off. I turned to see that the car behind had stopped near the track of blood.

Why on earth, I wondered, had I agreed to this blood-thirsty act? Zoyev had taken me off my guard, so quick was his decision to kill the sow, and now here I was, my clothes soaked with blood, implicated in his theft. A violent robbery like that can happen in any country, and I could have justified it if it had been performed out of hunger, but Zoyev was far from hungry.

He stopped and took out his field glasses to look at the men in the car. They had got out, and were now chasing the pigs themselves and shooting them as we had done. I had my suspicions that Zoyev knew who they were. We got back to Tashkent at lunchtime and went straight to his house, where we avoided being questioned by his wife. We got the pig out, almost frozen, its eyes still open and looking straight at me. Zoyev took a hatchet and split the pig in half, then in quarters, like a professional butcher.

'Here's your half,' he said. 'It's fifty-fifty this time, not like before.'

'I don't want any of it,' I said. 'I don't need it. I wanted the other food to give away to people in need. I don't want this.'

He insisted I should have some of it, and I knew why: he wanted me compromised, to make me an accessory to the robbery. I took my quarters, wrapped in paper and placed in a sack. Then we both had baths to rid ourselves of the gory mess. He loaned me another coat which I could return later when his wife had cleaned mine. Then he dropped me back near Nokka's house.

Almost as soon as I started walking, a policeman came up to me:

'What are you carrying in that sack? Show me your identity papers.'

'This is meat from a pig which has been slaughtered.'

He didn't like the look of me, and he asked me to open the sack there and then. When he saw the contents, he asked me to go to the police station with him. At the station he questioned me further, then took a knife from his pocket and sliced off a good joint of meat, the best cut.

'Does your Moslem religion permit you to eat pork?' I asked.

'Yes,' he answered.

'Then take the lot,' I said, handing him the sack.

'You stole it.'

'No, I didn't, someone else stole it and I won this part in a card game, but I don't want to take it home.' He took it.

I finally arrived back at Nokka's house in time for dinner. I didn't know what to say to her. She looked into my eyes:

'*Garinka*, what's the matter? What's happened? Whose coat is that?'

I begged her not to ask questions.

'I must have a bath,' I said leaving her. I bathed once again and once again changed my clothes. Pigs have an incredible amount of blood. We had an early dinner with a few drinks and went to bed. The family had accepted my sleeping with Nokka as a husband, though old Kapranov hated me because Nokka was his favourite daughter and now she was mine.

Normally, when she was about to go to bed, Nokka would put some Coty perfume on. I stopped her that night:

'There's no use putting it on tonight,' I muttered. She was surprised; usually we made love every night, and sometimes in the day as well. She came to me and caressed me, but I was unable to respond that night. She was hurt but, whenever she looked at me, I could see the face of the old woman. I thought she had probably had VD.

Here I was in bed with this desirable woman whom I loved. When a man really loves there is a mutual respect bound up with the sexual aspect, and one should never tell any woman that you have made love with another. By this time, Nokka had become desperate, kissing me everywhere, but with no response from me. Then she started to cry, saying I no longer loved her. I couldn't bear to see her suffer, so I poured out a large glass of vodka and despite my principles told her the whole story. Her reaction surprised me. She laughed and laughed till the tears ran down her cheeks:

'*Oti moi durachok*, my silly boy!' she gurgled.

Her long eyelashes were stuck together with tears. She started to kiss me again:

'Don't worry, make love to me. Love me.'

So far in my life I had learnt that when you confess to the truth you mostly get punished for it, but this was one occasion when the confession helped. We passed a happy night and in the morning, when I described the scene in the *chaihana* once again, we both laughed so much that her father banged on the shed wall with his hammer, shouting to us to stop.

11

Lowest Ebb . . . NKGB

At the end of January 1943 when I went out to buy cigarettes I was picked up by two NKGB men in plain clothes a few hundred yards from the *dacha*. They told me they had orders to arrest me, and took me to their headquarters.

We were shown into the office of a high-ranking officer, Krasnov. On the desk before him was that old acquaintance, my file.

He stood up, silent for a while, then said quietly: 'We know everything about you.'

'Whatever you know,' I replied, 'it does not entitle you to do what you are doing to me.'

He shouted: 'You mix with Polish officers when you go to the National Hotel for example. We also know that you have visited the headquarters of General Anders' army at Langjul.* Would you be prepared, in exchange for your liberty, to help us in whatever ways are in your power?'

I looked at him hard:

'What exactly do you want from me?'

'I will give you a list of people, all Poles. Two have become Soviet citizens. You already meet them at parties and in the ordinary course of events. All you have to do is to get into conversation with them – we will tell you what information we require, and you will tell us what they have to say. There is a note here in this dossier that you have an exceptional, almost electronic memory.'

* Head of the Polish army in Russia. His headquarters were near Tashkent. On the outbreak of war with Germany the Polish prisoners of war and internees were released to fight with the Russians, but the Russians always remained highly suspicious of these Polish 'allies'.

'What you are asking me is to become one of your informers in exchange for my liberty.'

Quickly he interposed: 'Why don't you think it over?'

'You know what, I'll leave the thinking to you; you are specialists in destroying people, and turning them into what you want them to be, but you won't succeed with me. You are taking the law into your own hands. I have nothing to fear. I will not agree to any of your dirty propositions.'

He continued to turn the pages of the file, looked up at me angrily, then started to read out all the information he had about me. They knew far, far more than I had feared. He paused.

'*Gavno*, shit!' I replied. 'We've been through all that before and I don't want to hear it again.'

His next remark I will never forget. It turned my whole world upside down. He looked me in the eyes and said:

'Your escape from Kandalaksha was so impressive and courageous we decided to follow you step by step . . . until now.'

Even now, as I remember the shock of that pronouncement, I get a pain in my guts. A silence fell upon us both. At last:

'Give me proof of what you are saying . . . names . . . dates.' I was trying desperately to gather my thoughts and play for time.

He thumbed through the files again.

'We had no evidence of your whereabouts until you arrived in Moscow. We lost track of you completely. We picked up your trail again when you applied in Moscow for the appointment of Health Inspector: they had to get clearance from security departments. That was when we found you again. You have retained your Polish citizenship, and we have co-operated in many ways with the Polish government-in-exile concerning their citizens in the Soviet Union, in Soviet prisons, or those free to work here, but as far as I know your name is among those declared to be presumed dead.'

I answered:

'Look for other victims – I have been victimized by you for too long.'

He got to his feet, called in another officer and stamped around the room:

'I told you, I told you he is an enemy.'

After a few minutes of exchanging notes between them, his colleague left the room.

'We have offered you your liberty, a career and a good life, but you have chosen death. Even if we are unable to rearrest you because of the amnesty granted to Polish citizens, you will remain here, charged with spying, because you are a spy.'

Minutes later I was in a cell with three other prisoners. One was Rachmaninov, the brother of the composer who was still alive at the time. He spoke a little French and let me know as soon as he could that the second inmate was an informer who spied for the authorities. His name was Schwablay, a German Russian from the Volga, aged about thirty-five. It was impossible to tell who might be an informer and who not because their brainwashing system was so effective that they could break anyone if they spent enough time on him, and turn him into whatever they wanted. The third prisoner was called Tabarov, a solicitor from Leningrad. One night he came down from questioning and crawled back into the room on all fours, groaning in agony. As I went to help him he placed his hand behind him. It was bloodstained. He refused the medical aid I offered. Later he told me that they had seated him on a kind of press, his legs in front, metal plates pressed against his sides. They had gradually screwed the sides together so hard that the lower bowel had emerged from his anus. They had wanted him to confess to false charges. His face was green, his lips blue. The terrible intestinal pains had made him cry like a baby searching for its mother's breast to ease the pangs of hunger. He took my head between his hands and put his face to mine. He sobbed and sobbed, I could understand him.

During the five days I spent with the other three I discovered that Rachmaninov had been arrested in Moscow, sent to several different prisons over the course of three years and had never yet been given a trial or convicted of any crime. The charges had been the usual counter-revolutionary ones.

He had often written to his brother in New York but, wherever he happened to be at the time, he was always told to write 'Moscow' at the top of his letters. They were taken to that city and sent from there. The composer would reply to the address given in Moscow, the letters were intercepted, and sent on to his brother, to wherever he was. He was always told to put the date later by a few days so as to give time for the letter to be sent from Moscow. Whether the great Rachmaninov ever discovered what was really happening, or whether he even suspected it, I don't know. The composer was an ardent supporter of the Russian people, especially during the war when Russia was suffering on such a tremendous scale. He sent donations towards the cost of trainloads of expensive medical supplies. And this was how the NKGB paid him back. They kept his brother in prison until he died.

On the fifth day in the cell I was called to see my interrogator Krasnov. He read out charges signed by Schwablay that I had made fun of Stalin and had called him a tyrant. I denied it.

'The honeymoon is over. You will see.' He telephoned a guard and directed him to remove me.

I was now taken to another cell. It was in complete darkness, without a bed or any furniture. It was so small that when I stretched my arms I touched the walls – thick, damp, with no windows, but a small hole high up on one wall covered by a grille. My first impression was of complete darkness, but there were a few rays of light at the grille and some snow there. The inside of the door was iron, with a small peep-hole. The first hours there I spent wondering how long they could keep me in such a place: I wanted to be one step ahead of them. The outside temperature was −10°C, but inside, due to the thick stone walls, it was much colder. It must, I guessed, be deep below the earth, no heating, no way of knowing what hour of the day it was ... no noises. The only sound I heard for the first twenty-four hours was when someone approached my cell and put the key in the lock. The cracking noise of the key made such an impact on me that I was frightened every time the door opened. The guard would come in with another prisoner who carried food: for me, half a pint of tepid water. In the stream of light from the corridor outside I could distinguish the head of a herring floating in the water. I rejected the food and declared myself on hunger strike until I was taken to someone in authority. The guard said nothing, just took away the food.

Minutes later the door was opened again and they brought in a narrow wooden board. The guard grunted:

'Here's your mattress. Have a good sleep.' Then he pushed a wooden pot through the door for my use.

'Try not to crap until the morning, otherwise the cell will stink all night.'

That first night I spent walking round and round the tiny cell, doing every exercise I could think of so as not to die from the cold. The 'mattress' was useless. Every time I stretched out on it my feet hung over the end on to the concrete floor. It was intentionally too short. There was no blanket. In the morning the guard came to take away my bed and brought me a piece of black bread, with some hot black coffee. I refused it but he said it was a rule that it should stay in my cell. I threw the coffee on the floor and placed the hunk of bread by the door. As he was locking the door I felt the urge to use the toilet, and told the guard so. He pointed to the pot.

'Use that. You can empty it tomorrow morning.'

'But the other guard told me differently last night,' I said.

'He was just kidding you.'

After almost twenty-four hours in the cell I knew every inch of the walls, every nook and cranny. There was much more light than I had thought at first. I passed my hands continuously over the walls. I sometimes stood, my hands folded one over the other, my head resting on them, and slept like that, standing.

I thought back to so many things: my home, my family, the war, the German bombings. Most of what I remembered made me sad, but at times my blood boiled. My brain was crystal clear, and sometimes good and sweet memories passed through my mind. I remembered how Nokka had said, 'Go away. . . . Now. . . . Run,' but one thing I knew, that I had never felt fear. I was only sorry I was in this cage, powerless to fight, to die fighting them physically in my own defence. That was the force of those beasts. I was entombed. No way to fight back. At times I thought they might succeed in destroying me.

The key crashed into the lock. It was the guard with the evening meal. I refused it without a glance. He came back with my 'mattress' for my second night in the cell. I told him I had used the bucket and wanted to take it outside.

'Keep it here till tomorrow, it will make you sleep better.'

A few hours later, it must have been the middle of the night, the key rasped in the lock and I was summoned up to see Krasnov.

We were alone in the room. I sat down.

The door opened, and four men like bulls came in. They wore holsters for guns but they were empty, not even Krasnov had one. These officers said they had come to meet me, and asked me to stand up. I stood and made immediately for the nearest corner. They looked at each other surprised that I had guessed why they were there. They closed in. I grabbed the chair nearest me and fought like a wild cat until I lost consciousness. They kicked me everywhere with their boots except on the head. As I crumpled to the ground, I knew I was prepared to die.

I woke in the same cell, completely naked except for underpants. I had not been unconscious for long. The cold brought me round quickly. When I rested my arms on the walls to sleep the guard opened the door and swished a bucket of water over them.

'We don't want your skin to get dry, do we?' he jeered.

Within minutes the wall was covered with ice.

The third morning in this living grave they followed the same routine.

Late in the evening I was taken out again for interrogation with Krasnov. Further questionings and beatings took place. Then back to my cage.

Next day, early, the door opened and I was handed a shirt and trousers and ordered to follow two guards.

We turned left as we went from the room, down a long corridor, and up some stairs where a man sat at a small table, dressed in civilian clothes, flanked by two armed guards, carrying rifles and bayonets. These guards were dressed differently from the others, in blue. They were military guards. The man at the table started to read out a paper he had in front of him:

'By special decree of the Court' – I don't remember the date he gave – 'you have been condemned to death for anti-Soviet activities, and spying for foreign powers. No appeal is possible. The sentence to be carried out immediately.'

He asked me to sign that I had heard the decree. I looked at him, then at the two guards with him, then at the two guards who had brought me there. It was dawn, the first light. The corridor was quite dark. I stood motionless and asked him to read it to me again. This he did. He remained sitting while the guards stood to attention.

'You are required to sign this,' he continued to stare down at the document.

'Give it to Krasnov and his friends. They will sign it for you.'

'You refuse to sign?'

'Yes.'

He wrote at the bottom of the document: 'Refuses to sign. The decree was read to the prisoner at 6.30 a.m.' He told the guards to sign as witnesses, which they did.

The military guards now had me in their charge, and we marched away to the right. An iron door opened in front of us. It gave on to a yard completely surrounded by high walls. The wall directly opposite the door was pitted with bullet holes, and there were some iron rings in it, presumably for attaching ropes. Six soldiers were lined up in the yard, carrying rifles with bayonets fixed. An officer glared at me balefully and shouted the order for me to be marched to the wall. The two guards stepped back. I was told to march to the wall thirty yards away. As I walked forward I had no doubt I would be shot. I had heard that some prisoners had been shot from behind, in the back of the head. I had also seen the bodies of men who had tried to escape and they had been shot in the brain from behind. I walked slowly. Death faced me. I thought only of my dead mother. The image of her face filled my vision. The officer shouted the order for the rifles to be brought to the ready. Just before I reached the wall he told me not to turn around until ordered. I stopped in front of the wall. He gave the order to turn. I turned.

There was Krasnov with someone else coming towards me. Krasnov, very grave and solemn.

'I can still save you. You will be able to work for us. All you have to do is sign the confession to all the charges made against you, and that you are prepared to work to the best of your ability for the government of the Soviet Socialist Republic.'

I looked him in the eye.

'Proceed. I hate you. I hate your organization, I hate your

151

system. I hate you all. You're not communists, you are traitors. You are destroying communism.'

He drew back without turning. I stood waiting. The officer shouted his orders to the firing squad.

'Aim! Steady!' Then:

'Fire!'

I saw the smoking muzzles of the rifles. . . . Suddenly Krasnov gave me a blow over the head with his fist which sent me to the ground. I had no idea where he had sprung from.

'You capitalist prostitute! You don't deserve a Soviet bullet!'

I stood up, a new-born man. What emotions had overcome me in those last few moments! It all seemed so improbable, but there have been many reports that this was a favourite trick of the NKGB and NKVD to get last-minute confessions. The victim would think his last moment had come and would be ready to confess to anything.

I stood firmly on my legs, which only minutes before could scarcely hold the weight of my body. My eyes turned to the firing squad: they were laughing and talking between themselves, their rifles slung over their shoulders.

Krasnov was no longer there; just as he had arrived from nowhere, now he had disappeared. Two guards came forward and I was ordered to accompany them back to the same cell which I had left such a short time ago unaware of the mock execution about to take place.

There I found a long wooden box the size of a coffin, lined with lead, holding a block of ice. Three guards tied me into a strait jacket and laid me down on the ice, strapping me on to it with several belts. The ice began to melt under the heat of my body. I tried to hold my head high away from it, but I was strapped down so hard I couldn't move in any direction. There was no longer any doubt in my mind: they intended to finish me in one way or another. It was hard to concentrate my thoughts. I was dying.

After several hours the ice under my body had melted enough to loosen the straps. It became difficult to breath. I resolved to make no sound. I found myself thinking of all those prisoners in the Death Brigade who had lifted the flaps of their tent and lain in the snow, freezing to death as they slept. I too will die when I fall asleep, I thought. A great fatigue came over me. I fought to stay conscious, couldn't hold my urine. In those moments I hovered between life and death. The cold, the hunger, the beatings and the mock execution were draining my life away.

The door swung open but this time it didn't seem to bother me so much, it seemed in the distance. Krasnov was in the cell with two others. He held a lamp high over my head and placed his hand on my icy face.

'He's dead!'

'Oh no, *Tovarisch*, I am not dead.'

To the guard in charge he shouted:

'You will face a trial and be condemned for this criminal act. Take him off immediately. Give him his clothes and a hot drink.'

As I regained consciousness and realized what was happening, I cried. As they dressed me, I could feel nothing, I was numbed. The guards helped me and brought me a hot drink which I accepted.

Krasnov asked:

'Hero, how are you feeling now?'

I tottered to pick up the slop pail and throw it at him, but I was hit on the head from behind. They left me.

I could still feel nothing in the lower part of my body.

I concluded they would kill me anyway. They wanted me dead, but they would have preferred me to kill myself. No doubt many had undergone similar treatment before me, and some had died as a result.

What else would they do?

No, no, I could not take any more.

I looked at the walls around me, every crevice and mark I recognized like a familiar landscape: there is where I placed my arms on the stone and leant my head against them, there is where I sat on the ground with my back against the wall, and so on. . . .

I decided I would take my own life, the life I had lived so fully, of which I had been so proud. I had always considered people who committed suicide as cowards, unable to face up to the realities and hardships of life, but now that the moment had come I knew I had been mistaken – it takes courage to take your own life.

There is a fatal moment before the act when judgement is suspended. The decision is taken, but how to accomplish it? I stood with my back resting on the wall searching with my eyes for some instrument, but I saw nothing which would further my purpose. It must be done, and well done. If I ran into the wall head first? The space was too small. I must find a way; I had decided to die but I would not give them the pleasure of killing me.

I took my left hand in my right, raised it to my mouth, and bit deep with all my strength into the vein. My sweet, hot blood spurted out like an oil jet. I held my arm down so that the blood would flow faster still. The blood splashed the wall of the cell, streaming down. I dropped the arm to my side and walked around the tiny cell. In the dim light I saw my red blood trickling and spreading over the floor. I kept walking, washing the floor with my own blood, sometimes shaking the wrist to make the blood flow freely, and pressing my left arm with all my strength to increase the volume. I grew weaker. I watched my life blood flow out on to the floor, indifferent to the pain. I could no longer keep my balance and staggered along the walls rolling round the cell until I slumped on to the ground near the iron door. I had succeeded in opening the vein and keeping the blood flowing so that it would not clot.

Suddenly, driven by some inexplicable force, I grabbed my left arm and lifted it high in the air:

'No, no. A man like you doesn't die like that. A man like you doesn't kill himself to save himself from torture. Let them kill me, I won't kill myself!'

The guard came running and crashed open the door. He had seen a stream of blood in the corridor outside. His first action was to deal me a heavy blow. I lost consciousness.

I woke up in the NKGB infirmary, my wrists bound. When I remembered how the cell looked I calculated I must have lost at least two litres of blood which had been replaced by a transfusion. I was given a short time to recover. Within twenty-four hours I was back in the same cell where I could smell the smell of my own blood, and see the stains although they had washed the walls and floor. Here I was, back again, extremely weak, but alive. My legs gave way beneath me. My pulse was irregular and, when I felt it, I could tell I had fever. The whole building seemed to be collapsing around me. In this cell, where a few hours before I had tried to take my own life, I stood with my head resting on the frozen walls. It was a relief. I burned with fever. I put my lips to the wall to feel the touch of the ice. It cooled the fire in my veins which was consuming me. I couldn't keep my lips there for long. There was the sweet taste of blood, my own blood. I repeated over and over:

'I will live, I will survive.'

They had put me back here to die.

I had only survived until now because I had kept moving and exercising for almost twenty hours a day. Now I no longer had the strength to move, and if I had stayed there a few more days they would have their wish fulfilled.

But I still could not understand why they wanted to kill me. What had they to gain from my death? Why had I been arrested in the first place? If they had seriously wished for my help, why had they used such barbarous means? I found no answer. Only time would tell – but would I live long enough to find out?

I fell asleep sitting cross-legged on the floor, my left arm held as high as I could with the other. They had not even given me the support of a sling on my arm which I had to keep moving to find the most comfortable position to ease the pain. They told me later I slept for six hours. I was woken with the light of the torch shining in my face. The usual guard, with the help of two others, brought me to my feet. We all went out of the cell and walked along the corridor to the bottom of the stairs. Through the windows I could see it was night, although I had lost all sense of time. I told the guards to let go, I would walk upstairs alone. These were back stairs which were used only by prisoners for special reasons. One guard said to the other:

'He doesn't want to be helped by an NKGB guard. He's such a proud anti-communist.'

As I struggled up the stairs I collapsed unconscious. Later I found out that I was taken to the prison infirmary then, on special orders, removed to a civilian hospital in Chimkent (Kazakstan), about 100 miles from Tashkent.

There I lay with very high fever, ill and weak, sleeping most of the day in a small ward, with two guards stationed outside the door. Only after a full week of treatment, and giving the doctors considerable concern for my survival, I was told I had had pneumonia and that I had been given further blood transfusions.

Every day I made good progress. There I was in a hospital bed, like a free citizen.

Until I found out more details from a nurse called Shura it was difficult for me to understand why I had been moved away from Tashkent where there were several hospitals. Again, I told myself : 'Wait and see and get strong.'

I looked from my bed at the window without bars and the idea of escape came to me. The medical staff were sympathetic. I told a nurse about my life, and a few days later she came to my bedside and told me that the police would soon be asking for me to be sent back to their headquarters. The doctors were trying to fob them off, saying I was not yet fit. Shura was my guardian angel. I decided to escape as quickly as possible.

There were guards outside the ward I occupied with two other patients. Without losing time I organized my escape for that same night. Usually clothes were removed from prisoner patients and a guard posted to stop visitors and gifts reaching them. I had no trouble in obtaining outdoor clothes thanks to the medical staff. The next step was to get out of the ward and into the nurses' service room on the same corridor. The guard spent most of the night asleep in his chair, so when my companions had fallen asleep I got up, dressed myself, covered my clothes with a white medical overall, and left the room; tiptoeing past the guard I went into the nurses' room where outdoor clothes had been left for me. Luckily the overalls were very large and I was able to put them over the suit. I opened the door. The guard was still asleep. I passed him and made towards the doors at the top of the stairs. They were locked. I went back to the nurses' room, to the glass-fronted cupboard which contained the medical supplies. There was a bottle of ether there. I would have to use it on the guard – otherwise he would wake up, sound the alarm, and I would be caught before I could reach the railway station which was an hour's walk away. I looked around before deciding what to do, then it came to me: forget the door, forget the ether, simply open the window and jump. If I landed safely I would then only have to get over a wall about eight feet high which gave on to the main road. I peeped round the door again to make sure the guard was still asleep, locked myself into the room, removed the medical coat, opened the window and clambered on to the window ledge, then dropped to the ground. I crossed the fifty yards to the high wall, ran back a little way, and took a run at it, shinning up one side so quickly that I overbalanced at the top and fell to the ground on the other side. I fell badly. The ground was frozen rock-hard. I moved away from the wall as quickly as I could but realized I must have twisted my right ankle. I had managed to get hold of some *valinki* boots, and dragged myself forward at a slow pace, limping. I turned back to look at the hospital: the outline of the building was quite clear in the cold starry night.

I intended to catch the express train to Tashkent which I knew left at 5 a.m., but I would have to avoid going through the centre of the town, so I took a side turning to skirt the built-up area. As I limped along I suddenly came upon a pack of wild dogs. They surrounded me. The first dog's shrill howls had brought the rest of the pack on to my heels. They pressed in closer and closer. They were painfully thin, starving. Their bones stood out. I was trapped. A shooting pain flashed up my leg. It was bitterly cold, and I was still weak after such a grave illness. But my boiling desire to survive gave me strength. I stepped forward firmly. At my feet I saw frozen lumps of horse manure, hard as stone. I picked up several. The dogs snarled and showed their teeth, their breath rising in the cold air. I shouted with all my strength first to one side then to the other:

'Get back dog! Get back, dog!'

The most vicious-looking one, with one ear half-bitten off, grabbed my boot with his teeth. This was the signal for all the pack to move in and tear me to pieces. It was still clinging to my boot when I hit the dog over the head, using all my remaining strength, with the lump of manure. Its screams of pain scared the others off at least for a moment. It was dying. Then I followed up my advantage by throwing the other lumps in quick succession at the other dogs. They backed away, snarling. I stumbled forward. Some had surrounded the dying dog, but others still sloped along behind me at a distance. I threw more lumps at them.

And that is how I owed my life to a horse which had passed by a few hours before and relieved itself at that spot. It was my lucky star again.

Half an hour later I was at the station.

I was fortunate enough to find some few hundred roubles in my pocket, placed there no doubt by some good soul at the hospital.

I enquired the departure time of the next train to Tashkent and was told I would have four hours to wait. Within minutes a train rumbled into the station. It was bound for Kuybyshev, in a north-westerly direction. I did not wish to linger in the town a moment longer than necessary, so I boarded the train.

After eight or nine hours, travelling in a compartment together with a mixed batch of people, I alighted at Aktyubinsk, still in the Republic of Kazakstan.

The escape and the train journey had in some way restored me to my old self – no longer frightened, and even happy in the small industrial city. Tashkent would have been too dangerous, and Nokka was being watched. After a good night's sleep I decided to go to the health authorities or to the Party Secretary and throw myself on their mercies, knowing that doctors were desperately needed everywhere. I had nothing to lose, and perhaps Krasnov would even be pleased to get rid of me. Furthermore I realized that, without identity documents, I would have no means of support or liberty to travel.

Before going to the offices of the Party Secretary, I wrote a letter to the head of the health department informing him of my problem and protesting my innocence of any crime. I asked for his help. I wrote that by the time the letter would reach him I would be at the Secretary's office, or perhaps even in jail.

My first meeting with the local Secretary of the Communist Party lasted over two hours. He was a local man, a Kazak. They have a different mentality from other Russians. It was a good sign when he listened to all I told him with attention, then expressed his opinion:

'I believe what you tell me, but you should not have disclosed so much.'

After making several telephone calls and visits to other offices in the building, the outcome was that I should write down my address, and return there the next day. I was advised not to disclose who I was or what had happened to me.

When I returned next morning there were two other officials in the room with the Party Secretary. I was to be allowed to remain in the city of Aktyubinsk if I agreed to remain for at least six months and to work in whatever job the health authorities gave me. Before leaving I signed a document accepting the conditions. That particular Party Secretary had handled my difficulties with tact and ability. As I was leaving he warned me:

'There are no charges against you in the city of Tashkent. Anyway, they haven't asked us to send you back. However, I would not advise you to go back there.'

Krasnov knew I was innocent. He had lost the game and must be content with preventing my return to Tashkent.

And so I started work with the health department in Aktyubinsk. They sent me to the labour camp nearby, where a certain Sacha Shermansky of Dniepropetrovsk, whom I knew, was the assistant camp director.

It was a great happiness for me to be free and to have work.

I made contact with Nokka who told me that she had been barred from leaving Tashkent and warned that if she should try to join me we would both be jailed.

The powerful arm of the NKGB can be seen not only in the killings and physical tortures, but also in the destruction of human feelings, and loving relationships between friends and families.

The Head of the 'Tovarisch' Organization had helped me:

Thank you Tovarisch.

PART THREE

Missions Accomplished

12

My Red Hospital

At the end of January 1944 I was informed by the health department that I had been appointed Chief Medical Officer on
a special trainload of repatriates organized for Poles and
Ukrainians due to travel to Kharkov, Dniepropetrovsk and Kiev.
I would certainly be obliged to stay in the Ukraine for some
time; I would take another post with the Ministry of Health, I
decided, until the final defeat of Germany, which looked as if it
would still be some months off. As a doctor I would be able to
obtain a travel permit for a visit to Moscow – and Nokka – quite
easily.

So I planned. But I had reckoned without coincidence. There
is a theory that all our lives are ruled by coincidence; and
certainly the odds against what happened next must have been
overwhelming. To meet anyone on purpose in the maelstrom of
war-time Russia was difficult enough; to meet anyone, of all
those millions, by accident was almost out of the question and
yet that is what happened to me – and it most certainly changed
my whole life. What if it had been Nokka herself? I sometimes
dream, even now, of how wonderfully different the next fifteen
years might have been. But it was not. I was never to see my
beloved Nokka again.

There were fifteen hundred people due to travel on that train,
and the station at Aktyubinsk was in a turmoil as we prepared
for departure.

As I stood in the open door of my carriage arranging the
placing of the four beds available for the sick I heard a woman's
voice:

'Is the doctor here?'

I turned and couldn't believe my eyes. It was Luba Sosnow
standing there below me, dressed in a heavy coat, her cheeks red

with the cold, looking up at me. I winked at her to stop her from saying or doing anything which would show that she already knew me. She didn't understand:

'*Garri, dorogoy!* Darling!'

She started to cry. I jumped down and put my arms round her, and kissed her, as we embraced. She was travelling on the train to Dniepropetrovsk. I told her to go into the wagon next to mine and gave her a hand up into the train. She stood and cried, telling me that she had lost her mother, had married and separated from her husband, a mining engineer, and that he had their baby daughter living with him and his family in Karaganda in Kazakstan. I stroked her and tried to calm her down, but she took my hand in hers and started to kiss it. She had stopped crying when we saw a young NKVD lieutenant standing on the ground outside the compartment, the *nachalnik* in charge of the whole 'echelon'. He said we would be leaving within the hour if all went according to schedule. I asked him inside and, when he saw Luba, he said:

'Luba, what are you doing here?'

He could see she had been crying.

'I came to see if I could be of assistance to the doctor. He says he needs help.'

I hadn't mentioned work to her but I backed her up:

'Yes, that's right, we are short of medical staff.'

He seemed to regard Luba with a proprietary attitude. He asked her where her luggage was. I told the male nurse to go with her and bring it to the compartment. While they were gone the lieutenant said:

'I brought her along but she is not really authorized to travel on this train. She's my girl friend.'

'Well, I have the authority to take her along since she is a doctor of medicine. If she's your girl, she can still be your girl, it won't make any difference, but I think you had better look for another – there are plenty on the train. She was crying because she was telling me that she had picked up an infectious disease and needs treatment.'

He changed his tune immediately:

'I understand. She's a good-looking girl. Lucky she is going to be a doctor, isn't it?'

That got rid of him. He left at once. Why did I do it, I wondered later. I was not the least in love with Luba, but I had lived in her home and had known her mother. I felt then, when I took her in with me, that I owed her something. I was pleased to see her too, of course, and sympathized with her recent misfortunes.

That night on the train we sat talking for hours. Her mother had died on the Russian island of Sakhalin, to the north of Japan, where she had been living. I wondered how such a strong woman had died so young. It was only a year since it had happened, and Luba started to cry, so I asked no more questions about that. She had separated from her husband because of his mother who had been too interfering, but she felt nothing for him now. Her only aim in life was to get her daughter back. We had no trouble with the passengers the first night. She was sleeping in the same compartment but we had separate beds and I didn't touch her because I could see she was depressed and unhappy. Furthermore, there was no desire on my side, only pity.

Early next morning I woke to find her sitting on my bed crying. I hate anyone to wake me up unless it's for some urgent reason, and I let her know how I felt:

'Why did you have to wake me up?'

'I have to talk to you, I haven't slept all night.' I tried to turn over and get back to sleep.

'I have to ask you a question,' she persisted. 'What would you do as a doctor, if you had two patients both likely to die, an older person and a young child, and the only medicine you had available was enough for one of them. To which one would you give the medicine?' Wondering what was behind her question, I said:

'That is something I could only decide at the time, with all the medical facts before me.' Then it struck me. 'Why are you crying? Was one of the patients your mother?'

'Yes, yes. My mother had dysentery. She lost so much weight. She was fighting for her life for three weeks. I had only a few grams of sulphonamide. I had to decide whether to give it to my mother or keep it in case my baby should become ill. I kept it. My mother died.'

'You made the right decision. I doubt if a few grams of sulphonamide would have been enough to save her anyway, if she was so ill. Don't blame yourself. Go back to sleep.'

She stared at me with her bewitching green eyes, put her hand on my face:

'Are you in love with some woman?'

'Yes.'

'But you aren't married?'

'No, I'm not married. Go back to bed.'

I could not get back to sleep again, and I sensed that she could not either. Even now I don't know why I did what I did then. Was it because she was sad, lonely and depressed? I don't know. Nature followed its course. But what I already instinctively felt was that this woman was poison for me.

Next day we were stationary for fifteen hours before we arrived at Kharkov. Luba had succeeded in getting what she wanted from me. She would never be the woman who could respond to me completely in the sexual sense, but she was pretty, had a good figure, a bronze skin and kept me entertained with her talking. Before we arrived at Kharkov she had persuaded me to leave the convoy at Dniepropetrovsk and come with her when my mission was complete. At every station along our route the number of passengers had decreased until now there were very few left. We had been lucky to avoid any outbreaks of epidemic diseases, so we were able to leave the train at Dniepropetrovsk station on the Wednesday morning. We went directly from the station in a *droshky* to Prospect Karl Marx where she had lived before. We knocked on the door of the house where she had spent her early years; a woman opened it. She asked what I wanted but, as soon as she spotted Luba, she quickly slammed the door shut. She had probably recognized her from the photographs dotted around the house. All Luba's (and her mother's) personal belongings and furniture were still there since, like most refugees, they had thought they would return to their home in a few weeks at the outside. The woman had slammed the door because Soviet law at that time stipulated that once Luba, the former occupant, stepped inside the house, she had the right to evict the squatters who had not lived there before the war. Luba leaned on the doorpost:

'Oh please, please, let me in. I only want to see the bed my mother slept in, and the chair where my father used to sit ... please, please ... have pity on me. Let me in. I won't stay, I swear.'

Her pleas met with no response. She threw herself at the door and hammered on it, first with her fists, then with her head. All her pain erupted:

'Oh, have pity on me, my mother is dead. I will never see her again. Only let me see the bed where she slept!'

She banged her head so hard on the door that I had to restrain her. I tried to pull her away. People passing in the street turned to look at the tragedy. She was crying ceaselessly now. She threw herself down on to the steps:

'Oh mother, I kiss the threshold you stepped over; oh mother, have pity, forgive me. Oh mother, I wish you could see me now: they won't let me into the house.'

Her tormented cries had by now attracted a crowd, which gathered around the steps. I tried in vain to control her. I shouted to the woman inside to open the door, but it was useless. I was unaware that she had telephoned the police. I tried to force the door with my shoulder – not one of the bystanders would help me. Luba was still on the ground, crying. Suddenly the lock gave way. The woman inside was alone. She shouted for help. Luba made no attempt to get up and go in, but I went in, some of the people were lifting her from the steps. She had reached the door when a police car pulled up outside. The woman was shrieking:

'Don't let her in. She lived here before. My husband is a policeman! Once she comes inside we shall never get her out!'

Luba and I begged her just to let us see the rooms, but she was unmoved. The police forced us into the car and took us to the police station. They almost charged me with breaking into the property but because the officer-in-charge was a very humane and understanding person we were released when Luba undertook not to return to the house or go near it without official permission and signed a document to that effect. Luba asked if one of the policemen could go to the house and bring her a few of the photographs of her parents, but they refused. We were relieved to leave the police station with at least our freedom intact and went straight to her mother's sister, an old lady bent with arthritis, who lived with Lucia her daughter, a doctor of economics. There we went through another tearful scene, with much crying and shrieking. Such events were a common occurrence during those years, but I could not bear to watch it and hated every minute of it. There were only two bedrooms in the apartment, so Lucia slept with her mother and Luba and I occupied the other room. They all talked and talked about friends and relatives, what had happened to them and where they were now, which ones had died at the hands of the Nazis. Their stories were not unique in any way. Their grief was not the only grief, but it was typical of millions. Few families escaped the death toll. The only good news was the retreat of the Nazis before the Red Army. Complete victory would only be a matter of time.

Through Luba I met a lot of people in the medical world in Dniepropetrovsk. She had been attending the Dniepropetrovsk Institute of Medicine before the German occupation, and had only one year more to finish before graduation, although four-year students like her had been given permission to practice during the war emergency because of the acute shortage of doctors.

So the final year's courses had not yet been organized and she would have to wait several months before taking up her studies again, though she had put her name on the register of students. I went to the offices of the Ministry of Health where I had been registered many years before. They gave me work immediately as the head of the District Hospital of Sofiyevka, not far from the city of Krivoy Rog. In normal times this hospital had three hundred beds in five blocks. Luba was also given permission to work as a paediatrician and in general medicine there until the commencement of her course.

I was called to the office of General Kucharave, head of all medical services for the whole province.

'There is a typhoid epidemic raging in the area,' he told me. 'At the moment the doctor in charge at the Sofiyevka Hospital is a surgeon, Zaikin. He can remain in his surgeon's job if he proves useful to you, but if he gets awkward, send him to hell, or do what you like with him. There will only be three of you doctors. Don't expect any more – I already know they had twelve doctors there before the war, so don't write to me about it. I want you to get the epidemic under control.'

He lifted the telephone: 'Send Dr Kozlova in here!' She was my immediate superior in charge of rural hospitals, an epidemiologist. Our meeting lasted no more than twenty minutes. General Kucharave talked rapidly through one corner of his mouth while puffing on a cigarette. He told me to get my wife – i.e. Luba – and myself immunized against typhoid. I told him straight away that she was not my wife.

'Well,' he said, 'she probably will be very soon.'

Dr Kozlova told me she would want a report from me every three days. I made it plain to General Kucharave that, since I had left Dniepropetrovsk, I had been arrested and imprisoned and sentenced by Soviet law.

'Balls to the law,' he said. He was an aggressive type. 'Anyway, what's the problem?'

'I shall have to take command over Soviet citizens and they might resent being ordered around by an ex-prisoner and foreigner.'

'You have paid for your crimes, whatever they were,' he said. 'The staff there now, including Dr Zaikin, stayed there all through the Nazi occupation and co-operated with them. So don't you worry about what they or the medical staff might say. You have been appointed by the Chief Medical Officer of the whole province. You will have to face the party members there too. Once Kiev confirms your appointment you can treat them in the manner they deserve, good or bad. Don't start getting hang-ups about having been in a labour camp.'

As he shouted, he moved about and fidgeted. Luba shrank away from him. Dr Kozlova was noisy and aggressive too. I tried to bring the interview to a close:

'Very well, General, I will do my best.'

It was now late February 1944, still very cold when we arrived at the railway station outside Sofiyevka early in the morning. There was no one waiting for us, nor had any message been left for us. It was some time before a sledge arrived driven by one of the hospital staff. While we waited we kept ourselves warm throwing snowballs and swinging our arms around our bodies. We heard the bells of the sledge in the clear frosty air before we could see it. We piled ourselves and our luggage on board. As we drew near the hospital the driver pointed to some red buildings on a ridge above us.

'See those red blocks up there – that's the hospital.'

There were a number of buildings; almost like a town. But, as we got closer, I could see that many had no roofs. He went chattering on about the widespread epidemics, and the food shortages – especially for the hospital staff. When I asked him why he had arrived so late he answered that he had been told I would arrive at eight in the morning.

'I know the times of the trains, and that early one never stops here. I got to the station at the time Dr Zaikin and Chevchenko told me.'

It was still not long after eight when we arrived at the hospital. A separate flat had been assigned to us with two bedrooms, but it was bitterly cold. As we went in, a rat scampered across the floor and out again through the broken window. The driver dumped our luggage on the floor. Luba and I looked at each other in dismay.

Only a few hours later I called a general meeting of the hospital staff and the health services, and made a general inspection of the large area of about fifteen acres covered by buildings. One was for the doctors' residence, one for outpatients, two were hospital blocks with two to three hundred beds in each, and the other housed the kitchens, laboratories, stores and morgue. One building had been completely gutted by bombs, and others had had their roofs damaged. In peace time it had been a famous hospital staffed by ten to twelve doctors but, since the recapture of the city of Dniepropetrovsk on 25 October 1943, nothing had been done to repair the buildings or re-establish the services. Most of the former staff had been sent to the front, where many had been killed.

That first night Luba and I had no choice but to sleep in the freezing apartment. We thought it best to give each other a triple dose of anti-typhoid vaccine, but we must have been over-enthusiastic because we both developed high fevers and lost consciousness at times during the night. We woke shivering and weak. Our beds were wet with sweat as though a bucket of water had been thrown over them. It was not till the afternoon that we managed to get up and Luba found with horror that her foot had been bitten by a rat. We could only hope that she had not been infected with typhoid.

There was more than one type of typhoid epidemic: there was the abdominal or intestinal type, transmitted mostly through the water supply, the exanthematous, which could be contracted by direct infection of the blood stream, for example through the bite of a louse, and a recurrent group, which, as the name implies, would return whenever there was an internal infection. The latter type was the most common here.

There were many cases of venereal disease too, mainly gonorrhoea, and syphilis. During the German occupation the Nazis had deliberately spread some of the infections, and syphilis had been deliberately introduced into the bloodstream of patients when they received treatment for some other ailment. Patients sent to hospital would contract typhoid in the hospital itself through using cutlery and other utensils which were not sterilized. Another source of infection was the food which was often brought into the hospital by anxious relatives: the containers and cutlery were not properly sterilized before they left the wards. In short, there was a complete breakdown of the elementary rules of hygiene due to the inefficiency of the hospital administrators. The most basic precautions were ignored. Most of the remaining staff of fifty or sixty who had stayed there all through the occupation now feared arrest for collaborating with the Germans and as a result were totally preoccupied. For instance the representative of the Ministry of Health would run from one department to another without changing her overalls wearing a stethoscope around her neck. Already the epidemic was in full swing, the morgue filling up with corpses every day. Drastic measures would be needed to eliminate it.

During the first week I went to see the *rayispolkom*, the local Mayor, and the Procurator General, Leonid Markoff. I explained the gravity of the situation: the entire hospital area would have to be declared out of bounds if they wished to contain the epidemic and prevent it spreading to the surrounding countryside. Many of the local people used a path across the grounds as a short cut, including the chief of the NKVD, Captain Babenko, whose office was only fifty yards outside the grounds. This would have to stop. Furthermore, we urgently needed supplies of food, both for the patients and the staff. They said they would do their best but I should not expect miracles: they had no fencing but would put up some barbed wire around the hospital buildings.

I assembled the entire medical staff of the hospital and the surrounding districts, which came under my jurisdiction, within an eighty-mile radius of the hospital. My reason for calling them together was, I explained, to emphasize the dangers and to remind them of their duties: I would expect their full co-operation in the plan I had evolved to fight the epidemic. I promised that within ninety days there would be no new cases of typhoid in the hospital or near it if they carried out my instructions to the letter. I would have to be very strict in spite of the fact that some of the staff there were twice as old as I was, and more. My instructions had been printed and were given to all of them. They would have to send me daily reports on the numbers of new cases. As they filed out, I heard someone call me a 'young sadist'.

One of the biggest problems was to locate the new cases of typhoid and get them into hospital. Often they didn't know what was the matter with them and, when they were told, they tried to refuse to go to hospital because it and the staff had such a bad name. This was understandable but not very helpful.

My solution to the problem was to organize 'epidemic teams' consisting of one nurse and one assistant. We worked out a plan to cover the rural areas and to include every household. The teams had to visit every dwelling to see if there were any sick people who had not sought medical aid. Whenever they found cases they made a mark outside the door and put up a warning sign: NO ENTRY: TYPHOID. These teams told the people how to proceed, how to disinfect their clothes and household utensils, especially cutlery, plates and drinking vessels: all the most elementary methods of curbing the out-break. Once a case had been notified, the house was visited by a representative of the public health department and a notice placed on the door to this effect. Every time the epidemic team visited the house they had to sign the notice and write the date of the visit.

Three weeks later the hospital had been totally fenced off. At intervals of fifty yards signposts were erected forbidding entry except to patients and staff. The place looked like a concentration camp from outside. I did not like it myself, but it was the only way to impose total isolation. The local people co-operated except for two *nachalniks*, Babenko of the NKVD and an NKGB officer. They continued to pass through the grounds on sledges: their drivers would jump down, open the wooden-framed iron gates and drive through, ignoring the signposts. Sometimes the hospital doorman would protest, but without conviction. I understood the poor fellow: those two represented the two most feared forces in the Soviet Union. But I had a letter prepared for the doorman to hand to them the next time they came through in which I stated that the restrictions applied equally to them.

Next morning came the first confrontation. Babenko made his usual entry into the grounds as I was on my early rounds of the hospital between 8 and 9 in the morning. He ordered his driver to stop and beckoned me over with his hand. I ignored him: I cannot bear to be called in that way. Then I heard the horse pull up behind me.

'Didn't you see I was calling you?' Babenko asked.

I ignored his question:

'What are you doing in the hospital grounds? Do you need medical treatment?'

'No, I don't,' he said. 'I am Captain Babenko, chief of the NKVD. I want to talk to you. Will you come to my office?'

I said:

'Is this to be an official interview?'

'Make sure you come.'

'If you wish to speak to me, you will have to come to my office because I am extremely busy. I do not want to see you or your driver coming through these grounds! Ever! If you persist in doing so I will take steps against you.'

As I turned to walk quickly away I saw a young boy who worked with the horses we used. He had overheard the conversation and stood transfixed, like a statue. I turned back again:

'And would you be kind enough to tell the chief of the NKGB that this rule applies to him too? As a message from me?'

I turned on my heels. After all, I had no reason to be frightened of either the NKVD or the NKGB. I was working eighteen hours a day. The measures I had instituted were beginning to pay off. The supplies of food improved. The patients were permitted to receive certain items, but no containers or utensils or clothes were permitted to leave the hospital. New patients started to come in of their own accord, and slowly their trust in the hospital and its staff was re-established. The local people would now open their doors and welcome my epidemic teams. In my capacity as Health Inspector I was empowered to impose fines for any unsanitary practices. I could fine officials in charge of food stores which were dirty or vermin-infested 500 to 1000 roubles, and they had to pay it from their own pockets.

Sometimes I would take one of the horses and ride out for three or four hours into the rural areas, visiting houses to see how the regulations were working. The results pleased me. The horses, however, were too slow for me; on making enquiries I discovered that Babenko had taken away the fastest horse, a mare called Bistra, and replaced it with another. I mentioned to the municipal secretary of the Mayor that I would get it back, and he laughed at me:

'That's provided he wants to give it back to you.'

'You will be the one who will order him to return it to the hospital,' I told him. We left it at that for the time being.

There were three problems which remained: firstly there was no wood with which to make coffins, and the earth was frozen so hard that the graves were too shallow. Sometimes dogs would come and scratch away the earth and even drag off human bones and pieces of flesh which were later found in the streets. Those dogs became carriers of typhoid. The second problem was to find enough food, especially for my epidemic teams. They often travelled long distances, staying away from their homes at night. They needed to eat well. Lastly, I myself was over-worked and run down.

The first problem I resolved by having all the corpses burnt. There were no proper crematoriums, and sometimes we had to burn five or six bodies daily. We had them placed side by side, then another set of bodies was placed on top facing the opposite direction, like matches. Petrol was thrown over them and set alight. I ordered the destruction of all dogs found on the streets. As for my rural epidemic teams, I forced the secretary of the Mayor to arrange for places for them to stay when they were out on visits.

As far as my own health was concerned, I told myself I would not give in. I would liquidate the epidemic. I would continue with my work even if I had to die. I loved my work: I felt so much compassion for all those who were suffering and dying.

The decision to have the bodies burnt proved most unpopular: it was not easy to tell relations that they could not bury the body of their loved one. They cried, and cursed me. Sometimes they threatened to kill me. But the epidemic died down.

The medical staff were afraid of me because I used to check up on them day and night. They would never know where I might appear next. At three in the morning I would go into the wards and sometimes find nurses sleeping. One of the best-looking nurses, Zoya, would even be making love with a patient if he wasn't too ill! If I found the toilets unflushed or in a dirty state, or patients with long dirty nails, I would warn the staff that if I found the same faults the following day there would be trouble.

On one inspection I came across an unemptied bedpan full of infectious faeces. I asked Zoya if she had left it there for inspection for some reason. She turned red and said: 'No.' In full view of the patients I threw the contents on the floor, pulled off her nurse's cap, and told her to clean it up. No wonder they hated me, but I didn't give a damn. I knew that they would soon understand my reasons and come to like me. I had to put out the raging fire of that epidemic. Some of the staff wrote complaining about me to Chevchenko, and even to Dniepropetrovsk, but only the NKVD and the NKGB dared to oppose me. Even there, however, once they saw that my methods were paying off, they began first to respect me and then to admire the work we had accomplished. The rate of infection was dropping slowly but surely. My whole life was dedicated to this task, to stem the epidemic, to reorganize the hospital, and by doing this to win the confidence of the people in their hospital, staff and patients alike. Meanwhile, I tried to improve the living conditions of the staff, especially their food.

When Babenko had told me to come and see him in his office I had ignored him. Then I received further summonses on three successive days, all of which I ignored. On the fourth day I was holding consultations when his personal assistant arrived. He clicked his heels and saluted:

'The *nachalnik* Captain Babenko has ordered me to bring you forthwith to his office!'

I answered that I was in the middle of consultations and had more patients to attend to, and asked if this was an arrest.

'No, it is not an arrest, but as soon as you have finished here you are to come with me.'

He was made to wait in a cold waiting room for over an hour while I took somewhat longer than usual to examine the remainder of my patients. Then I went with him, taking an assistant nurse with me. Babenko was pacing up and down but as we came into the room he rushed quickly to sit at his desk. He told me I was very bossy, and asked why I had not been to see him.

'I have no time to sit around scratching my balls,' I said, 'and if you are looking for someone to scratch yours, you'd better look for someone else.'

He jumped up like a gorilla, stood in front of a huge portrait of Stalin, and started to talk a load of rubbish.

'You were ordered not to use the hospital grounds as a short cut,' I interrupted, 'and yet you persist in doing so. I have an epidemic on my hands, with people dying every day, and you have the audacity to call me here to threaten and tyrannize me. Now I am going to give you some orders: first, bring your assistant and show me every prison cell in this building, I want to inspect their state of cleanliness. Second, never come through my hospital grounds again unless you are ill. And, finally, you will return the horse called Bistra which you removed from the hospital and replaced with a much inferior animal. If you do not carry out my orders I will impose the maximum fines on you.'

'You should be anxious to co-operate with the head of the NKVD,' he faltered in reply. I had broken him.

We proceeded to three different cells which we found to be

dirty, unsanitary, and lice-ridden. A statement was drawn up by witnesses, including the occupants of the cells. I left the prison without seeing Babenko again. Next day he received an ultimatum to put all the cells into a decent state conforming to the strict standards of hygiene. A further inspection would be made and, if the prison was in the same filthy condition, the maximum penalty would be imposed.

The short cuts stopped. Bistra reappeared in the stables. Babenko did not attain the standards of cleanliness required in the prison, and a fine of 500 roubles had to be paid from his salary.

Naturally Babenko became my bitterest enemy, and he searched for evidence to be used against me, but I knew I had the full support of the Party Secretary to carry on my fight against typhoid.

Every day I used to ride out on the magnificent Bistra, a tall chestnut mare with a white star on her forehead, and white socks, a long mane, and a most intelligent expression. I loved her and she used to gallop so fast that I couldn't get my breath – I had to keep my mouth covered. She was invaluable to me in my work.

At the end of April I called a meeting of the entire hospital staff. I knew that I was not popular with many of them : I had sacked some people for inefficiency. I was hard to others, and I demanded very high standards and very hard work. Chevchenko tried to humiliate me during the meeting. I told her to use less lipstick and to stop wearing a stethoscope around the hospital as she had no right to use one, not even on animals, let alone human beings. She was a party member and she owed her job to that.

During the meeting a Dr Staviskaya sat in the front row. She was in charge of a children's home caring for about a thousand children. She sat with her legs open, a plump good-looking woman, but she wore no knickers and, although this invariably excites me, it was hardly the time or the place to show it. I told her the children in her care had second-degree scabies and, if she did not know how to cure it, I would send her a full barrel of ointment. She replied that she knew quite well what to do.

'Alright. I will give you one week, and then if I find kids with scabies I will make you clean their sores with your tongue.'

There was an immediate murmur of protest among the staff. But all that mattered to me was results. There were fewer and fewer cases of typhoid. Every day we saw the fruits of our efforts. I had to be hard with the hospital personnel. I had to develop a new side to my personality. I never smiled. In normal conditions one achieves more from people by showing kindness and consideration, but in those circumstances we had no time. We had to save lives.

Since all the staff had collaborated in one way or another with the Germans and knew that one day they would be charged and sent to labour camps, they had allowed their standards to fall drastically. My job was to restore standards. They called me a sadist and tyrant behind my back, but gradually they changed their attitude. It was difficult but I managed to obtain clothing, living quarters and bonuses for good work. But extra food was the hardest. The local authorities laughed at me when I asked them for this for the staff. I remonstrated:

'Why should you and your people and the *komsomols* and bureaucrats sitting in offices get special treatment and shop in special shops where they can get whatever they want, when my medical staff, who work day and night, and ride out for miles in the snow and cold, risking their lives while you sleep in warm beds, go hungry?'

One morning we fought about it so much I lost my temper:

'If you are unable to supply food for my staff, I will resign,' I threatened. 'I know all about the special deliveries of food you are getting from the *kolhozs*, so tell me now' – I hammered on the desk of the Party Secretary – 'yes or no!'

The Secretary stood up, pale with anger:

'Never in my life, in my twenty years as Party Secretary, has anyone had the audacity to hammer on my desk.'

'Oh, come on,' I said, 'will you get me the food or not?'

'You deserve everything we can get for you, you are so dynamic, and the results of your hard work are excellent. I will do my best for you. We shall have to see where the surpluses are. Just give me a few requisition orders for potatoes, flour, maize, meat, oil, sugar, salt and heating fuel, and I will do the rest.'

In the end I got food not only for the hospital staff, but for others too, including party members. I had my ways and means. I could even obtain wood for the coffins now, but we no longer required such large quantities.

The hospital staff began to say : 'Good morning Doctor' when they saw me in the corridors.

My next fight was against venereal disease. I opened a VD clinic of which I was personally in charge. I was getting three and a half doctors' salaries for doing four doctors' jobs. Our first mode of attack was to make a routine check of all hospital patients for VD, whatever their ailment.

Dr Zaikin, the chief surgeon and head doctor of the hospital, lived with his wife and two small children in the hospital premises, but he was afraid to enter the typhoid wards. During the first two months at the hospital I was often involved in disagreements with him. He was quite a good surgeon but a hopeless administrator with little or no force of character. More than anyone else a doctor of medicine needs to have a warm personality. In many ways a very sick patient is like a baby : he draws strength from the impact of the doctor's person-ality, and gets relief from the doctor's words as well as his actions. This is what Zaikin lacked; his expression was invari-ably gloomy and patients would say that just to look at his face made them feel like dying.

I put through a request to General Kucharave in Dniepro-petrovsk to have him replaced, though I knew it would be diffi-cult to find a surgeon, and, to make matters worse, Zaikin had himself become ill with typhoid abdominalis. He was in isola-tion in a room of his apartment while I coped with his work. I had not had much experience of major surgery at that time, so a plane was put at our disposition to send patients requiring major surgery to Dniepropetrovsk. They sent out a new consultant to the hospital, a beautiful blonde, Dr Parchomenko, whose hus-band was a professor at the Dniepropetrovsk Institute of Medi-cine. She was tall, blue-eyed and looked more like a film actress than a doctor of medicine. I was able to call her in for any case I found necessary.

They also sent two qualified male nurses. They had been demobilized, one called Peschenko with the rank of lieutenant, and the other, Krilov, a second lieutenant. They often embarrassed me by clicking their heels when I gave an order, but their experience and discipline proved invaluable. I put Peschenko in charge of the epidemic teams and he was able to check on the house calls they made, thus relieving me of that duty. Krilov worked in the hospital. Shortly afterwards a Major Ravinsky, a surgeon, still wearing military uniform, arrived. He looked a sick man himself, but he took over all the surgical work including the patients on whom I had operated. He was satisfied with their condition, which was a relief for me. The only person who criticized me was the gorgeous Dr Parchomenko who said I had taken too many chances and might find myself in trouble with the law for taking risks. Perhaps she was jealous of what I had achieved, but otherwise I had a good relationship with her. Our eyes would often meet, and we understood each other.

By May, there were only sixteen cases of typhoid left, all hospitalized. The days passed very quickly. The typhoid cases ceased coming in altogether, the block where the typhoid patients had been housed was empty. I had a white flag put up over the block. I was no longer the sadist. They had a new name for me: 'The Epidemic-Slayer'.

When I went to Dniepropetrovsk General Kucharave called in his department heads and many doctors to his office to meet me, and told them he was recommending me to the Ministry of Health for a special award for my outstanding work in the epidemic. As we left his office, he put his arm round my shoulder and led me out to the corridor.

'I'm just going along here a moment,' he indicated the toilet. 'Come with me.'

Inside, he said:

'We can talk here without fear of being overheard. You have done a tremendous job, and I really admire you for it, but I have to tell you that we have had a constant stream of complaints about you from Sofiyevka. Babenko has started preparing material to have you arrested. He doesn't know that he is going to be transferred in a few days' time. Fuck them all! Do your job, and I'll back you up.'

After my return to Sofiyevka there were no more typhoid cases, although we continued to be watchful. I used to ride out on Bistra to the black spots where typhoid had been rife, but everything appeared to be safe. One day on our way home Bistra stopped suddenly. At first I couldn't think why. She just turned her head to look at me, as if pleading for help. She had galloped about thirty miles that day. I remembered she had a weak leg, so I jumped down to examine it. I was alarmed to see pus oozing out from her shin. It appeared to be a bone infection. The local veterinary surgeon had been looking after the horses, but I had not been told how serious her condition was. I walked her the five miles back to the hospital without remounting. She even refused the pieces of sugar I used to carry for her. I put my cheek against her mouth and it felt dry. I tried to reassure her:

'Don't worry. We'll get you better, you'll be alright. You'll have a good rest and you will be alright.'

That evening the vet reported to me that she had a high fever and her leg was in an appalling condition. His advice was that she should be put out of her misery that night, but I begged him to wait for a few days to see if she improved.

I walked back to our flat in the dark. There was more bad news – the very worst. Luba told me that she had heard from the Procurator General that a warrant for my arrest had been issued, but they could not use it till they had obtained the signature of the Procurator General of Kiev, since my official appointment had been made there. She was crying with despair.

I couldn't understand:

'Why did they do this? Leonid Markoff is my friend. I saved his daughter when she had typhoid. We met often, why didn't he warn me what's been going on? What are the charges?'

I downed a large tumbler of vodka, then made the rounds of my patients who were in a ward which had been set aside for my own cases. There were twenty-five beds there. Only one, an elderly woman, was seriously ill, with cirrhosis of the liver. I hadn't been there for two days, and the nurse said they had all been asking for me. When I couldn't come Dr Ravinsky or Luba would do my rounds for me, but they always asked for me because I made them all laugh. I went into the ward where the men and women were divided by a screen. The old woman was holding a big cross in her hand. Her face looked as though she had died already.

'How are you, mother?' I asked.

Her pulse was weak and irregular, her body cold. As I stood listening to her heartbeat I asked her:

'What's the matter, little mother? You want to die?'

She answered in a broken voice:

'Oh, leave me in peace to die, doctor. I'm tired, I can't fight any longer.'

'No, you will live. Let me hold the cross and I'll tell you a story.'

She handed me the cross.

'You will live, and you will still make love one day with a fine young fellow.'

She laughed in her creaking voice:

'Not even you believe that!' she said.

'Yes, yes I do. You wait and see!'

I managed to cheer them all up, and left instructions with the nurse concerning their treatment.

It took me an hour to reach Markoff's house.

He was surprised to see me and somewhat embarrassed. His wife, who usually kissed me, was distant too. But I kissed her, and lifted his daughter high in the air.

'Leonid Markovitch, I have to talk to you.' I took him by the hand and led him into one of the bedrooms.

'Have you anything you want to tell me?' I asked.

'No,' he answered.

'Why are you going to arrest me then?'

The first thing he did was to produce a bottle of vodka. We both drank a lot. Then he told me that Babenko had been gathering evidence against me and, according to Babenko, the Party Secretary supported him. He himself had defended me and, strangely enough, the Chief of the NKGB had done so too. He had been playing for time since he knew that Babenko was to be transferred. Then he would allow the matter to lapse.

'Look, I'm your friend, I would have had the guts to tell you if you were going to be arrested. I know you have the party officials in your favour. You would be bound to hear anything like that long before it happened.' He was right. I knew all the party officials extremely well, and some were my patients. Often they gave me information I needed for my work.

All the same, I couldn't sleep that night. I had calmed Luba's fears about my arrest, but the plight of Bistra was worrying me. I finally got to bed at around three in the morning, and was just getting off to sleep when a nurse tapped on the window to tell me that the old lady with cirrhosis was dying. I rushed out and was at her bedside within minutes but it was too late. She was dead. I could never take the death of any patient lightly, although I knew that her case had been a hopeless one. At the autopsy we saw that her liver had atrophied to the size of an egg. I was too disturbed to go back to bed again, so I went to the stables to have a look at Bistra. She was standing holding her lame leg off the ground. She hadn't lain down because she knew she wouldn't be able to stand up again. I offered her sugar lumps. She looked at me, her eyes full of gratitude, but it was hopeless. I whispered words of comfort in her ear.

The next day was a very difficult one: a young prisoner committed suicide at the NKGB headquarters. He had hanged himself. They had tried to revive him but let several hours elapse before calling me in. They had probably been afraid to report the death for reasons that became clear later. When I arrived his body had already been transferred to the morgue; I caught a glimpse of the Chief of the NKGB, sweating and apprehensive, before I left, angry at having my time wasted, for the stables.

There the vet told me that Bistra would have to be destroyed, and the sooner the better. We stood looking at her together. I told him to give me time to walk away before he shot her. There was no argument about it now, she still had a high temperature and could not go on standing on three legs indefinitely. The other animals were moved out, and I went into her. It was so sad, I couldn't console myself with the thought that it was only a horse. I strode quickly back to my room and poured myself a vodka. Slowly I lifted the lace curtain and saw the vet go in to her with some other assistants. They closed the doors. The shot rang out.

The newly set-up VD clinic was my responsibility. We had not yet had time to concentrate our efforts against VD, but leaflets explaining what it was and listing its symptoms had been circulated. Anyone who needed help was urged to contact us and told they would be treated confidentially. As I was taking the surgery that day – there was a four-year-old girl with gonorrhoea – I could hear someone outside pacing up and down in squeaky new boots. I asked the nurse to look outside and tell whoever was walking about to sit down. She opened the door, looked out, then closed it quietly.

'It's the Chief of the NKGB,' she whispered.

I went out to him and asked what I could do for him. He said he wanted to see me alone, but not in the consulting room.

'Why not?' I asked. 'There is no notice outside to say what kind of clinic it is. Please come in.'

He sat before me, frightened and unsure of himself. I asked the nurse to wait outside. He embarked on his troubles:

'I'm a family man, the father of three children. My own future and the future of all my family is in your hands. Not only do I think I have a venereal disease, but to make matters worse a prisoner has died by his own hand while under arrest. He is here in the hospital morgue. He was beaten up by some of the other prisoners before he died. I have no choice but to beg your help, although I know you don't like our organization.'

I told him to pull down his trousers. From the examination and from the symptoms he described I saw he was suffering from a cystitis. I took a smear and told him we would inform him of the result. In the meantime he should follow my instructions.

Then he asked if we could both go to the morgue. I made no objection. There I inspected the corpse. I dictated the report of my findings to Peschenko stating that the dead man must be between twenty-five and thirty, that there was external bruising consistent with beating and kicking on the ribs, face and head. The deep marks left by the rope around his neck were also described. We came to the internal examination and, when I was about to make the incision in the thorax, I heard a thud behind me. The tough NKGB man, used to watching all kinds of human suffering, had fallen to the floor unconscious. He was

given first-aid before we could conclude the autopsy and complete the report, which gave the cause of death as hanging. The
report would be seen by General Kucharave, but I made no
comments on the bruising since the death of course had been
due to suicide by hanging.

In spite of his protests Dr Zaikin was transferred to a hospital
ward. He had wanted to remain in his apartment, but I told
him it would be a very bad example if he refused to be moved
into the hospital proper. His family had not contracted the
disease. When I went to visit him he said:

'Garri Semionovitch, I have decided to stay here in Sofiyevka,
and I want to write to General Kucharave to tell him so. Would
you mind writing the letter for me?'

'You, a Soviet graduate, want me to write the letter for you?
Why?'

'I just can't seem to put the thing together, and you have such
a forceful way of writing letters. I think you would do it better
than I would.'

'I'm sorry,' I told him. 'I can't do it because I have already
written to ask for your transfer elsewhere.'

His wife was there and they looked at each other, flabber-
gasted.

'Why did you do that?' he asked.

I said: 'You are a good surgeon, but you're lazy and un-
co-operative.'

I left them then, and did not see him again. He left three
weeks later.

Relations with the medical staff of the hospital improved all
the time. They had come to like me. There had been very few
alterations to the personnel and, in the case of Dr Zaikin, everybody realized my ruthlessness was justified. At a brief meeting
I told them not to be too complacent, that the epidemic teams
should continue their visits to every house and take notes of the
numbers of occupants, their sex and age, and ask if they were
suffering from any skin disorders or VD. They distributed the
leaflets about VD which I had had printed. I personally went
through all these reports. Dr Staviskaya, the good-looking doctor in charge of the children's home, was at the meeting. She

still sat with her legs open but she now remembered to wear her under-clothes. One of the staff expressed their satisfaction and thanks to me for the respect in which they were now held by patients. I told them they had all earned that respect. Before closing the meeting, I announced:

'We have made progress in every sphere of hospital life, and rebuilding of the bombed blocks will start soon. We shall be able to accept patients with a whole range of diseases.'

As they filed out they shook my hand, something they had not done before. As Staviskaya went out I told her how well she had done to clear up the scabies among the children – and that I was pleased to see she was now wearing black pants.

13

The VD Clinic

The Venereal Department proved most successful, even though we had only the most primitive types of treatment available for gonorrhoea and syphilis.

Every case of venereal disease is of interest to a doctor. If the patient comes for help voluntarily that's one thing, but often we had a fight with the patients before they would even admit they were infected. The day I discovered the child who had gonorrhoea I asked the mother to undress. She was reluctant, and asked why she should undress. I told her that her child had gonorrhoea and had most probably caught it from someone living in the house, from the sheets or other contact. It transpired that the child slept in the same room as her mother, and there were no other people living in the house. She had not had intercourse with anyone since her husband had left to go to the front. When I asked if she had ever had the symptoms of the disease she said:

'No, never.'

But when I examined her it was quite clear from whom the child had caught it. Both mother and child were hospitalized immediately and the house disinfected by one of the epidemic teams.

The Chief of the NKGB turned out to have gonorrhoea too, not cystitis. When I told him I would have to examine his wife, he said he had not made love to her for a long time and that the symptoms had only recently appeared. I had to know who the woman was, but he was loath to tell me.

'Be reasonable,' I said. 'I have a duty to help you and whoever else is involved.'

'Oh no, please don't force me to tell you,' he pleaded.

'You have your methods of getting confessions out of people

and brainwashing them, and so have I. Unless you tell me the name of the woman, I will put you in hospital in an isolated VD ward.'

With a dramatic gesture he drew his revolver and held it to his temple:

'I have my pride. I would rather shoot myself here than be put in hospital and forced to give the name of the woman.'

I was not impressed. I stood up and went round to him, put one hand on his shoulder and slowly pulled the gun down with the other.

'Alright, I won't put you in hospital if you will tell me the name of the woman. She made you ill and she can do the same to many others.'

In the end I won him round, and he told me. She was the local judge, a very tough woman, with whom I had had a few exchanges over administrative problems. I gave the NKGB man treatment, and saw his wife too, and soon the family was alright.

I invited the judge to come and visit me. She didn't turn up the first time but when I repeated the request she came, an aggressive, plain woman of thirty. Most VD patients preferred to be examined without the nurse present. As she sat down, she got the first word in:

'I know why you have asked me to come here.'

'Undress please, and get on to this couch. I shall have to call in the nurse to help me with the examination.'

Within minutes she was on the gynaecological couch with her two legs wide apart in the air. The picture was all too clear: she was in an advanced stage of gonorrhoea.

From her and the NKGB chief I was able to trace five others who had had intercourse with one or the other of them.

There was a high-ranking local government official, who had caught it from the judge. In view of her condition I had wanted to put the judge in hospital, but now it appeared that some local 'big fish' were involved, and I decided to give them treatment in the outpatients' departments. I had to be careful too about appointment times, so that none of them should bump into each other. It wasn't easy. Sometimes I had to give them very late appointments when all the staff had left.

At that time, it took two to four weeks to cure a case of gonorrhoea. The mother of the little girl patient had caught hers from a German soldier. It was an advanced case too, and if she hadn't brought the child to me there could have been a very ugly ending to her story. From two other patients we traced fifty-seven cases of syphilis. One was Bibikov, a man in his sixties with a little grey beard, toothless. When he came for examination he made the usual request for the nurse to leave the room. He had come in from the country. I told him the nurse would have to stay. He winked and pointed to a basket he was carrying which no doubt contained a gift for me. The nurse had her back turned.

'Thank you,' I said. 'I'm afraid I cannot accept your gift.'

It was the custom for these simple good people to bring a gift in kind for the doctor as a mark of their gratitude, perhaps a chicken, or eggs. Later I discovered that it was better to accept these gifts with good grace, because they were truly offended by a refusal. There was no law or rule against this practice.

'Mr Bibikov,' I asked. 'What's your problem?'

'He's become very ill,' he started. 'I've tried to cure him myself, but nothing I do helps him. I tried wrapping him in onion leaves, and I tried frying onions and putting them on his head, but he only got more swollen.'

He then started worrying about the nurse, intimidated by his surroundings. She looked at me and half smiled. I winked to her not to say anything.

He went on:

'He's really naughty. I've bathed him too, in hot and cold water. Someone told me I should bathe him in horse's urine. I even did that, but it didn't help.'

I knew from the start that he had been referring to his penis, but he had described it in such a way that he had aroused my interest and I encouraged him to continue in the same vein.

'Before I examine you I shall have to write this all down. Please continue.'

'Alright. Well, I've even bandaged him, but he won't get better.'

'Now,' I asked, 'who exactly is it you are talking about, your son?'

'No, no. It's him.'

'Your brother?' I asked him.

'No, it's him, him.' He looked down to his trousers. 'Doctor, don't you understand me? He got sick.'

'Perhaps you can explain it better to my nurse. What do you mean when you say he got sick?'

He scratched his chin with one hand, and with the other pointed to his penis.

'You will have to show him to me if you want us to help you,' I said.

It took us ten minutes to undress him and remove the many bandages he had wound round his penis. It looked almost like a wrapped baby. When we had nearly finished removing the bandages we could see the gauze was sticking to the open wounds. The poor man tried to hold back his cries of pain. Under the bandages he had a very small penis and an extremely advanced case of syphilis.

'You have syphilis,' I told him.

'My God, what's that?' he asked.

'You made love with a woman and she infected you.'

'God have pity on me,' he cried – he was wearing a large cross – 'What are you saying to me?'

It took us one and a half hours to get a confession out of him. He had made love with a milkmaid on the dairy farm where he worked.

We put him in the hospital and sent Peschenko to the farm to examine the workers there, especially the milkmaid. They brought her back with them. She was a stout, healthy-looking, wide-faced Slav type of around thirty-five, with a strong body. I told her we had asked her to come to the hospital because we knew that she was in need of medical attention. This she strenuously denied, saying she was as strong as an ox and had never known a day's illness.

'Nevertheless, I must examine you,' I told her.

Luba was present at the time. Most of the doctors had altered their work schedules to include a certain number of hours with VD patients who attended the ordinary outpatients' clinic where no one was too embarrassed to attend. At first we had opened a clinic specifically for venereal diseases, but we quickly learnt that we could get far more co-operation and many more patients by mixing them in with general outpatients.

This woman stood up to twenty minutes of questioning without admitting anything. In the end we called in a doctor who knew her. He lost his patience with her and shouted at her :

'Undress, bitch, or we will have to do it for you !'

I added : 'Your friend Bibikov is ill with syphilis, and you won't leave here until we examine you too. If you resist further we shall call in the police and have you put in prison.'

I had never threatened a patient like this before, but I knew that if I let her go she would never come back for treatment. I had learnt one thing at least from the NKVD, how to make threats. She consented.

When at last we were able to examine her we found she was covered in sores, some of them a quarter of an inch deep, a most severe case of syphilis.

I told the nurse to call in Luba who had been waiting outside. The woman was still protesting :

'You see ! There's nothing wrong with me. I'm perfectly healthy.'

I asked Luba to fetch a mirror. We all three stood round her while I held the mirror so she could see.

'Look,' I shouted, 'see how healthy you are !'

'That's only a little scabies. It just itches from time to time.'

The other doctor started to insult her, but I asked him to leave the room now. I made her undress completely. Her belly was covered in sores which had running pus. As she dressed, I told her :

'You are ill with syphilis, and you infected Bibikov.'

'Good God, what did you say ? What is syphilis ?'

It took a long time to explain it to her, then another hour to try to get her to give us the names of others she might have infected. I even told the nurse to telephone the police. She did all the milking at the farm, and at that time it was all done by hand. I shuddered to contemplate what harm she might have done. When she realized that I was serious in my threat to have her put in prison if she refused to co-operate she gave in. It transpired that she had infected over twenty men with the disease. The other thirty-seven cases involved were not directly attributable to her, but were passed on through her contacts. She had been living with a German soldier, she said. It took us a month to contact all these people and get them to the hospital for examination. Others had left the district and were far away by then. I had never experienced a case where as many as fifty-seven people had been infected through one person, and the number was probably even greater.

At that time it took up to two years to cure syphilis. The standard treatment was salvasan and bismuth. We had to keep the syphilis patients in the hospital for six to eight weeks before we could release them with a negative blood count. They were able to lead a normal life then, but with constant repetition of the treatment under medical surveillance.

There was another memorable case; the Secretary of the Communist Party in the district told me that a very high-ranking party member needed speedy and discreet treatment, because he had a most important job and was too ill to work.

Proshko was a man over six feet and lost no time when he came to see me:

'You know why I have come. Help me.' Without further preamble he undid his trousers with his right hand, which had three fingers missing, and showed me his penis.

'Look at it! I have quite a discharge. Just look at it. I have to carry it, but I can't use it. If you can help me, I will be your friend for life. Otherwise, just take a knife and cut it off. I'm ashamed. All my underwear gets filthy. It's utter misery. I'm a married man with children. Help me!'

I had him put in hospital and ordered him a special diet. He was given the usual treatment and, in addition, to speed matters up I imposed a high-fever therapy. Unfortunately his wife had been infected too, but his children were alright. I cured them both. When he left the hospital I told him:

'You can go and drink a bottle of vodka, then you must come back to see me in twenty-four hours. Don't make love with anyone, your wife or anyone else.' I knew who had given him the disease. Next morning I was woken at 5.30 a.m. by the sound of shots from a hunting gun. Then in the half-light of dawn I saw Proshko standing outside the window. He held the gun aloft in one hand, and his penis in the other:

'Look! No discharge!'

I rushed out and led him inside. He was very drunk, still holding his penis:

'Look, there's nothing. I'm perfectly alright! I'm cured. Let me give you a kiss!'

I think he was the only man who ever kissed me on the mouth.

'I'm going to pay you, pay you handsomely, with this gun. I'll bring you the first *zaichik*, the first hare I get, and you will eat it. I've drunk more than a bottle of vodka.'

I kept him there until eight o'clock and then sent him back to the hospital with Peschenko with instructions to boil all his underclothes for a long time, under his own supervision. Proshko became my good friend as will become apparent later.

It was particularly satisfying work with the VD patients, because more than most patients they were desperately anxious to get better again as quickly as possible.

It was late spring. The world looked beautiful, I was happy with my work, but my thoughts were concentrating on how I would get out of Russia. All the news was good now. The Second Front would open any moment. If the war ended soon I wanted to be sure that I was registered as a Polish citizen. A special NKGB bureau had been set up for this purpose. I decided to go to Dniepropetrovsk as soon as I could register, but Luba had been keeping me awake at night with her crying, pressing me to fetch her little girl, Sonia, so much that I had promised to go to Karaganda in the middle of June with or without the health department's permission.

14

⌐⌐

Enter Sonia

That permission was not forthcoming. General Kucharave told me he could not deny me anything, but Professor Fesenko and Dr Kozlova had raised objections about the possibility of further outbreaks of typhoid during my absence.

Kucharave was sympathetic:

'What you want to do is very humane, to return a child to her mother. I know you are impetuous, and if you should decide to go there under your own steam, I will certainly not penalize you for it later.'

This was the green light I had been waiting for. I thanked him and went to see Liebermann, his second-in-command. He had been the head of the Ministry of Health in Dniepropetrovsk in 1939, 1940 and part of 1941. He had been removed from the post because of his Jewish origins. He was told that the Nazis had been responsible for new outbursts of anti-semitic feeling, and that it would be better not to provoke trouble by retaining Jews in the highest posts. I personally had never accepted this theory and had often had arguments with the local party chief in Sofiyevka on this point. I considered it nonsense. The Red Army and the Soviet people had crushed the German occupiers and thrown them out. Why should we not destroy every trace of their dirty prejudices? It was Stalin who had initiated his anti-semitic policy before the end of the war by gradually ousting Jews from positions of authority. Of course it was done with the utmost care, and excuses were always given, but the machine was in motion already. Now, with hindsight, my fears then regarding Russia's Jews have been only too tragically confirmed.

The Allies landed in Normandy on 6 June 1944, and a week later I went to the special NKVD and NKGB office for registration of Polish citizens, so that I would be free to go as soon as the war ended. Luba asked me to put her name and that of her child on the list too. The person in charge of the office was a woman who had given birth to a son only two months before. She was very pale – so pale that I invited her to come to spend the holiday in August with us at Sofiyevka. She told me her husband was an NKGB officer, and asked if both of them could come. I didn't think she would take me up on the holiday but she did. As it turned out I was glad when she did. Her name was Viera, and she was to become a loyal friend. I went back to Sofiyevka and found everything in order and running smoothly.

So, now, obviously, was the time to set out to Karaganda on what was bound to be a very long and arduous journey as public transport was irregular, and delays were frequent due to the surveillance of military police and NKGB checks for deserters, German spies, and collaborators on the run. I was only just beginning to realize what a formidable task I had set myself.

I was to leave on 17 June and the night before neither Luba nor I could sleep. She talked continuously about this, that, and the other, but especially about us. Though I had been living with her ever since our arrival at the hospital I was never in love with her, but I had become used to her and often felt pity for her situation. I didn't want to marry her, as I planned to leave the Soviet Union alone, though marriage was a very simple matter of registration at the *Zaks* (registry office) and the payment of one rouble. She cried so much that night I think a sheet would have not absorbed her tears. She told me:

'If you bring my child back, you will always be the first in my heart after Sonia and my mother and father. I don't believe in God, I'm a true *komsomol* but I will believe in something if you bring her to me. But, oh, if they arrest you, it will be all my fault. Oh Mama, Mama, give me the strength to get through the next few days. How will I live waiting to hear from you? What have I done for you to make you risk your life for me?'

I calmed her down. She described her husband and mother-in-law and Sonia because she had no photographs. She told me her mother-in-law went to a certain shop every morning and described its location. She was a chain-smoker with a pock-marked

face, a long nose, and blue eyes, an ugly-looking woman. She
had the address of the house where they lived.

On the way to the station next morning, Luba handed me
three letters, one addressed to the Secretary of the *komsomol*,
the Communist Youth Movement, in Karaganda, whom she
knew personally, one to the Secretary of the Communist Party
in Karaganda, and one to her husband. I asked her to read out
the letters to me. The one to the Secretary of the *komsomol* was
a straightforward request for assistance to me in my mission.
But the one to the Party Secretary read as follows:

'In fulfilment of my duty as a Communist I wish to inform
you that my ex-husband, Michael Kagan, secured his release
from the army by using documents signed by doctors which
were not based on the facts. He is perfectly healthy and there
is no reason why he should not be on active service now.'

She gave the names of the doctors who had signed the documents.

I stopped the horse and cart.

'You have given me goose-pimples. Would you really be
ready to put the father of your own child in prison? And the
doctors who helped you?'

Now I began to understand what a bitch she was. I had lost
all respect for her. She started to cry. I tore the letter to the
Secretary of the Communist Party in shreds:

'That's not my way of doing things.' A fine sentiment that I
am afraid I had to betray, at least in spirit, later.

As we pulled up at the station she leant forward and kissed
me. By the way I returned her kiss she sensed the damage she
had done with the letter. In Yiddish – I had never heard her
speak a word of Yiddish in her life, although I knew she understood it – she said:

'Go with God.'

Five days – and three trains and eight police checks later –
I reached Karaganda, a centre of heavy industry and coal
mining, at around six in the morning. I had only 200 roubles
left, having over-spent on bribes and food during the trip. Here
I was in a completely unknown city, almost penniless. I took a
droshky to the address Luba had given me and en route noticed
a line of women waiting outside a food shop: one of them was

smoking. She fitted Luba's description of her mother-in-law, so I got down from the carriage and told the man to wait. Mrs Kagan had already noticed me, but I went up to another woman near her in the queue and asked her if she could help me with the address of a lodging house. She hesitated and tried to think, but in the end was unable to help me. I had taken out a packet of very good cigarettes which were difficult to obtain. I lit one and blew the smoke in Mrs Kagan's direction.

'Oh, what an aroma!' she exclaimed. 'I haven't smelt a cigarette like that in years.'

I handed her the pack:

'Please take one. I have more.'

Within seconds the packet was empty. They all wanted one. Mrs Kagan was quietly observing me the whole time. She had taken two cigarettes. I said to her:

'Throw away that one you're smoking. Try one of mine now.'

'Oh no,' she said, 'I want to save it for after my meal.' She looked at me curiously:

'That's a fine jacket you're wearing. You're a stranger, aren't you? What brings you to this city?'

'I came here to do a favour for someone, a woman. I have to go to see the Party Secretary first, then I have to leave the city and take a child with me.'

My heart thumped wildly when she asked:

'What is the name of the family, and the child?'

I said: 'Just a minute, let me look at the paper I have here in my pocket.'

I took out the letter addressed to the *komsomol*.

'It's Kagan, Michael Kagan.'

Her face turned grey. The others stayed quiet and watched her.

'Well, what is it? Has this Mr Kagan died? Do you know him?'

The old woman took out the cigarette she had intended to save till after her meal and lit it from the stub of the last one. Everything went quiet.

'Is this child's name Sonia?' she asked.

'Yes, I think so, let me have another look.' I took out the paper again and studied it.

'What a coincidence,' she said. 'I am Michael Kagan's mother.'

The women, who had been whispering among themselves, stood back to let Mrs Kagan collect her shopping first so that she could come with me. She told me to pay off the *droshky*, as she and her son would be able to bring me back. We walked the quarter of a mile to where she lived in a five-storey building. I was ashamed that I had been forced to act as I did towards the old woman. I had to do it that way because if they were to discover I had any relationship with Luba I would never get the child.

It was getting light as we walked up the stairs to the second floor. She rang the bell and said:

'Open the door, Sonia, my treasure. It's me, with an uncle.'

The door swung open to reveal a little blonde child, a girl of three, with blue eyes, and a mouth like her mother's. She smiled as we went inside. I shook her hand. Her grandmother said:

'This uncle has brought you a present from your mother.'

I had bought a packet of sweets from a soldier on the train who was on his way home from Germany. As I handed her the sweets I said:

'These are from your mother.'

She took the sweets, all smiles.

A man's voice came from another room:

'Who's there, mother?'

'Luba has sent a friend of hers with a message.'

A man came out of the bathroom, wearing trousers and vest, with shaving cream still on his face, tall, good-looking, blue-eyed, in his late twenties. He had a polite well-educated air:

'Welcome to our home. I'm Michael Kagan.'

That memory fills me with both pleasure and pain, mixed.

His mother waved us all into the sitting-room and asked us to sit down. She said she would prepare breakfast. It was a small apartment but comfortable and well-kept. Sonia went off to the kitchen with her grandmother, chattering and asking questions.

Michael wiped the shaving cream off his face and sat down to talk to me. He lit a pipe and drew on it:

'What news do you have of my home town?' he asked.

I went straight to the point:

'Your ex-wife Luba has been working in the same hospital as me in Sofiyevka. She has asked me to come here to bring her child back to her.'

I handed him the letter Luba had written. It was sealed, and I did not know what she had said, but it was not hard to guess that whatever she had said it was causing him considerable stress. He drew in hard on his pipe:

'She hasn't changed at all. But I won't give you the child. I want to keep her with me for another six months.'

'I'm sorry,' I said, 'but that is out of the question. You will have to hand her over. I regret the fact that I had to come to your home, for what I have to say will be most unpleasant. But I think it best if I am frank and open. . . .'

We were interrupted by his mother who came in and told us that breakfast was ready. We ate, and while we ate the child Sonia gazed at me with her oriental ice-blue eyes. She was wearing a little blue dress with a white collar. The old woman had winked at me not to mention her mother's name at the table. She was smoking one cigarette after the other.

Michael had healthy-looking red cheeks, but now he looked most unhappy. They had been prepared to be friendly towards me, but I could understand that my purpose had caused them great unhappiness.

The mother called in a neighbour in her fifties who took Sonia off saying:

'Come, play with Caterina for a little while.'

She lifted up the child to carry her out. Sonia continued to gaze at me over the woman's shoulder. I would not fail, I resolved I would take her to her mother.

'Now we can talk,' Mrs Kagan said. Her son passed her the letter from Sonia. She put on her glasses, read it, then took a cigarette.

'Now I know why I had those bad dreams. There was a policeman who hit me over the head with a stick. How can she write such terrible things to my son?'

I told her to be reasonable. I could only remain there two days longer and I wanted an amicable arrangement agreed to by all three of us. I proposed that Mrs Kagan should travel with the child as far as Dniepropetrovsk. Michael remarked:

'You talk as though it's all settled. I do not want Sonia to go away, or my mother. There is no point in your staying here.... Here is my answer.' He tore Luba's letter into pieces and threw them in the fire.

'Perhaps if I let you both discuss it further?' I suggested.

They talked for another forty minutes without arriving at a decision, then Michael said he would be late for work.

'I'm truly sorry,' I told him, 'that I have got to give you some more bad news. Your wife told me that you are a deserter and that some doctor friends of yours helped you to get demobilized. She gave me a letter to give to the Secretary of the Party if you refused to send her daughter to her.'

'I know that already,' he said darkly, 'she put it in her letter.'

His mother interrupted:

'Come back here at three, and we can talk again.'

I left the apartment thoroughly ashamed of the part I was playing. I had never used threats for my own gain or advancement or to save myself. They didn't know it but I was acting from a very weak position. My documents were not in order. I had no real authority to make the journey. I was engaged in a battle of wits.

I walked to the bus stop with Kagan, having left my things at their flat. He asked where I would go until the afternoon.

'I shall call at the Party building to see the Secretary.' He looked surprised.

'It's for other business, nothing to do with you.'

He pointed out the building and took me to the door to see if they would let me in, and to hear what I would say.

'The Party Secretary is expecting me,' I said, 'please give him my name.'

It was bluff, of course, but they let me in, and I said goodbye to Michael. He said he wouldn't be home before five, but that I could go there earlier if I wished.

I had forced myself in to see the Party Secretary, and now I had to stay and talk to him for an hour. He offered me tea. I told him I had come to Karaganda to collect a child, and would be leaving there in a couple of days with the child and another person. I would need his help to obtain reservations for a sleeper on the train. I took out my travel warrant and asked him to stamp it on the back, to confirm that I had paid him a visit.

'Of course,' he said, 'I will do what I can to help you, although I don't think you will need my stamp. You should go to the local health authorities for that. But now that you have come here, never mind, I will stamp it. My secretary will make arrangements for the sleepers.'

I thanked him and left the building. If all Party Secretaries were as clever as he was, they would have no party left by now. The stamp on my travel permit was now an endorsement of the legality of my purpose. On the way there I had had a lot of explaining to do every time my documents were checked. Now I had something the authorities would respect. Furthermore, it would have been impossible to obtain couchettes without his help, so my visit had proved fruitful. As I walked around the city I wondered if the Party Secretary would start having second thoughts about me. The very nature of my mission made me feel uncomfortable, but I still thought I would win through. I returned to the apartment much earlier than expected, at mid-day. The mother was there, and so was Michael with a young woman.

'It's just as well you came early. We have had a talk.'

Michael wanted to know whether in fact I had been received by the Party Secretary. I showed him the back of the permit with the stamp. It was the most convincing of arguments.

'I never tried to take Sonia away from her mother. I only took her because Luba kept telling her I had died in the war. Sonia! Come here, tell uncle what your mother always told you about me.'

She confirmed what he said, then left the room with the young woman.

'Now she knows I'm not dead. I want to keep her with me for another six months or a year. She will be that much older and will not forget me. Then I'll give her back to Luba.'

'I'm sorry,' I told him, 'you won't be able to do that. I must go back to Dniepropetrovsk. If you refuse to send her I will have to ask you to come with me to the Party Secretary this afternoon.'

The mother smoked one cigarette after another.

'Michael, I can't let you go to prison,' she sobbed. His eyes filled with tears too. He took her in his arms:

'Don't cry, mother.'

'Michael,' she pleaded, 'the child will have to go back with him.'

I felt like a murderer. To her I said:

'You will come with the child to Dniepropetrovsk. I'll pay your return fare. You can talk to Luba. You will stay in your home town for a holiday. I wouldn't dare to take her on such a long journey alone.'

'Well,' Michael conceded, 'that would make a difference, I suppose.'

We then discussed the couchettes, which I said I could arrange. I didn't have enough money to buy the rail tickets, but I would manage somehow. I felt so guilty and upset that I refused their invitation to lunch. If I stayed I felt I would break down.

I went to the market. I had a square gold doxa watch which I sold for 1,500 roubles. It would be enough for the tickets and travelling expenses. Through the Party Secretary I obtained couchettes for Mrs Kagan and Sonia on the train leaving at dusk the following evening for Moscow direct. By four in the afternoon I was back at the flat and placed the tickets on the table.

'So you do have influence,' Michael said. 'Did Luba give you the money to buy the ticket for Sonia?'

'Yes, she did, and she also asked me to invite your mother to come with us.'

'She's a clever bitch,' the mother said, 'she knew Sonia wouldn't go with you anyway all by herself.'

The child rushed over to me:

'Oh, yes I would go with him. I want to see my mother. I love my mother. Then I'll come back to Karaganda, grandma. Then Papa will come with me, but Auntie Ninotchka won't be able to come, will she?'

Whether Michael had married the girl I had found him with I didn't know, but they were certainly living together.

While Mrs Kagan went out to do some shopping, I stayed with Sonia in the sitting-room. She sat on a high window-seat, playing with a cat. On her return the grandmother made tea while Sonia chattered away in such a sweet voice that she made me forget for a moment what I had done. I was looking at the pictures on the wall when I heard a strange noise from the direction of the window. It was the screech of a cat. The child looked pale and shaken.

'Where's the cat?' I asked.

'I threw him out of the window.'

When I asked her why she had done such a thing, she explained that it was a naughty cat which sometimes scratched her. The door bell rang. Someone had brought up the cat, bleeding from the nose and ears. The old woman placed it in a sack:

'What have you done, Sonia? Why did you do it?'

The child didn't seem at all affected by the drama, and only repeated that it scratched her sometimes. I took her hands in mine. There were no signs of scratches. Her hands were Luba's hands in miniature.

Next evening, after all the packing and preparation, we all five of us stood at dusk on the station platform: Michael, his mother, Ninotchka, Sonia and I. Other passengers milled around us, all with their own preoccupations and worries. I felt isolated and different from them all. It had been a warm day, but my fingers were cold when I raised them to my face. My pulse raced. I felt everyone else must be normal, but not me. How had I succeeded in taking this child away from her father? My soul troubled me.

My thoughts were interrupted by the whistle of the train. As it drew nearer Mrs Kagan pulled me back from the track. The hour had come. Michael had been holding Sonia in his arms and talking to her. He stroked her hair and kissed her many times. He stood a little way away so I couldn't hear what he said to the child. Then, out loud, he said:

'Sonia, I have a surprise for you. I've bought you a present.' Ninotchka opened a brown paper parcel, and held up a little velvet cape, blue lined with red. Michael placed it around the child's shoulders. As he tied the cord he said:

'There we are, *dochka*, my child.'

Then he held her high in the air. All the people in the station turned to look at her.

'Straighten your legs, and hold them out. See, you look like an angel . . . you're flying to meet your mother.'

He lowered her to kiss her. The old woman was crying. Ninotchka had tears in her eyes too. Michael had managed to hide his grief at that moment.

'Goodbye, my child. Don't let your mother tell you I'm dead any more. I will see you soon.'

We all got on to the train. I don't know if Michael is still alive, thirty-five years later, but he has certainly not seen his child since. I would like to see their reunion. How fine it would be for a man to meet a grown-up daughter for the first time, and for a daughter to find a father.

The train was packed. As it slowly moved out of the station I lay on the lower couchette (Sonia and her grandmother shared the upper one).

'You did the right thing,' I thought. 'After all, if she is a good mother, a mother has more right to a child than the father.' I had acted well.

The further we got from Karaganda the more at ease I felt. Eva Markova Kagan constantly attempted to strike up a conversation with me. She had her suspicions, something told her that she had not been told the full facts, but there was nothing she could do about it. Sonia was bubbling with life, interested in everything. When she went to bed, her grandmother told her to give me a good-night kiss. She opened her blue eyes very wide, put her little arms around my neck and gave me a smacking kiss. It made me feel very happy. At that time I had no desire to acquire a wife and family, but the child was giving me a glimpse of the joys of family life.

On the whole the trip back was less arduous than the outward journey had been, in spite of the three- and four-hour waits at some stations. Sonia seemed to have become very attached to me. I tried to amuse her with stories and games, and she would sometimes sleep head to toe with me on the same couchette to give the old lady more room. Unfortunately, food for three was costing more than I had calculated, and my money ran out after the first three days. But I solved that problem too – and with a bonus. There was a soldier on the train who had brought a rocking horse with him from Germany to give to his daughter, but his wife had left him, taking the child with her and he didn't know what to do with it. Sonia sat on it, and started to cry when I told her it belonged to the soldier. The soldier had been watching me:

'I quite like that jacket you're wearing,' he said. 'I bet it's not made in this country.'

He was right. We had moved to the end of the coach to talk, and I did a deal, a swap: my jacket for the rocking horse and 200 roubles, enough to see us through. Both Sonia and I were overjoyed at the deal. She kissed me many times for it. Eva Markova only realized that I no longer had the jacket when we arrived at Moscow. As we walked out of the station she suddenly noticed:

'Where's your jacket? You must have left it on the train.'

'It's too late now. It's probably gone,' I replied.

There would be a five-hour wait for the train to Dnieprope-trovsk. I decided to see if I could find Nokka but, when I told Eva Markova and Sonia to wait for me, they were both dismayed. Sonia started to cry. Through her sobs she pleaded:

'No, uncle, stay here. I don't want to be alone without you.'

'But I shall only be gone for a couple of hours to see some friends,' I reassured them. But she repeated:

'Don't go, don't go,' and burst into tears again. I drew her head on to my shoulder to calm her down.

Eva Markova didn't like the idea either:

'So many people get lost and separated from each other on stations during the war, you know. And without you we'd be lost. Please don't leave us, for pity's sake.' Then she started crying too. That made the child worse. Passers-by stopped to listen and ask:

'Why are you crying, child?'

Life had already taught Sonia a trick or two:

'This uncle has taken me away from my father to take me to my mother, and now he wants to leave us.'

It was hot there on the station, and now many pairs of accusing eyes were fixed on me. I led the pair of them off to another place. We sat on our parcels, and I pacified Sonia by rocking her on the horse.

'Alright,' I conceded, 'I won't leave you, we'll all go together in a *droshky*.' I did not want to lose this opportunity, I didn't know when – if ever – I would get back to Moscow. When the driver asked where we were going I remembered I had left the address in the jacket I had sold. I could recall the name of the street, but not the number. I told him to go down the street, and I would recognize the house when we reached it. We must have been an unusual sight with all our luggage and a rocking horse on the driver's seat.

We found the house. I got down and rushed up the stairs, but no one answered. Then I went next door and asked if Nokka was still living there. She still lived there but was out at her mother's house. I asked where that was but the neighbour didn't know. After consultation with her husband and another woman they came to the conclusion that Nokka's mother lived with Tanya, and that was fifteen miles from the city.

As we were talking, Sonia ran up the stairs, tugged at my trouser-leg, and urged me:

'Come on, uncle, let's go!'

It was an agonizing moment of decision for me. I loved Nokka more than any woman I had known, but I had lived all through the war with the idea of leaving Russia. I still intended to go, and perhaps it would be kinder to her if I didn't try and find her. I wanted to thank her for all she had done for me; I knew she had sent me many parcels in prison which I had never received, and she had even sold her fur coat to buy things to send to me. I wanted to show her my gratitude, to hold her, to kiss her. As I stood on the landing, the neighbours watching me through the open door, I asked:

'Is Nokka living here with her husband?' – to find out if she had a man.

'No, she's alone,' the woman answered.

'Please tell her Garri was here.'

I kissed the handle of her door. I'm leaving her a kiss, I thought, the last. I will never see her again. I thank her for everything she has done for me. Sonia interrupted my thoughts:

'Come on, uncle, please, Granny is all alone downstairs.'

I explained to the neighbour:

'This child is my friend's, and she has her grandmother down-

stairs. I have to leave now. We are taking the train to Dniepropetrovsk tonight.'

As I approached the *droshky* I could hear Sonia in an excited
voice saying:

'Mama Eva' – she sometimes called her grandmother this –
'Uncle kissed a door handle.'

The *droshky* ride had made further inroads on our meagre
finances.

At the station I stood until the very last moment on the
platform, watching and waiting. She might have come home
and received my message. I tried to catch a glimpse of every
figure in the moving crowds, and at times I thought I saw her
coming toward me. Several months later I found out from
Koch's son, who was then living in Moscow, that Nokka had
received my message, but had not known whether to follow
me to Dniepropetrovsk because she didn't know if I would be
staying there or travelling further. As I kissed the door handle
I had thought:

'This is a piece of metal which the woman I have loved most
in my life has just touched.'

So it had come to the end. I was never to see Nokka again.

On the way to Dniepropetrovsk Eva Markova kept trying to
worm any information out of me concerning my relationship
with Luba, but I gave nothing away. She had enough worries
already, poor woman. We arrived next morning. She wanted to
go straight to Sonia's new home, but I managed to persuade her
to come with us to Lucia, Luba's cousin.

When we knocked at the door and Lucia and her mother saw
the child they fell upon her with hugs and kisses. Sonia no
longer remembered them, got frightened by all the excitement
and started to cry. I took Eva Markova to one side in a room and
told her the truth about my close ties with Luba.

'I knew it, I knew it' – she lit a cigarette – 'there isn't a man
in the world who would make such a sacrifice for a woman if
he didn't love her, but I'll tell you one thing. You won't stay
with Luba.'

'Why do you say that?'

'You will see, later. The child is here, she has the right to keep her. I can be at peace now that I know you will look after her. She'll be happy with you.'

Then she started to cry. Pangs of guilt rushed through my body. I offered to take her with me to Sofiyevka to see Luba. I shook my head:

'I'm so sorry.'

'Don't blame yourself, young man. You are good. Perhaps you think me old and stupid, but don't worry, I understand. You told me you had forgotten your jacket on the train. I knew all the time that you swapped it for the rocking horse.'

'Why did you ask me about the jacket?'

'I was thinking the whole way that you must be her husband. But I wanted to know what kind of a man you were too, to know if you were sincere. Well, my mission is finished. I'll leave now and go and see my old home and neighbours.'

Lucia offered her a bed. I advised her to stay, not to be alone, and I would get Luba to come and see her in a few days.

'I'll stay here a few days then. These are good people. But Luba will never come to see me.'

I took Sonia with her small bundle and rocking horse to the station to see the times of trains. If there was a suitable train we would leave directly. The old woman kissed the child.

'Goodbye, *dochka*. Don't forget your father and your grand-mother.'

'But you are coming with me, Granny.' Sonia started to cry.

'You go with uncle now. I will come in a few days.'

First we went to the Ministry of Health and we were lucky enough to be offered the use of a single-engine plane by Lieber-mann. It was normally used as an emergency transport for patients. There were two passenger seats. Sonia kept looking around to make sure the horse was there. She started to cry in the plane and I had to distract her by lifting a little flap on the floor of the aircraft and showing her the ground rushing past. Then the poor child vomited. Fortunately it was only a twenty-minute flight. At Sofiyevka we circled several times around the hospital before landing. We saw Luba and others waving to us from the field nearby. We landed and bumped to a halt. The door was opened and everybody ran towards us across the billowing grass. Sonia was pale. Luba shouted:

'Sonia, my Sonia, my life.' She kissed her hands, her face and even her little dress. Both she and Sonia cried, and some of the onlookers cried too. I didn't cry. I still had the picture of the child's father as he lifted her high in the air imprinted on my mind. I could still hear the spitting noises of the great steam engine. I stood silent. Luba, dragging Sonia by the hand, rushed over to me and kissed me. I had left Sofiyevka thirteen days before. In that time I had broken up one family and brought another together again.

As soon as I got back to Sofiyevka I made my hospital rounds and listened to the reports of the staff. Everything had been going smoothly. There was one disturbing case, a little girl of six who had been admitted with meningitis. I went to see her and found her to be in a grave condition. She reminded me a little of Sonia. I took a special interest in her, and assured her distraught mother that we would do everything in our power for her.

Luba was ecstatically happy to have Sonia. The child looked well and thrived on the fresh air and sunshine of the country-side. We had to put certain areas out of bounds to Sonia because of the case of meningitis, and often I had to stop her from following me around like a little puppy everywhere I went. I think her open affection for me often made Luba jealous.

I couldn't persuade Luba to go and see Mrs Kagan in Dniepro-petrovsk, so I decided to visit her myself. When I suggested that I should take Sonia to see her grandmother, Luba refused to let her go. I had prepared a parcel with honey and other food for the old lady to take on the long journey back.

'Why are you doing all that?' Luba asked aggressively. 'What she needs is a dose of strychnine.'

Mrs Kagan was very happy to see me and thanked me for the trouble I was taking with Sonia. She asked a thousand questions, all about Sonia: how she had behaved when she saw her mother, whether she had sent any message for her. All my replies were aimed at making her happy. She was touched when I gave her the honey for her cough, and the other medicines and things I had prepared for her.

'You're a good man. God help you. Please look after Sonia.'

When she came to the door to say goodbye she reminded me with a wry expression:

'Garri, Garri Semionovitch, remember what I tell you now. You will not be happy with Luba. You will not stay with her.'

As I walked away from the door I had no doubt in my heart of hearts that she was right. My visit to Dniepropetrovsk had been very short as I was worried about the meningitis case. Back at the hospital this particular anxiety was soon laid to rest; for after several days of intensive nursing care we could see that the girl would be up and about within a week; and fortunately no other cases were reported.

Luba had changed overnight. She no longer cried, but she did find a new hobby to practise: jealousy of any nurse or attractive female I chatted with or was even merely polite to. I had given her no cause for such behaviour. But her jealousy became an obsession and infuriated me because it was unjust.

Another move of hers also alarmed me: she had started to tell Sonia to call me 'Papa' instead of 'Uncle'. When Sonia talked about her father in Karaganda she would say:

'Alright, Sonia, but now this is your father here.'

What she was doing was very wrong, and I told her so. But she was an expert at getting her own way so that not only did Sonia quickly get used to calling me Papa, but Luba also had the child's papers altered to Sonia Urban.

I, of course, loved the little creature from the moment I had seen her. She played with me and went riding with me, sitting in front of me on the saddle. She loved galloping with the air whistling past her face and would catch her breath. She would ride around on my shoulders and I would carry her like that for miles and make myself tired. Her presence brought light and happiness into the lives of all around her.

One morning I received a telegram from General Kucharave summoning me to Dniepropetrovsk. At a meeting with him and Dr Kozlova I was presented with a commendation written personally by the Minister of Health in which he expressed gratitude for the 'untiring and dynamic fight' I had led for the 'general good of the people'. They gave me a special monetary award too.

General Kucharave went on to say that, in view of the success we had had at Sofiyevka, he was thinking of transferring me elsewhere, to Sinelnikovo, where they had several problems. Since Luba would soon be resuming her studies, that autumn would be a particularly good time for me to move. I would hold the same post as Health Inspector, but without additional work as a hospital doctor.

'There's an enormous pig, fat as a barrel, called Perpelica, who is the undisputed boss there,' explained the General. 'He's been there all through the German occupation, and the representative of our Ministry, Rikov, is on good terms with him. The reputation of the medical staff, especially regarding prevention of epidemics, is very low. No one respects them. I think you are the man to instil some order there. We are afraid that there will soon be an outbreak of epidemics there if something is not done quickly. We shall give you all the information about our various departments and hospitals in the area. You will be working in the clinics, but for the time being you will have to leave the hospital to Perpelica. I'm afraid a clash between you will be inevitable sooner or later. We shall be sending you a replacement at Sofiyevka, then in October you can go to Sinelnikovo.' He smiled. 'Before you leave,' he added, 'the personnel secretary of the Ministry of Health would like to see you.'

I told him I would do my best to carry out what he hoped to accomplish, but that I would like to take my two experienced and reliable personal assistants with me.

'That will be a matter for the doctor who replaces you to decide.'

I didn't much like the answer but was not unduly worried. I would find a way of taking Peschenko with me. I took my leave.

Then I went to the 'Iron Door' where the personnel secretary handed me application forms for membership of the Communist Party. He let me know what an honour it was to be asked to join the party and that I had been highly recommended.

'I am very touched by this mark of trust, but I think I should speak to the General Secretary of the party before I fill in the forms.'

I did not go to see him, but instead wrote a letter thanking him for the great honour, saying that I was greatly moved, but adding that, since I was still a Polish citizen, I felt I had not yet done enough to deserve membership, that I would increase my endeavours for the general good of the Soviet people, and that I would apply later.

From the Ministry of Health I went to the emigration office to see how my application was progressing. The beautiful Viera said:

'Don't worry, you will be the first to obtain your permission. Now, don't forget I shall be coming to visit you in two weeks' time with my husband. The invitation still stands, I presume?'

I had always found her attractive, but now she looked even better.

'Of course. We shall be expecting you. I want you to come.'

'Did you say you wanted me?' she asked, looking me straight in the eye.

'Yes, you and your husband.' We understood each other.

Back in Sofiyevka I told Luba the news of my transfer. She was pleased about it, since the journey from Dniepropetrovsk to Sinelnikovo was a short one. I imagine she was pleased to think I would be seeing no more of the attractive women at Sofiyevka. There were still several weeks to go before the move, and we decided not to inform anyone of the date because I didn't want them to relax their vigilance in any way.

When Chevchenko handed me a letter from the Ministry of Health naming my successor, I decided I would call the medical staff of the whole district to a meeting before I left.

We were having lunch one day when a nurse rushed in screaming at us to dash up to the hospital as fast as we could.

'They've brought in a lot of injured people on a cart,' she panted.

I jumped from the table and ran. They were mostly children of different ages, with various injuries. Even the sides of the cart were stained with blood. All the relatives were crying and trying to console the suffering children. They wheeled them into the casualty ward. A woman came forward, took my hand, and pleaded:

'Doctor, doctor, you saved my child before, for God's sake save her now.'

It was the mother of the little girl who had made the

miraculous recovery from meningitis. I went to the cart, jumped on the side and started to remove the bodies which had been flung on top of each other. I found the little girl and lifted her off in my arms. She was still alive. One of her hands had been blown off, and she was bleeding from a wound in the chest. Her clothes were soaked with blood. I ran into the surgery with her and shouted for an emergency reception centre to be set up by all available doctors. A nurse started preparing the girl for surgery – then she died. I had tried so hard to save her life before, had spent sleepless nights worrying about her, and now she was dead. Her face was chalk-white, spattered by a couple of small bloodstains. The sight paralysed me for the moment, she looked so much like an older version of Sonia.

The catastrophe had been caused by a German land-mine which the children had tried to dig out. Two of them had been killed instantaneously when it exploded. The other staff were coping with the rest of the casualties; I was very shaken. As I left, I found the girl's mother standing outside crying. She took my arm, and looked into my face.

'I know. She's dead this time. You couldn't save her.' Her cries of grief followed me down the corridor. She sobbed to the other bereaved parents:

'She was destined to die. They saved her once, my only child. I have no one else. My husband died at the front. Oh God, how will I live now?'

She lifted her arms, and looked up:

'Why did you take her away from me?'

Her lamentations were still ringing in my ears as I closed the door of our apartment. I could see the child's face as she lay in high fever, her head held backwards, and then, later, covered in blood as she was on the cart. I went into the apartment still wearing my white medical overalls.

Sonia ran to me. I hadn't known what I was doing: I never, never went into the apartment wearing hospital clothes, it was a strict hospital rule that the medical staff should change when leaving the hospital into clothes that had not been in contact with patients.

I slumped into a chair and pushed Sonia away from me. She

213

ran into a corner, put her fingers in her mouth and burst into tears:

'Papa, you're ill, you're bleeding.' She thought it was my own blood.

I was worried because I had received a notification from Dniepropetrovsk that General Kucharave wanted me to remain in Sofiyevka in view of the meningitis case we had. I had sent them a full report in which I gave my opinion that the danger had passed and there could be no cause for concern about an outbreak of meningitis. Fortunately Sinelnikovo had greater political significance for Kucharave at this juncture so the suggestion was not followed up.

We always had plenty of patients but now it was routine hospital work. I dreamt only of the day I would leave Russia and be able to search for my family. Until now my busy life had kept such thoughts in the background.

All the news we heard now was good news – censored, but good. Our holiday visitors arrived, Viera looking even more feminine and attractive in civilian clothes. She had extraordinarily well-formed breasts, and if she had not had such a nice husband I would have made love to her. They went back at the beginning of September, and by then we had all become firm friends. Viera told me that they had received 12,000 applications from people wishing to return to Poland in the district of Dniepropetrovsk alone: not only Poles, but Jews and Ukrainians who had claims to Polish citizenship. We were only waiting for the complete collapse of Nazi Germany.

Then came the less good news – not of defeat or retreat – but of treachery and massacre. We heard the story of the Warsaw uprising. I felt in my bones that it would fail, that no one would fight to save the Jews in the ghetto, except for a few distinguished exceptions. From the time of Christ the powerful influence of the Catholic Church has been exerted to turn even schoolchildren against us. Even now, when there has been considerable progress and relaxation in the Church's attitude, largely thanks to Pope John XXIII, the Vatican has still not recognized the state of Israel, and anti-semitism remains a profession out of which some people, and some nations, make a living.

News started to filter through of the massacres that had taken place in the concentration camps. The Allied governments and the Vatican had known about this, but they had all closed their eyes. The Jews were abandoned in the Warsaw uprising too. On 29 July 1944 the Soviets had broadcast to the exhausted and discouraged Jews in the ghetto urging them to rise against the Germans. This they did with outstanding courage. But under personal orders from Stalin the Red Army waited on the far side of the Vistula and watched the massacre from a distance. Many courageous Poles fell there too, alongside the Jews.

I didn't want, when the time came, to take Luba and Sonia with me out of the Soviet Union. Luba was unmoved when I told her she must never take Sonia away from her father to a place where he would never see her again. She just said we should wait and see. She was banking on my growing love for Sonia. It was amazing how quickly the child was forgetting her father and grandmother: Luba and I were her whole life.

The day came for the meeting I had arranged for the entire medical staff: doctors, nurses, epidemic teams and my other workers totalled over one hundred. After the heads of the various departments had given me their reports I gave my own assessment of our present achievements and goals, and stressed the precautions which must be taken before the onset of winter against the possibility of another typhoid epidemic. At the end I said I had a further piece of news which might give some of them pleasure, namely that it would be my last meeting with them. I told them where I was being transferred and who would be the next Inspector. I trusted that they would give him their complete loyalty.

The meeting went very quietly until a middle-aged member of the staff, Bichkoff, asked if he could speak. He had come back from the front, and he spoke briefly of the achievements at the hospital, and of how I had imposed a hard and strict system of discipline. He said that they would be losing not only the man who had known how to eliminate a raging epidemic, but who had looked after their interests too, and succeeded in getting them decent food and better conditions. He choked with emotion and had to fight back tears – he was loudly applauded, and on that note the meeting ended.

I was going out when I was waylaid by members of the staff who persuaded me to accompany them to the clinic hall. I knew, of course, that something was afoot – but was not prepared for what I found: the hall festooned in garlands and flowers, Luba there and all the hospital and office staff. So the news of my departure had got out, and they had all joined in preparing a farewell party for me. I was touched – but determined not to admit it.

There were many more speeches now, all sentimental and touching. Chevchenko spoke the longest, and Peschenko was supposed to say something but when they called him up to the platform he broke down, in tears, unable to speak. I quickly led him off and got the two accordionists to strike up the music for dancing.

In my speech I thanked them all for the excellent party they had given and for all their help. I asked them who had organized it all. 'Dr Parchomenko,' came the surprising but flattering answer.

'Who supplied the keys of the clinic hall?' I continued.

'Dr Chevchenko,' was the answer.

'Right,' I shouted, turning to Peschenko, 'tomorrow you will collect a fine of ten roubles from Chevchenko and twenty roubles from Dr Parchomenko. Tell them it is not permitted to hold meetings for purposes of social enjoyment according to the decree for the control of epidemic diseases!'

They all applauded, some collapsed with laughter and the gorgeous Dr Parchomenko asked leave to reply.

'It will be my great pleasure to pay this fine, especially as it's the first time any one has dared to fine me. There's just one question I would like to ask: why did Chevchenko get away with a ten-rouble fine, while I have to pay twenty?'

'You are a consultant. You can afford more,' I replied, as I led Peschenko away trying to comfort him, and promising I would send for him to come and join me in my next post. He embraced and kissed me – a true representative of the warm-hearted Russian people.

And so ended, on this sentimental note, my life at the first hospital I had ever run. During the past few months at Sofiyevka we had received no letter or word of any kind from Sonia's father or her grandmother Eva Markova. I still do not understand why.

15

Kruschev's Party at the Kolhoz

It was the third week of October when I arrived in Sinelnikovo, where I presented myself to Comrade Rikov at the Ministry of Health offices. He was not a doctor of medicine, but a member of the party. He welcomed me and expressed his satisfaction at my appointment. He showed me round the offices in the building; mine was at the back, an uninviting small room overlooking the garden. Rikov's office was much larger than mine. He kept talking incessantly, telling me I would have good living accommodation; I could tell he was nervous and apprehensive.

'If my home is going to be as attractive as my office, there will be trouble. You will have to give me a better office, this one won't do. I have to invite people here, they're not going to respect my position.'

Fortunately for him, the house proved better than the office.

Luba went off to Dniepropetrovsk to resume her studies and to live with her aunt and her cousin Lucia. Sonia was to remain with me under the care of a kindly middle-aged woman, Ekaterina Andreyova, in whose house we were living.

Although Rikov was technically in a post superior to mine, he had probably been told what kind of a person to expect. I broached the matter of the office one morning when I heard that Peschenko would be arriving at the end of the week. I said:

'I think I'll have his desk there,' and indicated a corner of Rikov's own office.

'What do you mean, there?'

'It will give added authority to the entire health department if I occupy the larger office. Since you have been unable to provide another, I shall be taking yours. You may have mine.'

I had never even sat in the back office since my arrival. I had avoided doing so, using Rikov's office right from the start. His face turned green and then grey.

'Well, you really have a nerve, don't you? I had heard about you before, but I never thought you would have the guts to sack your boss and take over his office.'

'I know you are a patriot,' I retorted, 'but you have everything disorganized. You're far too slack. That is why they have sent me here. I shall need your office if things are to be corrected.'

'So I must be your first victim? Do you think you are being fair?'

'Yes, of course it's fair. If you don't like it, keep your office and I'll go back to General Kucharave and tell him they will have to provide me with a decent office.'

The discussion ended amicably. I took over the office. We remained friends, and agreed to work together. What is more we stayed friends till the day I left that town.

The city and surrounding districts of Sinelnikovo were larger and more densely populated than Sofiyefka.

I started by paying a visit to the local Party Secretary and asked for their full co-operation. He said that they had been anxiously waiting for my arrival, that they had heard about my previous work, and that they would do all they could to help me.

Peschenko, who had become a dear friend, was also about to arrive. I met him at the station and got him a room in the same building as myself for the time being. He held me in great respect, but I too depended on his help completely. He was my right-hand man, thorough and disciplined. I had never known him to lie or conceal anything from me. I trusted him as much as I would have trusted myself; his only weakness was that he sometimes gave in to sentiment.

I had prepared a circular to be distributed to all officials. The hospital would figure largely in the general measures we were planning to take. I informed Dr Perpelica that I would be visiting him one morning at 9 a.m. When I arrived with Peschenko, a nurse received us with the news that the doctor was busy operating. We waited for the great man in one of the patients' waiting rooms. From what they had told me, both

General Kucharave and Dr Kozlova hated him. First impressions explained why; his appearance was disagreeable in the extreme : a short fat man with a small reddish-blond moustache. He shook hands with me and ignored Peschenko. Then I introduced him as my assistant. They shook hands.

After visiting only a few wards I had seen enough. In my capacity as Health Inspector I had a statement drawn up to the effect that the patients were found to be in a generally unhygienic state, with dirty toenails and fingernails and dirty linen. General standard of cleanliness : 'unsatisfactory'. In the kitchens the conditions were even dirtier. When I asked the patients about their food they said it was bad. I told Peschenko to continue with the description of our findings and waited behind to speak to Perpelica alone. We went to his office.

'You are probably eating the patients' food,' I told him.

'Why do you say that?' he asked.

'A surgeon who starts operating at six or seven in the morning would never become as fat as you are on a normal diet. Or are you ill?'

His face broke into a wonderful smile, with two dimples :

'You amaze me. How dare you speak to me like that?'

'Go back to your work and let me have someone to show me round every corner of this hospital.'

It took us the rest of that day and the whole of the next to make a thorough survey of the state of the hospital. The report we made concluded that the hospital was filthy and in consequence presented a danger to the health of patients and visitors alike. I gave Perpelica a week to have the building thoroughly cleaned and imposed a fine of 1,000 roubles on him, to be deducted from his salary.

He was obliged to sign the report of our findings, and he wasn't smiling any more. As we were leaving he became much more conciliatory in his attitude, offering to place the hospital at my disposal if it should be needed.

'Thank you,' I said. 'Try to get the situation under control in the time I have given you. Otherwise I shall ask for your transfer from here.' He shook his head from side to side, wobbling his chins, trying vainly to think up excuses :

'Oh, no, I want to stay here. I'm a good surgeon, but I don't like dealing with these administrative problems. I will be grateful for help in that direction.'

We helped, but it took us six weeks to clean up the hospital. Eventually we became good friends. It was true – he was a good surgeon. I even got him to lose weight.

Sonia was growing happily. Luba and I, as I have explained, were living apart although she came over from Dniepropetrovsk every weekend and sometimes during the week, staying the night and returning the next day.

One evening Peschenko came back very late from a trip with two nurses from the epidemic teams. They knocked on my door, and I let them all in. We all drank and ate and I told them they could stay the night as it was so late and bitterly cold. I slept in the same room as Sonia, and I let them have the other room. At about one in the morning there was a loud banging on the door. Luba had arrived unexpectedly. When she saw those nurses she exploded: it was one of the biggest rages I have ever seen:

'Here you all are fucking each other while my innocent little girl sleeps in her bed.' I begged her to calm down. The nurses dressed trying to explain as they did so what really had happened. I insisted that they should not leave. The noise had woken up Sonia who started to cry.

Luba was like a wild animal. She pushed the poor women, half-dressed, through the door into the snow. They were deeply humiliated because it was so unjust. The landlady who lived upstairs had been woken and switched on her lights. Sonia still sobbed. I took her in my arms to comfort her. Luba was like a wounded tiger, pacing up and down. I found no words. Luba tried to pull the child away from me, but Sonia resisted shouting:

'Papa, papa!'

Then at about four in the morning Luba quietened down, and Sonia fell asleep, exhausted. I told her:

'Until the day I die I shall never forgive you for what you have done today, never, never, never.' I should have beaten her, but I could never do that to a woman. 'I certainly won't take you with me when I leave Russia.'

She tried to undo the harm she had done by cajoling me and pleading, even trying to make love. I dressed and went out to walk in the fresh air for more than an hour. She left again early that morning. Within a week I was unfaithful to Luba for the first time. One cannot be faithful to a woman one does not respect.

At the end of February 1945 the local Party Secretary sent for me. He talked to me for a couple of hours, telling me how surprised they were that they had received no application from me for membership of the party, especially in view of the high recommendation I had had. I gave him all the usual excuses: that I did not yet deserve such an honour, that I intended to go to look for my family after the war, and that would mean leaving the country which would certainly not please the party.

'No, that doesn't follow at all,' he said. 'We all have a high opinion of you and trust you in every respect. Now, there is something else I must tell you, which is still at the moment highly confidential. When the war ends, which we expect very soon, this area has been chosen for some special victory celebrations. They intend to hold them at the first *kolhoz* established here in the Ukraine, the 'Lenin' *kolhoz*, which is about fifteen miles from Sinelnikovo. Delegates from the Soviet Republics will be coming here, together with the Party Secretaries. Nikita Kruschev, as Chairman of the Ukraine Praesidium will be the host. We expect that it will take place in June or July. General Kucharave has asked me to appoint the most able man I can find for this job. That is you. We shall need sleeping accommodation for all the delegates in the *kolhoz*, and you will be closely involved in the preparations as far as public health and hygiene is concerned. The celebrations will go on for a week, with speeches and banquets and dancing. We shall need to have medical facilities prepared for any kind of emergency, and you will be responsible too for the hygienic storage and preparation of food. The last thing we want is a case of food poisoning, intentional or unintentional. You will receive all the supplies and powers you require. There will be a lot of drinking which will no doubt lead to disputes and physical violence. Here is a file with details of the sleeping accommodation required. I shall provide you with further information as I receive it.'

He warned me not to discuss the plans with anyone except Rikov, who already knew about it. I left him, wondering whether I would be able to cope with such a heavy responsibility.

The secret of the celebrations could not be kept for long because of the extensive preparations required. There was even speculation that Stalin himself might be there.

Luba for the time being was not making any scenes, and even seemed to be making an effort to be amiable. Sometimes Sonia would say to me, 'Kiss Mummy.' Whether Luba had instructed the child to do so I don't know, but she must have sensed that Sonia was the link which kept us together.

My love for Sonia, indeed, was so strong that, against my better judgement, I allowed Luba to persuade me that it would simplify matters if we were married. We merely went to a registry office, signed a document and paid a fee of one rouble. Administratively it helped; emotionally it made a sounder base for Sonia. But the ceremony, or rather the lack of it, meant very little to me; I never considered myself as married to Luba in the true sense.

But, of course, as she must have foreseen, it did mean that I wavered in my determination to leave them both behind when I eventually managed to leave the Soviet Union.

A few weeks after my 'marriage', I visited Dniepropetrovsk to see how my application for emigration was progressing. The beautiful Viera always looked deep into my eyes and laughed whenever she spoke to me. I said:

'If you weren't wearing that NKGB uniform I would think I was looking at a beautiful woman.'

'Under this uniform is the body of a woman.' She flirted openly with me until I kissed her there in the office. Even her uniform couldn't hide her superb figure. It was a long kiss and she could feel how excited I was.

As I held her in my arms I said:

'We must behave like reasonable people. I like your husband, he's a good man, and you're happily married.'

'That's what you think. He's a Georgian. We are quite happy but he's always going away and he is certainly making love to some woman wherever he goes, so why shouldn't I do the same?'

My heart said 'yes' but my head said 'no'.

To delay matters I asked if she could get exit permits for Sonia and Luba too. I was rather surprised when she said it could be done easily.

'Well, you are married to her, and by law you can take her with you.'

'But what about her marriage and the child of that marrriage?'

'Luba has presented a divorce certificate issued by a *zaks*, together with a letter signed by her first husband which states that he is willing to allow her custody of the child.'

It transpired that Luba had been to see her several times, and had had dinner with her.

So Luba had been making sure of her preparations without telling me! I took Viera in my arms again without compunction and didn't leave her place till early next morning. As I walked toward the Institute of Medicine I met Luba arm-in-arm with a doctor wearing an army captain's uniform. They were looking into each other's eyes before Luba saw me. She let go of his arm quickly:

'This is an old school friend of mine. We studied medicine together too.' As we three stood on the bridge together I wondered if all three of us had been unfaithful to someone the night before. At that time I didn't give the matter much importance, but had reason to remember the incident much later in my life.

At the beginning of May 1945 radio programmes were often interrupted to give the latest news flashes. Some of the nation's greatest leaders spoke, including Batka Stalin. The climax came on 7 May with the announcement of the unconditional surrender of Germany. My pulse raced as I listened. Freedom was in sight. The Soviet people, who had suffered such terrible losses, were overcome with pride.

A wave of happiness swept over Russia, but the relief the people felt was mixed with tears. They cried openly in the streets, some in joy, some in grief on hearing the news of the death of husbands, sons, and parents. My heart cried too. I was full of compassion towards them. I must get back to Poland to see if any of my family had survived.

224

The victory celebrations at the 'Lenin' *kolhoz* had been fixed for the first week in June, and the arrangements had to be made by the last week in May. There were to be two surgeons in attendance, including Dr Parchomenko, the lovely blonde consultant I had met in Sofiyevka. In addition five doctors and twenty nurses would be there to staff a full-equipped ward and private rooms for the most important visitors. It was strange to think that even on this joyous occasion we had to prepare for emergencies. I had been told that it was necessary because there could be fights and accidents when the delegates drank too much, as they surely would.

Two days before the celebrations began I was called to the office of the Party Secretary of Sinelnikovo. Many high-ranking party officials were in the building, including the entire city council of Kiev and the head of the NKGB there. They questioned me from all sides:

'Have all the necessary preparations been made?'

'Yes.'

'Could two emergency operations be performed simultaneously?'

'Yes.'

'Have you the space to hospitalize patients after surgery?'

'Yes.'

'Have you sufficient medical staff?'

'Yes.'

'Have you complete supplies of medicines?'

'Yes.'

'Are the doctors already in residence?'

'Yes.'

The local NKGB chief intervened:

'No, the surgeons are arriving tomorrow by a special plane.'

I said: 'If I said "yes", I meant "yes". They arrived today on a plane provided by the Ministry of Health. I asked General Kucharave to send it.' I looked at the NKGB chief directly: 'You are not always informed about everything.'

The NKGB official from Kiev said:

'Why did they have to go there today? Tomorrow would have been in time.'

'That's my business,' I answered.

'Well, I want an answer from you,' he insisted.

'It was just to be absolutely certain that they would be there with time to spare. They need to go over the buildings and equipment well beforehand. I shall make it my own responsibility to make sure that they are fully acquainted with the facilities. I considered it preferable that they should not leave it until the last minute.'

A man in civilian clothes, whom I later discovered to be another high-ranking party official from Kiev, spoke up:

'You're perfectly right. You speak like a Bolshevik. Are you one?'

'Perhaps I speak like a Bolshevik and party member, but I am neither.'

'What are you then?'

'I am just doing my work, and I am honoured to do it. I do it with all my heart. You can be sure that all the preparations for which I am responsible are made and in order.'

Rikov, who really should have been responsible, was not present. They said I could leave. The interview had made me apprehensive: I was only just beginning to realize that I might be the scapegoat if anything should go wrong. They might even arrest me.

I returned to the *kolhoz* and didn't leave again until the party was over. My main concerns were two: food poisoning, and injury or death resulting from fights. For the first I could certainly be held responsible, but how could they blame me for injuries or surgical operations which would be the concern of the surgeons?

It was too late now. The die had been cast.

On the first day delegations arrived by every method of transport: by rail, cars, small planes, horse-drawn carts. They were to eat in a specially constructed wooden dining hall, at long tables which would seat two to three hundred people. Each delegation had a table about seventy-five feet long, comprising three smaller tables. They were covered with white cloths and dotted with Russian flags, and the flags of the various Republics. At one end of the hall was a smaller table set on a platform for the use of the Praesidium of the Ukraine, and all the Party Secretaries, who were to sit near the Chairman of the Ukraine

Praesidium, Nikita Kruschev. The walls, inside and out, were hung with slogans and decorations, pictures of Stalin and of war heroes.

Outside, a police cordon had been set up around the *kolhoz*, staffed by the NKGB and NKVD, and about five hundred soldiers were on duty. The dining tables for the members of the *kolhoz* were in another hall, and more tables were put out in the open air.

Military orchestras took turns in providing a non-stop musical background. Special transports had arrived loaded with food of every variety and in great quantity . . . and drink too. Even before the official opening drunks were roaming the streets.

Entertainment was to be laid on by opera singers, acrobats, orchestras, jugglers and gypsy musicians. Each delegation brought with it entertainers from their own Republic, who performed on a specially constructed stage.

Sleeping room was found for everyone, except that we had overlooked beds for the medical staff. This had been Rikov's responsibility. We managed to find some space for them at the last minute.

The hot weather had not improved the quality of the meat which no longer appeared to be fresh. It was to be served to the important visitors, and was under my personal supervision. It was unusually hot that summer, and we did not have good storage places for it. If I did not pass the food as fit to eat an alternative would have to be found and we would have to admit our mistake. If the meat was cooked and served and proved to be the source of food poisoning I would be shot without ceremony.

I took another look at the meat. It certainly looked over-ripe! I had several pieces cut from different parts and had them cooked, boiled for twenty-five minutes. I tried a few pieces but, unwilling to trust my own judgement, I asked someone to fetch some of the doctors. It was then that I realized that I didn't know where to find them, where their quarters were. I hurried out and bumped into Dr Parchomenko with a dozen of the medical staff. I asked them all to try the meat. They weren't willing guinea-pigs, but they tried it and said it wasn't bad. So I gave permission for the cook to go ahead and cook it after it had

227

been washed and sprinkled with salt and vinegar. There were no fatalities.

On the opening night the sounds of music drifted through the summer sky as fireworks shot into the air.

In the dining hall I was making my last-minute checks, when a party of plain-clothes' policemen came in and went to the top table reserved for the Praesidium. Then I noticed a little bald man standing with them. He laughed and talked a lot and showed protruding teeth with gaps in them – it was Nikita Kruschev himself. He was inspecting the beautifully decorated hall and examined first the tables, then the cutlery. Suddenly he saw me standing nearby, and beckoned me with his finger. I was wearing a white medical overall at the time, as were all the other medical staff. Perhaps at first he thought we were kitchen staff, it would have been understandable. I looked behind me to see who he was calling, then he said:

'Doctor, come here.'

I went up to him and his party.

'*Sdrastviti*, welcome,' I said.

'Did you not see that I was calling you?' he asked.

'No, I didn't think you were. I thought it was someone else you wanted?'

'Well, it was you I wanted to speak to.'

I replied: 'If you were calling me, I don't like to be called by a beckoning finger. Even a dog wouldn't understand you.'

He laughed: 'How would you make a dog understand then?'

'There are several ways of calling a dog, but only one way for calling a human being – by his name or title.'

'That's alright with me.' He laughed again. 'What they told me about you is true. I heard about the meat you tried on yourself and the medical staff. It means you take your job seriously. Why did you have to taste the meat? Why didn't you just throw it out?'

'Do you want a sincere answer?' Then I told him the truth: 'If I had thrown it out I would have been arrested; and if someone had got poisoned I would have been shot. Anyway I hope you enjoy your dinner.'

He laughed again with great delight.

As delegates filed into the hall each group was greeted by its own musicians playing the music of their Republic. That inaugural dinner was the first of the many entertainments which took place in different parts of the *kolhoz* in permanent or temporary buildings and often in the open air. The events had been well co-ordinated.

When I visited the medical staff I discovered that Dr Kozlova had arrived from Dniepropetrovsk. I was trying to resolve the problem of sleeping space for the medical staff. I approached the head of the *kolhoz*, and he said:

'Why don't they use the beds in the medical wards?'

I couldn't accept this under any circumstances. I went to the building next to the wards, which happened to be a dormitory for soldiers with forty beds. I told the medical staff to go and sleep there. Outside I had a notice-board put up: DANGER: ISOLATION WARD; signed Health Department. The news was quickly whispered around the camp and within minutes everyone knew. There had been no luggage or soldiers' kit in the building, and the troops were accommodated in other parts.

Everyone started to drink heavily: delegates, petty officials, the *kolhoz* families, and the local people who had come in from the surrounding districts. The most frequent word heard on every corner was: '*Pey*. Drink.'

I didn't drink although my throat was dry and tickled. Listening to the good music and watching people enjoying themselves I felt how I imagine waiters must feel, only here eighty per cent of the waiters were NKVD agents specially trained for this job. The Ukrainian women wore peasant costume with embroidered blouses. We could see that they wore no brassieres as their nipples stood out clearly through the material. The men would carry them off to a quiet spot or else to one of the dormitories and make love, but not in the part where the delegates were. There everything was on a more formal basis.

I thought I would give Dr Parchomenko a personal guided tour of the festivities. As we made our way through the crowds we saw an officer pull out one of the breasts of a Ukrainian woman, kiss it and shout: '*Lublu tebia*, I love you.' A gypsy violinist was walking past and he grabbed him by the sleeve.

'Come on, play something nice,' he shouted, then he put his arm round the woman's shoulder. The fiddler started playing.

'Play me some of the war tunes to remind me of the times when I won these,' he said, touching the line of medals on his chest. Then the fiddler changed to a lovely war song. He had a marvellous voice which made me forget everything including my work. It was a very sad song about a woman who waits and waits for her husband to return from the war, standing in the window with a lamp for the man who never comes. As he sang the tears rolled down his cheeks. I couldn't understand how a NKGB officer could have won so many medals. I could not spend more time there. I had to continue on my rounds.

Dr Parchomenko said she would have to find a toilet. I told her there were some on the other side of the *kolhoz*, I would show her the way. Our path took us behind one of the blocks and she said suddenly:

'Oh, I think I'll do it here,' and she squatted down, still holding my hand.

She must have wanted to go very badly because the force of the jet sounded as though she had made a large hole in the ground.

It was a starry, clear night and I looked into her eyes:

'You must have been drinking a lot,' I said.

When she stood I could see I was right: she had made quite a mark on the ground.

As we walked back I took her by the waist and started to kiss her. In the distance the strains of the romantic music could be heard. It was a real pleasure. But nature is strange, we are all different, some men need more time, some less. I belonged to the former. I could hear people only twenty feet away round the corner, and she started to scream: 'Go on! Go on!' Someone would come round the corner any minute. It was a couple of soldiers. One of them coughed. The interruption meant that we didn't finish our pleasure. We walked hand in hand through the crowds; we passed Rikov and Dr Perpelica and came to a crater made by a 1,000-pound bomb, which had been fenced off. The fence had been torn down in one place. This was just the dark corner we had been searching for. I got through the fence. But then fell into the crater. Nadia Parchomenko started to shout for help. As I lay helpless at the bottom, Rikov and his friends came back in answer to her cries:

'He doesn't make a sound. That's bad.'

'He must be dead. Look at all those rocks and the rubbish in there.'

They went to fetch a torch which they flashed round while others went for help to haul me out. I can make a fair imitation of a dog yelping, so I had a go then.

Then I heard Rikov: 'To the devil. It's a damn dog.'

Then I groaned. Someone else said: 'There is somebody down there. Dr Urban, are you alright?'

'Of course I'm alright,' I shouted back. I was wondering how I could get Nadia down the hole and keep her there for a while. Eventually a rope was brought and they pulled me out.

'Why didn't you answer us when we were shouting?' someone asked.

'It was probably the shock of the fall. He couldn't speak,' another said.

I sneaked away with Nadia, and we positively ran to my room where we finished the work in hand. We were both mightily content. We had to continue on our rounds afterwards. We saw a very tall Russian holding down a woman over a table, shouting in a drunken voice:

'I love you.'

She was drunk too and moved her legs in bicycle fashion. The music went on all night and it was dawn before the people trickled away to their beds.

Next day the political speeches continued, and the following days were much the same, with dancing and celebrations going on until the early hours.

It was a picturesque event of great significance for the Russians: telegrams signed by Stalin and other high-ranking party officials were read out in which the valiant sons of Russia, both the soldiers at the front and the people behind the lines, were congratulated. Every morning the fields and the barrack areas looked like a pub after a busy night. The glasses ran out (most got broken), so they drank from bottles which were passed from hand to hand.

At the end of the last day we were able to confirm that the number of accidents and injuries had been extremely low with no fatalities and no cases of food poisoning. The heads of delegations for the most part left before the rest, the last to leave being the musicians who were giving their own party on the last afternoon. They entertained each other; and for me, now relieved of the heaviest part of my work, this was most interesting. One group would shout to another:

'To you comrades we drink, and for you we dance and sing.'

Then they would perform their songs and dances, which would be taken up by dancers and singers from another party: there was an enormous variety in the kinds of music and dance, there were even gypsy dancers and acrobats all performing in the open air. It was unforgettable.

Next morning when everyone had left I told Nadia I would be leaving Russia very soon. She kissed me and asked me not to go, or, if I must go, to take her with me. We left the members of the co-operative to their normal routine and went back to our usual daily duties.

16

⊂———⊃

A Volcano of Heartbeats

On 6 July 1945 an agreement was reached between the government of the USSR and the Polish government-in-exile which provided for the repatriation of Poles and Jews of Polish nationality who had not taken Soviet citizenship. It was the happiest day of my life. I heard about the agreement the next day from my NKGB lady-friend in Dniepropetrovsk, Viera. She wired me to come to that city – I was there in forty-eight hours. She was very formal at first.

'Garri Semionovitch, allow me to congratulate you with a kiss. You have permission to leave the Soviet Union with Luba and Sonia. We wish you great happiness in the future.'

She kissed me on the cheek. Her kisses, later, were very different. Her husband was away, and we celebrated together. I spent that night in Dniepropetrovsk without attempting to see Luba. But on my return to Sinelnikovo I found Luba waiting for me, much to my discomfort. She had come there the day before, not long after I had left, although it had meant missing lectures.

'I suppose you had a good time,' she smiled.

'You're right,' I replied shortly.

She asked why we couldn't go back to our old relationship, like we had been when I had first met her, when I had gone to fetch Sonia for her. Before I could answer her, Sonia jumped on to my knees saying:

'You are the same to my mother, aren't you? Like always?'

I often thought Luba must be jealous of the affection Sonia showered on me, but I now realized I was wrong. She liked to see Sonia show her affection for me: it tied me to her.

We left the child and went for a walk. We sat on a bench at the roadside. I told her that I would be leaving Russia very soon, and that I didn't want to take her and Sonia. She should finish

233

her medical studies, Sonia should see her father again. I explained that I didn't really love her and that we wouldn't be happy together.

She started to cry, then stroked my head:

'*Lubovmoya*, my love. Don't destroy what we have created. Let me bring my child up as a Jewish child. Have pity on us. Forgive me for acting so badly. I beg you, for the sake of my dead mother, for Sonia and for me.'

She held my lapels and brought my face close to hers. The people passing turned to look at us. She broke into a heart-rending storm of tears.

'All I want,' she sobbed, 'is for you to take Sonia and me out of the country. Once we are out we will go our separate ways. If you don't feel disposed to do it for me as a husband, surely you will do it as a Jew for another Jew. I know you have deep feelings: you're a good man.'

She knew how to touch my innermost sentiments. This appeal affected me. I said I would think it over. I would give her my answer at least a week before leaving. I tried to make her understand how unhappy she made me with her wildly jealous scenes, and asked her never to repeat them.

At the end of September I was asked to come to the Ministry of Health in Dniepropetrovsk.

When I went there I saw Dr Kozlova first. As I walked along the corridor I noticed that the placard which had been put up in recognition of my work in Sofiyevka had been removed from the wall, but that did not of itself much worry me:

'Well, it was up there for some time,' I thought. 'It had to come down one day.'

But when I went into Dr Kozlova's office she received me coldly. Usually she smiled. I sensed that there was a difference in her attitude to me. She told me that there would be a meeting in General Kucharave's office in a few minutes, and I was to go there with her.

The telephone rang. The General was ready for us.

In the General's office we found him together with the chief of the 'Iron Door' of the Ministry of Health, a *politruk* who possessed files on every member of the ministry staff.

General Kucharave stood up, then walked around the room

three or four times without speaking. Dr Kozlova smoked. The *politruk* flicked through a file. Finally Kucharave spoke.

'It's unbelievable how much shame and disgrace you have brought upon me, upon Dr Kozlova and the whole department. What has made you apply for permission to leave the Soviet Union?'

'I want to go and look for my family.'

'They must all be dead,' he dismissed my explanation.

'Well, I might find their graves and mourn over them,' I persisted.

'There are none. The Germans left no Jewish graves.'

'How do you know that?'

'I know. Your future is here. I want you to stay here. You are an excellent doctor and administrator and my best Inspector of Health. I even gave you special powers. I would never have believed you would pay us back like this.'

'Why are you making so much of a tragedy out of it?' I asked. 'You have no right to speak to me like this. The trust you placed in me and the privileges you gave me I have not betrayed. I have worked day and night carrying out my duties. You yourself have often praised me for my successes. Do you really believe that you will change my mind with your propaganda speech? You are very mistaken.'

He came close to me, pushing his face close to mine. He gnashed his broken teeth.

'Get out! Get out of here!' he bellowed.

I turned to go. He went back to his desk. As I placed my hand on the door handle I said without turning:

'General, thank you for the trust and confidence you placed in me. I never betrayed it at any time. I did the work you gave me.'

Less than six weeks later, as I sat in my office, a telegram was brought to me informing me that General Kucharave again wanted to see me in Dniepropetrovsk. It made me apprehensive: it was the end, or very near it. I had already spoken to Rikov about my fears and told him to take over his former office, which I was occupying. He refused, saying he was quite happy where he was. Ignoring his protest, I ordered Peschenko to move all my belongings back to the smaller office.

General Kucharave received me immediately when I presented myself at the ministry. He was alone, and asked me to sit down.

'You thought you would never see me again, didn't you? I've heard that you have earned yourself the reputation of a tyrant among your medical colleagues, but they call me worse: they call me a sadist. I must say I respect you for the work you have done. It's not yet too late for you to change your mind. Stay with us.'

I stood up.

'Please,' I said, 'my decision to leave this country is not something I can change.'

'Then I wish you luck. I personally will nominate you to visit some of the assembly points for the repatriates: it will be a highly responsible task, since the centres are the most likely places for any outbreaks of epidemics. It's something I want to avoid at all costs because, if there should be a flare-up, the fucking Polish government will say that it's our fault and that we are trying to impede the repatriation of their citizens. You will transfer to this work in two weeks' time, and you yourself will travel on one of the last railway convoys as Health Inspector.'

I thanked him for the confidence he had maintained in me, and assured him that he need not worry. He stood up and shook my hand. He called me by my first name:

'Garri Semionovitch: I have been hard on you, perhaps unjust, but I have to contend with immense pressures on me. I was seriously wounded in the war and it has affected my nerves. When you return to your country and find that you are disappointed, just send me a telegram and I will send out a plane to bring you here.'

I was lost for words.

As I left, he reassured me: 'You will be notified where you should report next.'

He was human after all! Only a good man, with deep feelings, could have spoken to me as he did at this, our last meeting. As I paced along the corridor, two scenes came to my mind: one was the previous meeting we had had, when he had thrown me out of the office, and the second was the image of him a moment previously, with tears in his eyes. How could these two sides to his nature be reconciled? I think I understood him: basically he was a good man, but in order to maintain his authority, he had to feign a hard, unforgiving attitude. So many of the civil servants in Russia, whilst bowing to the might of the Communist Party, had their very human and humane feelings at the same time. I understood his predicament. That policy of fear never paid off, then or now.

The last few weeks and months before leaving were very hard. Apart from occasional visits to the refugee assembly camps I had no job to keep me busy. My closest companion was Sonia: I told her stories, made her laugh. She would kiss me. She always had little cold fingers which I would pretend to bite. She was the oxygen of my life during this waiting period.

One morning, very early, there was a heavy hammering on the door. My first thought was that it must be the NKVD. Whoever it was was hammering with both hands. When I opened it I nearly fell down in surprise. It was my old gonorrhoea patient, Proshko from Sofiyevka, enveloped in a capacious black fur coat, on his head a fur hat with two long ear-pieces hanging down to his shoulders. He was carrying a pair of hares. He was drunk and fell upon me, kissing me:

'I promised, and I've kept my promise,' he blurted out. 'I came by the night train because Peschenko told me you would soon be leaving. I didn't want you to leave Russia and think I was some liar.'

He kissed me again, hugging me close to his snow-covered coat. I hauled him inside, and gave him a breakfast of a dozen eggs with bacon fat, washed down with a tumbler of neat vodka. He was so violent and frightening I sent Sonia to the other room with her great-aunt.

'You saved him. He's completely dry. Nothing comes out, never. . . . I can drink and fuck . . . and I owe it all to you.'

By the time he left eventually, an hour later, I was quite drunk myself, and felt extremely ill. When Lucia came into the room, the first thing she wanted to do was to throw out the two hares. It would be a hard job to clean them properly, she said, and in any case her family never ate game. And so, after all that, we gave the hares to some people downstairs, who knew nothing about the pledge Proshko had so handsomely, and so unexpectedly, redeemed.

In the New Year of 1946 I started to organize the repatriates' transport and inevitably got involved in several rash promises to would-be repatriates who had not obtained permission to leave.

By the last week in February, we knew the trains would be leaving very soon. An army officer, a friend of Viera's, would also be coming clandestinely, and I had of course promised her I would help. She told me he had fought in the front line, and had been decorated, but that he was unable to accept the anti-semitic line that government policy was taking, although he was not a Jew. I asked Viera why she had done so much for others. She answered:

'I don't know why I do it. I can't help myself. When I see someone in trouble I must help them.'

I was with her in her office at the time.

'And we should occasionally think of helping ourselves,' I said provocatively.

Her response amazed even me. She rushed to the door and locked it, ran into my arms and started to kiss me many times with great feeling. She said – she had never said it before – that she loved me and asked me to make love to her then and there.

'Not here, it's too dangerous.'

But my resistance weakened. We made love on her desk, her legs dangling over one end, while she held on to the corners. The desk moved with the motion so I had to hold her behind. It was not precisely comfortable so I lifted her, still engaged, into the corner of the room, against the wall. We could clearly hear a typewriter banging away behind the locked door, but I carried on and made my beautiful NKGB officer happy.

Next day I went to meet the NKVD officer, Wolodia Korsa-koff, who would be travelling with us. The train would cross into Poland and end its journey at Opole in Silesia, which had formerly been part of Germany, and the lieutenant would be in charge of security and checking the documents of the passengers. He was a young man in his early thirties, a Tartar, a cheerful type. I wanted to be on the best terms with him, because I knew I would have seven illegal emigrants with me, and indeed during the next few weeks we became very friendly. From Dniepropetrovsk, we would travel across the Ukraine, west through Ternopol, Lvov and Przemysl, just over the new Russian-Polish frontier, then to Tarnow, Krakow, Katowice and to Opole. From there we would go on to Waldenburg, a small industrial town formerly in Germany, now in Poland. A reception centre would be set up there by the Polish authorities, and they would decide the eventual destination of every passenger. The town was notorious for the large number of Nazi Party members and SS officials who had lived there. Their homes had been requisitioned for the use of returning Poles and Jews who were homeless.

At the end of February I made my last attempt to dissuade Luba from coming with me. We talked from early evening late into the night. I told her it was not too late to decide to stay in Russia. I didn't mention how I had got involved in promising to help illegal emigrants because I was afraid she would sell me out: I had not forgotten the letter written to the Communist Party Secretary in Karaganda which could have put her husband in jail. As usual, Luba's reaction was very strong. She cried so much her eyes and face became swollen. I gave in.

'Alright, I'll take you, but once we're over the frontier, you go your way and I go mine.'

She swore on her mother's grave that she would keep to this bargain. She fell to her knees and kissed my hands. I had to raise her from the floor to stop her kissing my shoes.

Two days before we left Russia I went to say my goodbyes to Nadia Parchomenko on Prospect Karl Marx. Her husband was there. He didn't appear to like the look of me. I don't blame him. I lied, saying that she been called urgently to see a patient. We went downstairs arm-in-arm, hand-in-hand, and walked together up the hill, talking of the good times we had had, how I had fallen into the crater at the *kolhoz*, what music and dancing there had been. Without noticing we had reached the top of the hill. By the time we had come down the other side we were covered in powdery snow. I remember I took some snow and rubbed it on her cheeks. We kissed.

'I envy you,' she said. 'I wish I could go with you in your pocket.'

On the morning of 1 March we all cried when we said our farewells to Lucia and her mother, a very old lady now. She had no illusions.

'We shall never see you again.'

'No, you won't,' Luba said, and took her aunt's face in her hands, 'you are my mother's sister – you have the same beautiful face. Let me kiss you.'

So we left and took a *dröshky* to the station, away from the main building, where the transport train stood. As we passed through this lovely city, I think we were both thinking we would never see it again. I was not sad. It held no good memories for me. I was not in love with either Viera or Nadia Parchomenko. Luba and Sonia, as it later turned out, would bring tragedy and suffering. It was to take me twenty years to discover the real Luba, and even now, as I write, I still do not know whether I have discovered her true nature. I felt sympathy for those who had to remain behind and extremely happy to be finally on my way.

The seating accommodation on the repatriates' train was more comfortable than I had expected. It was even heated. From the number of NKVD guards and dogs in the area it looked as though we were destined for Siberia. I was curious to know why such a heavy guard was required for such a harmless trainload. Wolodia, the young lieutenant, came up to me, very shaken, repeating that I was his brother and friend, and that he had come to warn me to take great care. He had undergone some unpleasant questioning because someone had tipped off the police that there were illegal emigrants on the train. If any person was discovered who was not entitled to be there, the whole trainload would be prevented from leaving.

'For God's sake, help me, you must help me.'

'How many have you got?'

'Only one.'

'Bring him to the hospital wagon,' I decided quickly. There were twelve beds in there.

'No, I can't do that, they would recognize him straightaway.'

Snow was falling lightly, making Wolodia's face even more pallid than it was.

'But we aren't leaving yet. Hide him somewhere else until tonight,' I suggested.

'No, I can't do that either. If the Poles find out, they'll hand him over, because he's a Russian.'

'Then you've no choice. Bring him to the hospital wagon.'

He went off. I followed him to his carriage. He was alone with his fellow-officer who knew about the extra passenger. Wolodia showed me how he had fitted a panel across the end of the carriage, specially made to look like the proper wall. The runaway was behind it.

'Better leave him there,' I said, 'don't shit your trousers, it's in the hands of destiny now.'

Until now I had not become involved with his law-breaking and should, of course, have informed the authorities about it. When I looked at the panelling again I suggested he have hooks fixed on it and hang up some coats there.

'That's no good. They all have dogs when they're searching and dogs always make straight for the fur to smell it.' But he set about doing it all the same.

Fortunately, there were fewer police around on the platform when I stepped out. The situation was no longer so tense. I approached the officer in charge of the NKVD at the station and asked if he wouldn't mind moving his police and their dogs further away from the train as they were causing alarm among the passengers. He obliged. I asked Luba if there had been a police search of every wagon. She had been passing through all the compartments to check that there were no sick passengers: I had appointed one person in every compartment to report any suspicion of sickness or fever to us. Luba said that the police had not searched. Late in the afternoon, as darkness fell, a man of about sixty, dressed in a military greatcoat, holding the arm of a woman, came up to me. She was in officer's uniform.

'I have come with this woman on Viera's instructions. There are just two of us.'

I looked at him, but asked no questions. I asked them to come with me to the medical compartment. He removed his coat and I gave them white medical overalls.

241

'Have you brought any luggage?' I asked.

'No,' he replied.

As he removed his coat I saw he was carrying a gun and a pair of hand-grenades. His uniform was that of a colonel, and his companion was a captain.

What was I doing? I had managed to avoid taking Wolodia's stowaway – but now this – a full colonel and a captain fleeing from Russia – not just illegal emigrants of Polish or Jewish origins. This would certainly mean the firing squad if I was caught. My heart leapt wildly. When Luba realized what was happening she started to panic about her own safety and Sonia's. A born egoist. I didn't realize it at the time but I discovered that all she cared about was herself and Sonia. I was merely the means by which they would get out of Russia.

I didn't know the exact departure time, but I could see that NKVD patrols were going into every compartment. I could see their torches and hear them talking as they walked along the platform. As they came nearer I went out to see what they were doing. They had asked all passengers for their papers. I had understood that all the exit documents had been lodged with the *nachalnik*, the head of the NKVD on the train. This was so, but every exit permit was made out in triplicate, one copy remaining with the passenger, one for the Soviet authorities, and one for the Polish authorities. What was going on now was an unexpected spot check. They must suspect something. I ran quickly over to Wolodia. He was trembling with fear.

'Something has gone wrong,' he said, stating the obvious. 'I'll bring my man along to your hospital compartment, and you can put him in a bed.' He was panicking now.

'He will have to move into your compartment.'

'Alright, then move him,' I gave in.

Things could hardly be worse, after all, even if we're discovered.

'Can you let me have a loaded gun?' I asked.

'What do you need it for?'

'In case they catch me. I'm in very deep now. I won't go back to a camp.'

He gave me two pistols. I noticed that in the compartment he had boxes with several weapons: machine-guns, rifles, and ammunition, probably intended to halt any Pole or Jew who might try to run away and stay in the paradise of Russia!

We hastily smuggled Wolodia's man across. From the hospital compartment I continued to watch the guards. There were three of them checking inside while one waited outside with an Alsatian dog. They were not well organized, and it was taking them ten or fifteen minutes to pass through each compartment. I went into the carriage where the guards were, casually, and said:

'Good evening, everybody,' in Russian.

'We speak Polish,' one man said, 'Good evening,' he added in Polish.

In a loud voice I replied:

'But you are still in the Soviet Union. You still eat Soviet bread, so shut your mouth and don't try to teach me how to behave. Are there any sick people, or anyone with fever, here?'

The man we had appointed to be in charge came up to me. I said: 'I have found a few suspected cases of typhoid, but we have isolated them now. I asked the local health authorities to take them, but they refused to let them off the train. So keep a good eye on them and report any suspicious symptoms to me immediately.'

The young police lieutenant who had been examining their papers came up to me and took me outside.

'*Molodiez.* You're our man. You are a true Soviet. Those Poles are all parasites – you did well to tell them so. I shall be glad to see the back of this blue-blooded *gavno*, this shit. And a good thing too that they wouldn't let the typhoid cases off!'

He gave orders for all the guards to end the checks.

'You will soon be on your way,' he said.

'Oh, but it will take a long time for you to finish your checks,' I protested.

'No, I'm finished.' He shook his head.

'Perhaps you would like to see the passengers I put in the hospital compartment?'

As we talked I could see three dogs outside Wolodia's compartment making a commotion, barking loudly.

'No,' the officer replied, 'I want to get them all out of the country, the sooner the better.'

There was a notice attached to the hospital carriage which read:

BEWARE, DANGER FROM INFECTIOUS DISEASE.

As he looked at it, he said:

'If they die on the journey take their bodies back to Poland. They don't want to stay here, and we don't want their dead bodies. The country is crawling with those parasites. You couldn't shift them even with cannon shot.'

He stood savouring the flavour of a Machorka.

'I forgot to buy cigarettes,' I told him.

He handed me the pack and walked away: 'Goodbye' he shouted over his shoulder.

It was bitterly cold as we stood outside the train. As he moved away, I saw Viera standing in the shadows, not far from him. The lights on the train lit up her face:

'I came just to see your face once more,' she said.

Luba looked out. Viera took my hand and shook it. I signed to her that everything was alright. She passed me a note. I quickly put it in my pocket. They left. Only a few minutes passed before their footprints were covered by snow.

I returned to the compartment. The long-awaited whistle blew, the signal for departure. All hearts beat faster. All had longed for that moment, and especially the ones who had risked their lives and freedom to be on that train. All those heart-beats collected together would have been like a volcano.

The train proceeded to Zhitomir where we doubled south to the town of Vinnitsa and into Ternopol. I noticed that machine-guns had been mounted on the top of every third wagon of the train. There were two soldiers on every machine-gun. When I asked Wolodia why this had been done, he told me that there were bands of anti-Soviet Ukrainians and even remnants of the German army in hiding in the forests. They had been attacking trains and killing passengers.

When we left the station Wolodia came into my compartment. He had changed into civilian clothes. He asked me to put him in one of the beds prepared for the sick. He said he had no intention of returning to Russia: he would leave the train with other Polish passengers at Katowice.

244

'How can you leave a whole train to return empty to Russia?'
I asked.

He explained that he feared his own fellow countrymen.

This incident illustrated to me the fact that the elite NKGB
and the NKVD were by no means united by the same aims. At
that time the NKVD had control of internal security inside the
Soviet Union, while the NKGB was involved with Soviet espion-
age abroad. NKGB officers were senior to NKVD officers.

Even today, perhaps even more so today, I am sure that at
least one in every two NKVD officers would jump at the chance
to go abroad and to stay abroad, if he was born in the Soviet
Union less than sixty years ago . . . and would not go back.

We reached Przemysl and were told we would have to wait
for at least four hours. Before the war I had known this city well
and had friends there, among them a doctor of medicine called
Turckel. I was delighted when I saw that he had been called out
to perform the routine inspection of the repatriates. The medical
staff on the station informed him I was on the train.

He came across to me in his white coat. We fell upon each
other with embraces and tears, like two children. He had known
my family. I could hardly form the words of the questions he
was waiting for me to ask: Who is still alive, who is dead, how
did they die? Very gently in a broken voice he told me that
there was no need for me to go to my mother's home town . . .
that everyone was dead. They had been massacred, over forty
thousand of them at the new Jewish cemetery.

I

PART FOUR

Bitter Pills and Germans

17

In Authority

Three nights later the train, skirting the Carpathian Mountains, and still carrying large numbers of refugees who had failed to link up with relatives on the way, thundered across the Pomeranian Plain, across lands that had long been German but were now part of reconstructed Poland. Next morning it drew to a halt at Waldenburg, a town in which we, the Jews and Poles, were now to play the unusual role of victors. Our long journey together was safely over – though my own little Odyssey had barely begun.

At every one of these stations at which we had stopped after the frontier there had been reception committees awaiting the train, and pathetic groups of people holding up placards bearing the name of their families. There were shouts and cries of joy from those who found relatives – a father who found a child, a son or daughter finding a mother, or brother finding brother, but very few of the Jews found anyone. . . .

The local Secretary of the Communist Party in Waldenburg, a Pole in his early forties, gave a speech of welcome. He told me that he had received word from the Ministry of Health in Warsaw that I had been appointed Chief Medical Officer for the town. A house which had belonged to a Nazi was put at my disposal, a lovely villa with well-equipped consulting rooms, the former home of a doctor.

As he handed me the keys the Party Secretary told me:

'You are now the lawful owner of this property, and you will soon receive documents to that effect.'

A meeting took place forthwith at the house and it was decided that the homeless Poles and Jews would be electing a committee which would commence the task of finding homes for the refugees. We would have to find accommodation for about four hundred Jews. The Party Secretary made no secret of his opinion that we were very privileged because we would be given houses in the centre of the city, and would receive supplies of food through the Polish Government and the International Red Cross. In March it was still bitterly cold, and I made it clear that there should be no delay in housing the displaced persons so that outbreaks of epidemics could be avoided. The Secretary reassured me that, the moment the Jewish committee was formed, we could start housing the people. The reception committee left, and I had a chance to look around the beautiful house. My heart was near to breaking when I looked at its luxury and comfort. I had forgotten that such homes still existed. The wardrobes and cupboards were stuffed with clothes, materials, linens, silver, glass, china, tea, sugar, chocolates, syrups and drink. I couldn't believe it.

Our belongings were pitiful by comparison. Luba unpacked ten pounds of butter, three pounds of honey, a pound of tea and a couple of pounds of sugar. I had four thousand roubles in banknotes, and one gold ten-rouble piece. It was the sum total of the possessions I had acquired in the Soviet Union – plus one wife and one child. Behind me I had left a legacy of a sentence which, thanks to the amnesty, I had not completed.

I opened my medical bag; there were two pistols given me by Wolodia who had left the train without further difficulties at Katowice, announcing that he had no intention of ever going back – so much for the NKVD – and the little note Viera had pressed into my hand. I had folded the note in a special way : I could see it had been opened. I re-read it :

'*Lublu tebia*, I love you. A happy journey. I wish I could be this little scrap of paper. I kiss you for ever – Viera.'

I still held it in my hand when Luba came in.

'She's a whore. I know you screwed her.' I hated her at that moment.

'If it weren't for her, you and Sonia wouldn't be here now,' I retorted angrily.

I destroyed the note and was hiding the weapons when the bell rang. I went to the front door. It was the Nazi doctor who had lived in the house. His wife was with him.

'For God's sake let me into the house,' he pleaded. 'I must take some important medicines and other things I left here. When they turned me out of the house I had no time to pack anything.'

I stood aside to let him pass and asked if he would like to sit down. I told him who I was and said I regretted that we should have to meet in those circumstances.

'You can take whatever you wish. You may empty the house as far as I'm concerned. Just leave me a bed and some sheets. I don't want any of your things.'

He and his wife had tears in their eyes when she said:

'May God bless you, you are a kind man.'

'If you are a doctor,' I asked, 'how could you have been a Nazi Party member?'

He gave me the usual reply: 'We were forced.'

'You may take what you like now, but if you need to come back again, please always do so discreetly before eight in the morning.'

I felt distinctly uncomfortable about taking over his house although I realized that perhaps a son or relative of his could have been responsible for killing people in my family. Oh no – I never wanted such an exchange.

As he left the house he bowed from the waist.

Luba unpacked our clothes and started to settle in. They even sent us a maid.

The Nazi doctor used to come to the house with a hand-cart early every morning to take away whatever he wanted until one day the Party Secretary happened to see him there. He took out his pistol and held him up against the wall in the hall. Quietly he warned him:

'If I find you here again, I'll shoot you like a dog.'

Then he remonstrated with me for being too easy with him.

A sub-committee was formed for rehousing, comprised of three Poles, with a local Jew, Lipshitz, as secretary, another Jew and myself. There was a list of properties to visit and every day they would go to the houses on the list, accompanied by a guard carrying a machine-gun. Big placards had been prepared which read:

'This house has been requisitioned by decree number so and so, dated so and so,' and signed by the Mayor.

I was present at the requisitioning of about forty houses. We spent five to ten minutes at each of them. Sometimes whole families were ejected. They were permitted to take a limited number of personal articles with them, but the rest, which usually meant the furniture, had to remain. Although these may seem harsh measures, they were of course benign compared to the brutality used by the Nazis when acquiring the houses: then the occupants were killed on the spot, or sent to death camps. At every one of the houses I visited the people there protested their innocence of any crime: some said they were Jews, or that they had risked their lives to save Jews, some said they had a Jewish grandmother. . . .

'Hitler appears to have been extremely generous,' was my rejoinder. 'He even permitted Jews to join the SS.'

One day, some time after the incident between the former owner of the villa I occupied and the Party Secretary, I noticed the doctor walking to and fro near the house. I went up to him.

'Oh *Herr Doktor*!' he said. 'Please, let me come inside, I want to talk to you.'

'Alright, come in,' I said, waving him in.

He seemed very frightened as I took him inside. First he remarked on some of the changes I had made, then with a trembling voice he gave the purpose of his visit:

'There are some old souvenirs of the family, especially of my dead mother, in the attic. Would you be so kind as to allow me to go up there sometimes to potter about and pray occasionally?'

Neither Luba, Sonia, nor I had even been into the attic. I thought his request not unreasonable and let him go upstairs. When he left the house I saw that the door to the attic was padlocked, although he had not carried anything out with him when he left.

During the next few days I was too busy even to wonder why he came with his wife, every evening at dusk and went up to the attic. But then I thought: if he has come to pray, as he says, it seems very strange because most of the Christians I know would go to a church. On his next visit I went with him to the door of the attic. He unlocked it, then stood and waited.

'Go ahead,' I told him, then followed him in. I could see that my presence had made him uncomfortable. Yet there was nothing in there unusual or strange. There were piles of trunks, cases, old pieces of furniture, old pictures and photographs.

'Well,' I said, 'please, show me where you usually pray.'

He looked at his wife as though asking for her advice. She shook her head indicating that he should disclose nothing to me, then she started to sob, quietly. Well, I thought, what's the difference if it makes them happy to be here and pray quietly. I went downstairs. Luba was there and asked me what I had seen. I told her.

'You had better not let them come here again. We shall have trouble with the local Communist Party.'

As they were leaving I went into the hall and asked him to hand me the key. He refused.

'Alright, come back with me and open the attic door for me.'

We all trundled back upstairs. He was most agitated, his wife too, as he fumbled with the key.

'Why have you asked us to come back?' he enquired.

I walked past him:

'I want to have another look at what you have in here.'

His wife answered:

'What we have here is of absolutely no use to you or the Polish authorities, it is nothing of value.'

They stood still as I looked and looked. I turned on the light and peered into the cases.

'I will not allow you to come here any more,' I said to provoke them.

She started to cry:

'Have pity on us, the most holy part of our lives is here in this attic.'

He interposed:

'If you will not permit us to come any more,' and he held up a capsule of cyanide, 'I shall die here and now, with my wife, and you shall watch us.'

I quickly grabbed the capsule.

'I want to know what it is here that is so important to you.'

He looked first at me, then at his wife:

'Mutti, we shall have to tell him.'

He beckoned me to one corner of the attic, lifted two floor-boards – it was very easy – and revealed a coffin. He slid the lid off to one side. There lay the embalmed corpse of a young man, dressed in an army corporal's uniform. The coffin had a metal lining and was covered with a thick transparent substance.

'It's my son.'

It was done. He had said it. He stood with one arm around his wife's shoulders and held her hand with the other.

'It's my child,' she said, 'we have kept him here for many years, and we always come to visit him.'

'It is as I said, no value to anyone else, only for us, our son.'

I took another look at the body and told him to replace the lid and floorboards. I put my hands on their shoulders,

'Come with me.'

We went out. When he locked the padlock he handed me the key.

'You keep it,' I said.

We all went downstairs into the consulting rooms, I poured them both a drink and took one myself.

'Tell me everything. Why is the body of your son upstairs in this house?'

'He was wounded at the front and brought back to a military hospital not far from here. When he had almost recovered they gave him leave to come home with us. It was such a joy to us to have him here. He was still a child, but he had seen such terrible things. He said he never wanted to go back to the front. He became a deserter. At first he went away to another town, then came back here. We hid him, but the strain was too much. He committed suicide. We could not hand over his body to the authorities, we would have been in trouble for hiding him. So we decided to keep him here.'

The longer he continued with his bizarre story the more sympathy I felt for them. Here he was, a Nazi doctor, ejected from his home, the centrepoint of his own personal tragedy.

'I do not intend to remain long in this town, but as long as I am here you may come with your wife whenever you wish to be with your dead son. When I leave I suggest that you have the body quietly removed and buried because others will move in here.'

254

I told Luba nothing about the incident. Ten days later, when she was out of the house, the couple came with a horse-drawn cart to move the coffin. They had brought four people to carry it out. Next day the doctor came to tell me that the body had been buried in the cemetery in the presence of the priest. In my consulting room he took my hand, knelt down before me and swore he had never done harm to a Jew or a Pole.

Another incident was equally harrowing.

We went to one of the better houses on our list one day, and the Polish members of the committee stopped at the door and refused to go inside.

'Why don't you go in?' I asked.

'The woman who lives here is the lover of a high-ranking Soviet officer.'

'It makes no difference,' I said. 'Come on, knock on the door.'

Usually we would give a gentle ring at first when we went to a house, but often there would be no answer. There was no reply. The guard who was with us banged on the door with the butt of his gun. Voices could be heard.

'Alright, I'm coming.' It was a woman's voice.

A very pretty woman of about thirty opened the door. The Poles hung back, afraid to go in. I went inside.

'Ivan, Ivan, come down,' she called, '*schnell*, come down.'

I looked up the stairs from where I stood in the hall. A regular officer of the Red Army came down the stairs, buttoning his flies.

'What is going on here?' he asked in a commanding voice.

I came up close to him, looked him in the eyes, and said in fluent, rude, Russian:

'You've screwed her. Button up your smelly trousers and fuck off!'

He was stunned. Before he could reply I said:

'And quick. I'm in the special NKGB service. Get out. Fast.'

He drew his heels together: 'Yes, *Tovarisch*!'

To her I said:

Frieda, or Rosemarie, or whatever your name is, open your ears and listen. This house is hereby requisitioned.' I told one of the party to read out the order. The paper trembled in his hand – they were still very much overawed and afraid of the possible consequences. I went up to her, and held up my open hand:

'Five minutes. You have five minutes to get out.'

She was a really beautiful woman, and I heard one Pole whisper to the other:

'She's a beauty. If that Russian could screw her, why shouldn't a Pole fuck her too?'

It was usual, whenever houses were requisitioned, to find hoards of treasures: objets d'art, pictures, silver and other items of value, since they have been occupied by high-ranking SS and SA officers or Nazi Party elite members, who had looted them from many sources. So the Poles always had a look round to see what they could take away in their pockets, holdalls or brief-cases – without being too obvious, since looting was against the law. They were always tempting me to join them in this looting:

'*Doktorku*, look, here. Here's something for you.'

But I would not give them the pleasure. The only time I took anything it was three pairs of silk stockings to give to Luba.

They thought that if I stole they would be able to sleep soundly but I told them not to fear discovery on my account. While they were looking around the house on the ground floor, we suddenly heard screams from upstairs. We guessed that somebody was trying to make love to the woman. I told the Pole in charge of the group to go upstairs and put a stop to whatever was happening there, but he only replied with a knowing wink. They were after all representing the authorities in charge, and I was there only as a representative of the Jewish committee.

The shouts continued. A man was bellowing: *Kurwa!* Whore!' and then she screamed:

'You Polish *schwein*! Pig!'

The situation was becoming too heated. I beckoned the head man in the group to come upstairs with me. As we neared the bedroom door, a Pole ran out covering his genitals with his hands which were covered in blood.

'My God!' he screamed, 'look what she has done to me!' On

the floor lay his penis. The woman rushed out shouting too; her face bruised and bleeding, her lip split open.

I rushed to the man to give him aid, then ran down stairs to tell the soldier to stop the first car and call the police. As I ran back I heard a shot from upstairs. I raced up the stairs to find the mutilated Pole holding his groin in one hand and firing shots into the back of the woman who lay dead on the ground. His friend had handed him a loaded gun.

He stood over her, unable to stem the flow of blood which dripped on to her body. His voice was weaker now:

'*Kurwa niemka!* German whore!'

His friends pulled him away.

Later he told how she had resisted him at first, but eventually he had worn her down and, just when she was on the point of giving into him, she had grabbed the knife and cut off his penis with one sweeping blow saying:

'No Polish swine will have me!'

After this terrible scene we found a little girl of about four years of age hiding in a wardrobe on the top floor. As we left a considerable crowd had gathered outside.

It was such a bloodbath we had trouble keeping the story quiet and in getting anyone to live in the house.

The committee became very unpopular and thereafter made its visits accompanied by three guards instead of one. As far as the occupants of the house were concerned this was not really necessary because the Germans would not have raised a finger against them. Once beaten they were cowards to the end.

I began to avoid going to the houses with the committee. I hated to see the people who were pushed out protesting and crying, and the fights between the new occupants over the food and furnishings they found in the houses. I heard that one family found a big saucepan full of gold teeth which must surely have come from a concentration camp. There were arguments over who should take the gold until the Polish security officials confiscated it. There were other finds of precious stones, and jewellery which could be easily transported when the Germans (who had collected them) could escape to the American Occupied Zone of Germany. Every day we heard stories that deep in

Poland they were still hunting down Jews and killing them.

I myself was planning escape. My plan was to get first to Leipzig, then to Eschwege where there was a displaced persons' UNRRA camp.

On my last visit with the housing committee we went to a large house with sixteen or so bedrooms. The Poles were reluctant to go inside because they had heard that there were some typhoid cases in the old building. Again I was obliged to urge them to go in. The door was opened only after we had hammered on it for some time. We all filed in, eight members of the committee and three soldiers. The declaration was read out. Four elderly Germans had gathered near us to show us a document signed by the Soviet General in command of the area which stated that they could remain there. The Poles blanched and prepared to leave. I said:

'Who is running this city? The Russians or the Poles?'

They looked at each other.

'The Poles of course.'

They proceeded to affix the notice to the door of the building. The Germans were given ten minutes to leave, and started to shuffle away. On the door of one of the rooms I found a notice in German which read: NO ENTRY. TYPHOID. The Poles refused to go inside. I went in to find an old woman in bed with a temperature and symptoms of the disease.

'Mother, I'm afraid you will have to get up from that bed,' I told her, reluctantly. She obviously had not long to live. One of the Germans had come into the room:

'We could push her out in the bed,' he suggested, 'it has wheels.'

I agreed at once. Another sick person was brought and placed in another bed too, and they were wheeled out. This took about fifteen minutes. In the meantime two Soviet messengers, on horseback, had come to the building and showed us an order, again signed by the General, to leave the occupants of the house where they were. The Poles dashed off, leaving me standing there alone. I turned to see that the old woman in the bed had died. I was dismayed but hardly shocked; after six years of war we had all, in central Europe, become hardened to death. When

I took her pulse to make sure she was dead I had one hand on the mattress: it felt very lumpy. I took out a penknife and split open the corner to find several little sacks filled with gold coins. Quickly I went into the hallway to find the other patient who was being pushed toward the door. I was convinced that the mattress would be stuffed with coins too. It was. As the other Poles had all disappeared, only the secretary of the committee, Lipshitz, was with me. The Soviet officer arrested us both and took us to the General's house. He was furious with me.

'Didn't I see you walking in the street with a Russian woman and blonde child?' he asked.

'How did you know that she's a Russian?'

'She is made in a certain way: large behind, and in front.'

'I suppose you are right,' I answered, 'I am told that Soviet bottoms are even bigger than Flanders mares'.'

He considered the conversation to be getting a little out of hand.

'You have been appointed Chief Medical Officer here, but you refuse to obey my orders.'

'Not when they apply.'

'But I am the General in command of this area, and everyone, I mean everyone, even the Polish government officials, does as I say.'

He had several officers with him.

'General,' I said, 'may I speak to you alone?'

He opened the door of his inner office.

'Come in.'

I followed him. A large portrait of Stalin hung behind his desk. He put his hand on the back of a chair, and a foot on the seat.

'What is it you wish to tell me?'

'General. I know why you wish to protect this family. They have a hoard of gold coins which probably belongs to you, and they are guarding it. But they are Nazis. They must get out of the house. You can keep the gold.'

This shook him. By now I knew how far I could go with all ranks of the Red Army including generals.

'You certainly learnt something during your time in the

Soviet Union. How many people know about the gold? The Poles? The guards who came to fetch you?'

'No one. Only you, me and the Germans.'

We took over the house two days later. That same evening the General and I drank three bottles of vodka between us. We exchanged experiences, and if anyone had recorded our conversation we would undoubtedly both have been shot by the NKGB.

The next day I told him I needed a favour from him, a *komandierovka*, or travel permit, for five people to go to the frontier zone. I told him I was anxious to see if there were any Jews still there.

'You mean you want to escape to the other side.' He looked me straight in the eye.

I knew far too much about him. He could easily have had me shot and be rid of me. But instead, he agreed to give me the permits. No doubt he considered that it would be an alternative way of disposing of me.

I told him I intended to leave in a week's time, but the Communist Party Secretary handed me the permits after only two days. They were made out in the names of Luba, Sonia and myself, and two other Jews who figured as my assistants. The reason for the trip was inserted as 'Health Inspection'. The permits allowed us to travel to Zgorzelec on the Polish-German frontier.

By dawn next day we, and the two other Jews with us, had been smuggled across the frontier between Poland and East Germany – the River Neisse. Although it was spring the morning air was cold. Our wet clothes clung to our bodies making us even colder. Sonia's face was blue. The two *mitschleppers* (hangers on) remained silent, moving when we moved.

We had come down the hill and kept to the right of the railway lines near the river. As the line made a wide bend before the station, we were shielded from the road and from the Soviet guards by an embankment. Luba and I took turns to carry Sonia, and every so often I would crawl up the embankment to reconnoitre the town. I spotted a Soviet truck patrolling the road, carrying several soldiers.

As we neared the station many railway lines converged. The

embankment gradually diminished so that we no longer had cover. There was a little railwayman's hut in the centre of all the converging lines. We made a dash for it and quickly piled inside. The maintenance crews had left working overalls and sweaters there which were at least dry. We took them and changed out of our wet ones, although Luba had almost dried off.

We had become worried about Sonia. Luba said she must go to the station to find a hot drink for her and went off about half an hour before the train was due. We watched as she walked along the platform. A German soldier came to her and started talking: he carried a rifle. I told the others to stay where they were and rushed over to Luba. Since she could only speak Russian and a little Yiddish the soldier was about to take her to the Russian headquarters.

I took the soldier's arm:

'*Genosse*, mate. Where are you taking that woman?' I spoke a Prussian German.

'The Soviet frontier police are searching for a woman with a blonde child carrying a doll.' He looked at me more closely, then:

'Which front did you fight on?'

'Stalingrad.'

'*Mensch*, man, you came back from hell,' and he offered me a cigarette. As I lit it, I said:

'*Genosse*, you must help me. That woman saved my life.'

'Of course, it will be my duty to help such as you.'

He appeared to be about the same size as me.

'Perhaps if we changed clothes I could get my people on to the train.'

'I don't think that would work. Everybody on the station knows me. If the Russians get the slightest whiff of this, they will have the train stopped further along the line and have you all taken off. Where's the child then?'

I pointed to the little hut: 'She is with two friends in there.'

'Well, it is safe enough there for the moment, but the workmen arrive at seven.'

Leaving Luba on the platform, we had strolled from the station along the road and were standing outside a small

261

K

gasthaus when a Soviet army car approached us. A bad moment, but the car went past. I asked him if he could get a hot drink for the child. He went into the house and emerged with a bottle of milk. He handed me some German money too.

'If they should ask if you have seen us, try to divert them by saying you saw us somewhere else, on the other side of the town.' I thanked him for his help. As I walked away he said:
'*Heil* Hitler!'

I turned back and returned his Nazi salute.

At the platform I found Luba and ushered her back to the hut to find the *mitschleppers* trembling with fear. If all of us now came out and walked over to the station we would certainly arouse suspicion. I told the other two to wait until the train pulled into the platform, then they should hurry across to board the train at the first available door. Luba, the child and I would move up to the end if all went well, and get on the train there. If not, we would catch the next one. A workman's woolly hat was rammed on to Sonia's head and her blonde hair tucked inside. The reverberating railway lines and the green signal announced the arrival of the train. As I watched from the little window I saw the German soldier engaged in conversation with a Soviet frontier guard. He was pointing in the opposite direction. Then the guard spoke to some others and they all boarded the truck. The train pulled into the station, coming from the same direction as we had taken, along the river. As the train shielded us from view we came out of the hut and followed our plan. The train was packed, but Luba and I managed to squeeze on at the front. We told Sonia to pretend to be asleep in her mother's arms. Luba found a seat. I warned her that if anyone should speak to her she should say 'speak Polish'. When I looked from the window I could see two Soviet guards walking along beside the train with two German guards and dogs. They were entering every carriage. I thought: God, we are finished, there will be no escape, everyone will be brought out and lined up.

I turned to a man who had attempted to start a conversation with Luba in Polish.

'She's not in a talking mood,' I explained.
'It's alright, I understood.'

To the Germans seated around Luba I went on to give more explanations:

'I'm German myself – was in the army in Russia. I have just returned to the Fatherland. This woman saved my life there so I feel I owe her everything. The truth is the frontier police are after us.'

They immediately stood up to hide Luba and Sonia. It was a long open carriage without compartments, so that a guard standing at one end could see all the passengers at once. Sonia was bundled under a seat and Luba lay down beside her, between a pair of seats facing each other. The other passengers sat on the seats and hid them with their legs. The guards did come into the carriage, but the area in the immediate vicinity of the stowaways was so congested that they were happy just to push a way through. When they had gone I looked out of the window to see my German soldier friend making a thumbs-up sign.

The wait at the station seemed interminable. At last the whistle blew, the wheels ground into motion. As I watched the station slowly sliding backward I caught sight of two frontier police holding my two *mitschleppers* by the arms. I nearly cried out. I had not seen their faces but recognized them from behind.

Once the train was under way the others helped Luba and Sonia to seats. I must admit that the Germans in that carriage were marvellous to us. Only one of them asked any questions.

'*Sind Sie Parteigenosse?* (Are you a party member)?'

'*Natürlich.*'

Then two or three of them drew themselves to attention:

'*Heil* Hitler!'

I was sure I wasn't the only Jew who had been forced to make the Nazi salute to save his skin or to fulfil a mission in Nazi-occupied Europe when the Germans were at the height of their power. How tragic that in defeat the Hitler myth lived on in their souls. Even now, thirty-five years after his death, Hitler's ideology still has its followers in many parts of the world, especially in Germany. However, I cannot deny that at that moment they helped me, no doubt because in their defeat and dejection they found solace in helping each other and of course because they believed I was German.

Had they known who I was it would no doubt have been a very different story. Despite a momentary flicker of gratitude it gave me great pleasure to trick them. Then and now every corner of that land is stained with Jewish blood as far as I'm concerned.

All the money we possessed when we arrived at Leipzig station consisted of the few German coins given to us by the soldier and some Russian roubles. We had abandoned the doll 'Pupee' before we boarded the train, and Sonia's woolly workman's hat had been exchanged for a beret given to her by a woman on the train. Somehow she had understood that she must be obedient as she had never been obedient before. I promised her she would have another doll or, if she preferred, perhaps she could have a horse like the one she had been given on the train from Karaganda. When I mentioned that city she said:

'Oh yes. That was when I left my uncle and grandma ... oh no ... it was my father. You are my uncle.'

Luba interrupted: 'I told you that you have a first father and a second father.'

I was unable to control an upsurge of guilt. My eyes filled with tears as I looked around the huge battle-scarred railway station, and the demolished buildings around it.

Sonia looked up at me:

'Why are you crying? There are tears in your eyes.'

'I was just feeling sorry for the people who lived here and whose homes got bombed.' But my thoughts were directed to that distant city in Russia and the station where her father had lifted her high in the air before he parted with her.

There was no time to dwell further on it. There were Soviet guards at every turn. To avoid questioning and arrest we must get clear of the station. As we went down the steps outside we were amazed to see our two *mitschleppers* rushing towards us. They said they had given the Soviet guards some gold roubles, and they had closed their eyes. All of us were overjoyed, and we repaired to a cafe nearby. We already knew that we would be unable to buy food without ration cards. I spoke to the manager telling him I had been in the army and the people with me had helped me, but we had none of us had ration cards.

He took us through to an inside room and served us hot drinks which I paid for with the few marks we had. Two men came in and started to ask questions about which regiment I had been in, what rank, and who had been my commanding officer. I was able to give convincing replies as I had spent much time with German army prisoners in the camps and knew a lot about the *Wehrmacht*. One of them lowered his voice:

'I am not familiar with these people you have said were in your regiment, although I did know a major in your battalion of the Panzer Division, you remember, the one with the monocle.' I nodded wisely. 'I warn you,' he continued, 'the manager of this restaurant spies for the Russians. He hands people over to them or to our own communist police.'

The two started to argue with each other, then one fat German said:

'I swear by everything that's holy: if you inform on these people, I'll kill you.' There was a pregnant silence.

'I want to get to the American zone,' I explained, 'to a town called Eschwege. It's across the frontier from Mülhausen.'

They talked amongst themselves, then came up with the proposition that they would go to the station, buy us train tickets to the frontier and find out the time of the next train. Until their return we should wait at the cafe. It did not take long before they returned with the tickets and information that the next train would leave in twenty minutes.

Early that evening we reached Mülhausen. We still had our two *mitschleppers* with us.. They said that I was their guardian angel and that I couldn't leave without them because they had brought us good luck too. It was God's wish that we should stick together to the end. We walked to the bus station and awaited the frontier bus for Eschwege. At that time it was, surprisingly, far easier to cross from the East German zone into American-occupied territory than it was to cross from Poland into East Germany: the Iron Curtain had not yet been drawn across Germany. It was routine for the Soviet and German police to check the *Ausweis Karte*, identity cards, which at that time bore no photographs, when the bus was ready to leave. On this occasion one of the Soviet guards looked inside,

'Look how packed it is! Let them fuck themselves!'

The *mitschleppers* looked at me with awe, almost as if I had personally worked another miracle. The guard banged the door shut with a shout:

'*Pojezdzai!* Go!'

He was the last Soviet soldier I ever saw. A genteel farewell. On that last stage of our escape Luba cried, and Sonia, without knowing why, cried too. When I looked around me at the other passengers I realized that we were not the only escaping refugees on the bus. It was the end of a chapter in my life: 1939–46.

Thirty-five years later I have forgotten much of what happened to me, though I have kept some old notes and cuttings, which are some help even if difficult to read. But when writing this the memories come flooding back as though it were yesterday. I cannot understand how my young body resisted so much suffering and punishment during those years. The effects on my physical health have remained with me: the torture, sadistic beatings and attempts at brainwashing have left deep scars, some visible, some spiritual. The cervical arthritis, and arthritis in other parts of my body, can be traced back to those years too. Thanks to an iron constitution and an overwhelming desire to do so, I survived, although there were moments when I had wished for death.

Injustices such as I suffered are still happening daily in the Soviet Union. The inhuman system has been denounced by fine men: Sakharov, Solzhenitsyn, and others. But the dissident voice is being raised only now. When I was there it was impossible for anyone to criticize the system openly, though there is no question that there were always those who disagreed with the totalitarian methods right from the early revolutionary days, genuine communist idealists who saw immediately that this was not the ideal society envisaged by Karl Marx and Engels. So my eyes turned back to watch the last Soviet soldier, the conqueror with his machine-gun. How could we guess then that thirty-five years later the Russian soldier would be pointing his machine-gun toward world domination, expansionism and imperialism?

As I have always said, the Russians are a great people with great hearts: I loved them and still love them. My only sorrow is that they haven't got the decent government they deserve.

We arrived at Eschwege around midnight and made straight for the UNRRA camp; Luba, Sonia, the two *mitschleppers*, and myself. We presented ourselves to two American military policemen:

'We have just escaped from the Russian zone.'

They took us to a special quarantine block where we were given baths, hot food and American cigarettes.

In Hebrew we say:

'*Moshia, Moshia* has come for us. Hallelujah!'

18

The Episode of Dr Base

At the end of the first week of freedom I was sent to work in the towns of Pegnitz and Creussen in the DPs' (Displaced Persons) camps. I was to remain attached to the UNRRA headquarters and was given a residence at 8 Bahnhofstrasse in Creussen, a house which had belonged to a Dr Lautner, a Nazi Party member. The house and the consulting rooms were put at my disposal in the same way as the Poles had done in Waldenburg. Ninety-five per cent of my patients were Jews, who had survived the concentration camps or escaped from the East.

Dr Lautner was an elderly man whose daughter, Hildegard, and son-in-law, Dr Heinrich Thiel, lived with him. I could have asked them to move out of the house if I had wished, but I knew it would cause him suffering, so I asked the military governor of Pegnitz, a US army officer, Captain Stematis, to find me other accommodation. I tried to calm Dr Lautner by telling him that I would not be in his house for long . . . he would soon regain his privacy.

When I thought about it, living and working among the Germans, now defeated and subdued, I found it difficult to believe what they had done. None of them seemed to know anything about the concentration camps. How could they have committed such crimes? But despite my initial reluctance – yes I can call it that – to accept stories that had originally seemed to be exaggerated Soviet propaganda, the facts and photographs were before my eyes every day. Creussen is a staunch Catholic town. The Governor at that time was a Herr Mehl. As I had been placed in a position of authority with regard to the DPs' camps, the local government officials tried to curry favour with me. Every one of them had been instrumental in saving Jews from the gas chambers, and every one of them loved the Jews. I would ask:

'How is it possible then that so many Jews were destroyed, shot or gassed?'

'We knew nothing of what was happening.'

One night there was an unusual celebration at Dr Lautner's villa. The house was ablaze with light, a rare sight in those days of austerity. Several of the UNRRA staff had assembled for dinner. A prima donna was to sing in honour of the occasion. Captain Stematis and his aide were there too, and a French officer, head of UNRRA at Pegnitz. For me her song went in one ear and out the other: I had my mind on other things. It sickened me to think that I was here listening to this German prima donna when only the day before I had been forced to plead for home for the victims of the Germans before Governor Mehl. But many people there in the room had suffered at the hands of the Nazis too, and it was impossible to apportion blame with any accuracy. I personally blamed all the Germans for the events of those war years except the small children and those born after the war. They were innocent even if their fathers had killed our fathers. How would we prevent such terrible years in the future? So ran my thoughts while I listened to the music.

Then suddenly we heard a terrific noise from upstairs which even the prima donna's voice was incapable of drowning. Dr Lautner's son-in-law had his apartment on the upper floor; I had only spoken to him once since I lived in the house.

I ran quickly up the stairs to his door which I found locked. I banged on the door repeatedly until his wife let me in. She was crying. Her husband was sitting at a desk, a gun before him.

'What's happened?'

'*Nicht, nicht, Herr Doktor,*' she answered.

I walked up to the desk and took away the gun. It was loaded and ready to fire. He sat pale and speechless. I understood that they had been arguing. I put my arm round his shoulders but he remained silent, only the voice of the singer continued unabated.

'Please tell me what happened.'

He took up his pipe, drew on it, then looked up at me:

'Oh God, how I wish I had had the courage to shoot myself

before you came in. My wife has been pleading with me not to take my life, but I can see no reason for me, an ex-army officer, to go on living. What future is there for us? Even here in our own house we are no longer the bosses. How can I live with such humiliation, while you and those Americans listen to that opera singer downstairs?'

'Well, there's no need to worry more on that score,' I said. 'I have some good news for you: I shall be moving out in the next few days. Come now, stop worrying.'

'I know. You will leave here but you will go to another house and make someone else unhappy.'

I remained quiet, looking at him.

'Do you object then to my presence in particular in your home? And to the presence of my people in this city?'

'Yes. But I'm not anti-Jewish. I'm not a Nazi – I was an army officer.'

I held out the gun to him.

'Come on, shoot me. You have the chance to kill a Jew.'

His wife was sobbing quietly:

'*Mein liebe, mein liebe* Heinrich.'

I kept looking deep into his eyes. Slowly he lifted his hand to take the gun. He placed it in his pocket. With all my force I hit him a back-hand blow across the face which tumbled him to the ground.

'You miserable defeated German aristocrat!'

As I left the room his wife rushed to him and from the stairs I heard him shouting from the window: 'Help, help!'

The guests downstairs had no idea of what had been going on up there. The incident held no particular importance for me: he was just a defeated German rat who was unable to face life any longer.

I left the Lautner house next day, and moved into a new residence. The Jewish people under my care liked me. I did my job. The American military authorities were satisfied too – I gave them no trouble. They supplied whatever I asked for, even an Adler car which I confiscated myself from an SS woman. She got 800 marks from me in compensation.

But there were those who did not like me and, of these, the most important was Governor Mehl of Creussen, a man who had at his disposition about six hundred homes which had been confiscated from notorious Nazis; a devout Catholic no doubt, but no lover of the Jews.

One day a pregnant Jewish woman called Bergman came to me and asked me to help her find a home. I told her to come back in a couple of days, I would speak to Governor Mehl. The town council offices were situated in a building on a hill over-looking the town, and approached through winding, picturesque streets. I went up to his office to speak to him about this woman.

As I entered he stood up:

'*Guten Tag, Herr Doktor.*'

I told him the story of the pregnant woman and suggested the house of a certain Zimmerman who had been a high-ranking Nazi officer. There were two assistants in the room.

'Dr Urban, I'm afraid you cannot have that house.'

'But, Governor, you know full well that we are legally entitled to use the house, and I intend to do so.'

'You must understand, Doctor. I am a German Catholic, not an anti-semite or a Nazi. The trouble is that, if I refuse to pander to every whim of the Jews, they now call me anti-semitic or Nazi. Our city of Creussen has always been a strongly Catholic town. Now one Jew after another is coming here. And they all need houses. If we say we don't like it, we are called anti-semitic.'

He had sat down part way through our conversation. I went up to him, grabbed him by the tie, and lifted him from the chair:

'But you are a dirty Nazi! An anti-semite! You just told me you aren't anti-semitic and in the same breath you said the town of Creussen was always a pure Catholic town before the war. Your own words condemn you!'

I shook him violently and threw him back into his chair:

'Herr Mehl! I give you twenty-four hours to put this woman into the home I allot to her. If you don't, I'll take you and throw you over this balcony. You Germans, especially those in your position, should help the Jews, who have remained, with all the resources at your command. They are just the remnants of millions. You should be trying to make amends for all the crimes

271

which have been committed against our people. You need not worry, no Jew will wish to remain here long. Every stone in this city and in this country has run with Jewish blood and Jewish tears. So you *Alte Scheisser*, you old shitbag, get on with it!'

I stormed out. Mrs Bergman happened to be coming up the stairs. I told her she would have somewhere to go next day.

When I got home I took Sonia to me and kissed her. She was so blonde that with her blue eyes she could easily have been taken for a German child. As I looked at her I thought:

'No. I will not let you grow up here to learn German speech and German ways.'

It was just a matter of time, I hoped, before I would be attached to the US army and then we would apply for immigration papers to the United States.

Next morning I found a German woman standing in the doorway crying. She had a parcel in her hand.

'*Herr Doktor*. Listen to me, please. Have pity on me. I am a German. I have no right to ask you to help, but it is not for me, it's for my child.'

I stood and listened to her story. She had always been a friend of the Jews. Her child, four years old, was dying of pneumonia and she was unable to obtain drugs which would save her. The parcel contained two lengths of cloth for me.

I told her what she already knew: that I had no right to attend German patients or prescribe medicines for them.

'So,' she cried bitterly, 'my child will die. My Rosemarie will die.'

She continued to sob, heartbroken. There were several patients waiting for Luba, all Jews freed from the concentration camps. They were sorry for her. I took her arm and led her to my car. We went to her home. As I went inside the first thing which struck me was the number of photographs of an SA officer. I asked her who it was. She said it was her husband who was dead. I observed: 'A Nazi, a killer.'

'He never killed anyone. They forced him to become a Nazi.'

The child was in an airless, dark room, breathing with difficulty. I heard the rasping, crunching noise as she fought for breath. I went to the window to let in fresh air. She had a burning fever. It was clear she would die if she continued without antibiotics.

She was extremely thin. I asked her mother why she was so emaciated. She told me that for two weeks previously her daughter had eaten almost nothing. When I asked how she had come to hear about me she said that a local German doctor had given her my name.

The girl was almost unconscious. Examination only confirmed my fears: she had double pneumonia. We went out. As I closed the door behind me the woman started crying again:

'Oh save my child! Save my child!'

She all but threw herself at my feet. I looked up and saw the photographs of her dead husband again; he was covered with war decorations: 'I can't help you.' I left abruptly and went about my duties. But the child's face remained fixed in my memory.

All the sulphur-based drugs were in extremely short supply and accounted for meticulously. Every milligram had to be signed for. They fetched enormous prices on the black market on the rare occasions they appeared. There were severe penalties for trafficking in sulphonamide drugs.

It was almost noon: I was unable to work or eat. I drove home and went straight to the surgery. I removed sufficient sulphonamide from the drugs cabinet for the girl's treatment, and divided it into the appropriate doses. On the way back my brakes failed, and I ran straight into a garden wall. I left the car where it was and ran to the woman's home. I injected the child and left other medicines for her with full instructions – the girl was in much the same condition as I had left her in the morning.

That afternoon at three I had an appointment with Governor Mehl. Normally his visitors waited in an ante-room. I walked straight to his room. He stood up.

'*Herr Doktor*,' he said as though nothing had happened, but he was trembling.

'What answer have you for me?'

'Nothing. Nothing has changed: it's like I told you.'

I went round the desk, lifted him from his chair and carried him to the balcony. He shouted for help, but I pitched him over the balustrade to the street, a drop of ten feet. I watched how he fell and the impact on his old anti-semitic German bones was not very great. Even while I watched him, he picked himself up: 'Where are my teeth?' he wailed.

I jumped over the balcony:

'You will settle this business for the woman by tomorrow.'

'I could have you arrested for this,' he fumbled as he pushed his teeth back in. 'I am telling you, I'm not anti-semitic. I want you to know that I am a good Catholic and I forgive you for what you have done.'

With the help of eight Jewish boys we moved Mrs Bergman into the Zimmerman house; they had a new lodger. But later that day Stematis came to my home with two military policemen to tell me that I had acted unwisely and contrary to the regulations of the forces of occupation. If he had not known me personally, that I was a decent man and had acted out of compassion, he would have thrown me in jail.

'Captain,' I reminded him, 'you don't yet have the authority to put Jews in German prisons.'

'You are wrong, I do have that authority and there are some Jews in prisons here in Germany right now.'

Of course he was right and I was wrong. The incident was closed for us both.

Little Rosemarie recovered. I visited the house five or six times, but those photographs never ceased to bother me. On the last occasion I went to the house I noticed that most of them had been removed. I asked what had happened to them and the woman said she had removed them because she understood that they reminded me of tragic events.

'You saved my child,' she said, 'and my child will know and all my family and friends will know that it was a Jewish doctor who saved her.'

I left the house. I was unaware that anyone else had come to hear about the child's case but, a week later, the head of UNRRA asked me about her. He asked me the direct question:

'Did you treat her?'

'Yes.'

He asked to see my drugs records and found her name on the list. I showed him the medical report card I had made out. It bore her name, the diagnosis, and in the space for 'Nationality' I had written 'German'.

'You know very well that you had no authority to treat that child: it is strictly forbidden, and you knew it. I shall have no alternative but to report you to headquarters.'

He did too. A few days later I was standing in front of a panel of medical officers and UNRRA officials. I put my case in five minutes. They decided that they would recommend my transfer to another town. I had little respect for them; I told them I would be happy to go.

I had to report to the UNRRA Fifth District headquarters in Munich to obtain my next posting: UNRRA doctor for the DPs in nearby Starnberg. The house of a Dr Base had been requisitioned for me. It was situated high up overlooking the city, in Heinrich Wiland Strasse. This Dr Base, a woman, had been an active Nazi Party member and was widely considered to be a fanatic. The house was in the most desirable residential district of the town along with other beautiful homes which had all been owned by Nazis.

Dr Base proved to be a nervous woman with a cruel facial expression and a twitch which caused her false teeth to click like a horse eating hay. She smiled at me:

'*Herr Doktor*, you wouldn't mind if I were to stay here in a small room with a bed, would you? I shall do my best not to get in your way.'

'I would prefer it if you moved out,' I told her directly.

'Why?'

'Because I don't like your face.'

Looking at the arrangement from her point of view, it is a shattering experience to witness someone else take over your home – it would have been better for her to have gone and lived somewhere else. But I, unfortunately for both of us, relented.

'I do not intend to remain in Starnberg for long and I do not wish to see you while I am here. You may occupy the cottage behind the house and use the garden entrance. That way there will be no need for any contact between us. Please do not interfere with any of us living in the house nor with the patients who will come here.'

Those patients were mainly Jews from the DPs' camp; many of them were strong enough to come up to my house to be treated. For by 1946 the Jews in Germany who had survived had started to regain their health and vigour, although the concentration camps left their marks mentally and physically. They were nervous, sometimes mentally unbalanced. When they came to me for medical help, invariably they would ask how they could remove the tattooed number off their arms. In addition to the houses requisitioned for them they were accorded other privileges.

Often the German authorities were obliged to close their eyes to incidents which in normal circumstances would have led to imprisonment. But their feelings of guilt and their fear of anyone who bore the tattooed number of the camp prevented them from taking action. Of course the Germans in the American Zone were healthier too. On my journey across East Germany I had seen the beaten hungry faces of the German population: in restaurants I had seen them draw a spoon from their pockets and when they finished their food they would lick the spoon clean. But here in the American Zone it was a different picture. They lived better; no one carried his spoon in his pocket. Many of the women, *fräuleins* or married women, had taken American soldiers as lovers. They got chocolate and cigarettes. We could see from day to day that they were making great strides towards the economic recovery of the country.

I earned enough for my requirements; I even had a few private patients. I had become accustomed to living with Luba; she had become slightly more reasonable; sometimes a whole week would pass without her mentioning the past and bringing up old jealousies. Sonia grew prettier every day. At that time she loved me more than I loved her, but even then she was the sun and moon for me. She gave happiness to my life.

One hot summer afternoon I heard Sonia crying loudly in the garden. When I opened the window to look I saw Dr Base walking quickly away from Sonia who was looking at her hand. I jumped from the first-floor window into the garden. Sonia's hand was still red. I ran after Dr Base.

'Why did you do that to my daughter?' I asked.

'She picked a pear from the tree. They aren't ripe yet.' She turned to walk away. I took her hand and squeezed it very hard.

I led her back to the fruit tree where the pear had fallen to the ground.

'Pick it up.'

'*Herr Doktor*, what do you mean? Are you crazy?'

I insisted. She picked it up.

'Now eat it. Go on, eat it!'

'It's too hard,' she protested.

I closed her fingers around the pear and brought her hand down hard on to a stone pedestal. The pear was shattered. Then with her empty hand I struck the stone again.

She screamed: 'That hurts!'

'If I ever see you again in this front garden, I'll kill you. If you touch my child with your dirty Nazi hands still running with Jewish blood, I'll cut off your fingers with a scalpel. Go!'

Sonia had stopped crying. She understood the situation perfectly. She broke into laughter. As I gave her a ride on my knee, she said:

'You know Daddy, the horse I had in Russia was much better.'

'But you forget you are heavier now, five years old.'

'Do you think we could get the horse again from there?' She didn't remember the names of the places in Russia but she could remember the horse she had loved, and probably many other things.

I talked to Luba about what she had said.

'She must be told the truth about her father. As a child she is as yet unable to distinguish between a blood relationship and other relationships but as she grows up she will understand. Then she will love me as a person who has given up so much for her.'

'No. She must forget everything about Russia,' Luba insisted. She was her mother but I knew she was wrong. As the years pass, it becomes harder and harder to tell a child about such things.

Dr Base continued to prowl around in the front garden. She would wait for me to go out, then come into the garden. She counted the apples and pears on the trees and felt them to see if they were ripe. She was playing a cat-and-mouse game with Sonia. One afternoon I came home to hear terrible screams and noise coming from the direction of the garden. Sonia had picked two pears and hidden them. Dr Base scolded her and tried to discover what had happened to the two pears. She dragged the child round the garden asking her where the pears were. When she found the pears Dr Base had hit Sonia on the back with one of them. When I arrived, Sonia was still standing there crying. I took her to Luba and ran to the cottage. The door was locked. I pushed with all my strength until I forced it.

'Don't you touch me!' she screamed. 'I've called the Chief of Police. They will be here any minute.'

I lifted her up and carried her outside and down the steps. She was shouting for help and thrashing her legs.

'The Jew will kill me!'

If she had not said that, I might not have lost my temper to the extent I did. I carried her to an ornamental pool where water-lilies grew, about four feet deep. I threw her in and held her down. She kept raising her head and shouting for help, and each time I pushed her back. The neighbours on both sides opened their windows and shouted at us. I raised her head to give her time to breath again.

'Drink, you bitch.'

She gurgled under the water. I pulled her out.

'The Jew will not kill you. I wouldn't dirty my hands with the killing of a Nazi animal like you.'

I pushed her down again. She must have swallowed two pints of water. I could see she would not be able to take any more ducking. I held her head between my hands:

'I shall hold you here until the MPs come to your rescue,' I shouted at her. Then I ducked her again.

'Come on, why aren't you shouting any more that the Jew will kill you?'

Then I saw her false teeth floating on the water. I dragged her out, placed her face down on the path, and gave her first-aid. She was breathing easily when I left her, and then got up and walked away. Meanwhile Sonia had run into a corner of the garden and watched the entire episode, biting her nails.

I went into the house to start consultations. Sonia ran after me. She whispered in Russian:

'There's another pear still hidden. Do you want it?'

She ran back to look for it, grabbed it and ran up to Dr Base and threw it at her.

When everything calmed down, about fifteen minutes later, we heard the sirens of the police vehicles. Suddenly the house was full of armed US military policemen who had arrived in three jeeps. They walked through the waiting room and burst into the consulting room, machine-guns at the ready. A lieutenant waving a revolver shouted:

'Up against the wall! With your arms raised!'

'There's no need to threaten me with guns!' I answered. 'I'm just a doctor practising his profession. I am not a gangster and you are supposed to be here to protect us!'

But despite my protests I was arrested and brought before the Chief of Military Police, a Lieutenant-Colonel Bludberg. As far as I recall he was the Military Governor of Starnberg too.

'Was all this done on your orders?' I asked as soon as I was escorted into his office. 'You know who I am. What do you intend to do now?'

The Military Governor wore glasses and he kept pushing them up the bridge of his nose, either from habit or nervousness.

'Relax, Doctor, relax. Would you like a drink? Whisky?'

I took no notice.

'You are not empowered to send troops into the residence of an UNRRA doctor, especially when he is examining patients, without the knowledge and approval of the UNRRA officer. You will have to answer for your actions.'

'And who will make me answer for them?' he flared up.

'I will, with the backing of the law.'

He looked at me, again offered me a drink, then poured one for himself.

'I refuse to drink with an American officer who collaborates with Nazis.'

'Now I can hold you responsible for statements like that.'

'You are the one in trouble. You have trodden on a man who will not permit himself to be trodden on.'

'Doctor, let me remind you of what you have done: you have acted in an altogether violent manner. In Creussen you threw the German Governor over the balcony, and here you have nearly killed Dr Base. You should go to the United States and use your talents for the benefit of your fellow Jews there.'

'That is my intention.' On looking back I see that he must have picked up that information from somewhere – the Russians were not the only ones to have a dossier on me!

'In that case if you intend to apply for immigration papers to the USA you had better be very careful indeed in your dealings with the United States authorities here, Dr Urban, very careful indeed.'

I looked at him in disgust. I could see he was an American of German descent, and it later emerged that many US army officers of this sort had helped to cover up for Nazi war criminals.

'You know, Colonel,' I said, 'I have been in Soviet concentration camps. They tried to brainwash me; boy, they taught me a lot. Now you, an Allied officer, are trying to threaten me and to protect a Nazi fanatic.'

I paused. I could feel my rage mounting. As I spoke he kept pushing his spectacles up his nose and topping up his whisky.

'You wear American uniform and yet you have the nerve to do this to a Jew. You are a traitor!'

I had to restrain myself from grabbing his lapels. Thank God I didn't touch him. They would have shot me.

An unpleasant pause ensued.

'Am I under arrest then?'

'Not at present.'

'Right, I will leave now if that's the case. It gives me no pleasure to remain in your company. I will be putting in a report to the higher authorities explaining why you are unfit to be a Military Governor here – or anywhere else in Germany.'

He smiled coldly.

'I will send for a jeep to take you back.'

As I left I remembered almost with regret the ferocious, but honest, manners of the Russian colonels and generals I had known.

Luba was waiting for me with a group of friends; she took me aside and told me that Dr Base had been taken away by ambulance, unconscious. I wondered what could be the reason, since she had appeared to be alright when I left her. Perhaps she was doing it for show. In any case it did not worry me – though our supper was not exactly a jolly occasion. After the meal there was a telephone call from the Military Governor: he wished to see me urgently back at his office in headquarters. Luba was fearful. I was none too happy myself. All the eventualities went through my head. I hurried to the Governor's office at headquarters (he had his living quarters in the same building). He wasted no time.

'Dr Base is dead. There will be charges brought against you. It may even mean a charge of murder.'

'Why did you call me here to tell me this news?'

'Because I am a friend of the Jewish people.'

'What do you suggest I should do about it?'

'Just disappear. I can delay any action being taken for at least twenty-four hours.'

'Why would you do that for me? If I am to be arrested it will be by the German civil authorities, not on your orders. But thank you anyway for your solicitude on my behalf.'

He wanted to prolong the interview but I left abruptly. On the way back I told myself not to worry; then I thought about the possible complications which could occur after an accident like hers. If death had taken place it was by no means a foregone conclusion that it was due entirely to the near-drowning. In any case, I reflected, he may not be telling the truth. He's frightened for his own skin. Why would he be so friendly to me? If I were arrested and imprisoned my accusations against him would lose all credibility. Let him go to hell!

Instead of going home I made for the city hospital of Starnberg. I gave the night porter a few packs of American cigarettes and asked if I might visit the morgue to see the body of Dr Base.

'But there are no bodies in the morgue at present, sir,' he said, 'and if there is a death in the hospital we all know about it.' He was probably correct about this since it was only a small hospital.

I went to the resident doctor, who knew me, and who, like all the Germans there, hated me. But I made him take me up to the bed of Dr Base. She was half asleep. I looked at the medical report, then felt her pulse. She was alright. She opened her eyes and recognized me.

'You will soon be back in your own home. I just happened to be here and went to the morgue to look for you!'

She replied with a weak laugh; her teeth were still loose.

I took the car and headed directly for the Military Governor's headquarters. The guard on duty telephoned the Colonel's apartments, but he was told that the Colonel had gone to bed and would not see anyone.

'Then please give him this message: Dr Base sends him her regards. I think he will see me now.'

The guard gave the message and then handed me the receiver. I told the Governor what I had seen at the hospital.

'I can't believe it. They telephoned me to say she had died.'

'It's not a good thing for a Military Governor to act so quickly on telephoned information.' He started to reply but I put the receiver down. I went home. It looked as if I was safe – but I wanted no more of Germany and the Germans. The next time they provoked me I might really go too far. I told Luba we would leave the next day.

It was not an escape: I am not the person to run away from any hardship, but the situation in Germany was still too explosive for me, and with my impetuous nature I could have paid very dear.

19

Goodbye, Good Riddance

We left Starnberg in the Adler convertible the following evening, without telling anyone. It was a clear night, the fresh air exhilarating as we drove along the excellent highways built for Hitler's regime by slave labour. Where would I be a year from now, I speculated? I realized that I had burnt my boats with the US authorities and with UNRRA by my departure, though I had been careful to leave keys and inventories behind. In any case, I fully intended to write a report on Colonel Bludberg, explaining my actions, and send it to the United States authorities – which indeed I did.

But I was under no illusions as to the price I would have to pay for writing that report: I would have to give up my hopes of emigrating to the United States. Where would I go? Where would I settle? From now on, I realized, I would have to provide for Luba and Sonia. I had given up the idea of parting from Luba, though that is what we had agreed before leaving Russia: quite apart from my growing sense of responsibility, Sonia had come to mean too much to me. It would be quite different from being a carefree bachelor.

My plan was to head for Belgium; there had been advertisements in the newspapers for medical posts in the Belgian Congo. The salaries were high, the positions seemed good. The immediate problem was to get out of Occupied Germany to the freedom from all military control in Brussels.

We spent the next day in Cologne walking about the streets. We were tired but I had to find some Jews who could give us information on how to get across. I was told it was not too difficult but we would need a pass – and in any case we would not be allowed to take the car. I noticed two big Dutch trucks standing at the roadside. The two drivers stood nearby chatting. I

went up to them and asked them in Dutch if they could give us
a lift to the Belgian frontier, or whether they were going direct
to Holland. They said they were in fact going to Holland but
they could drop us at the point where the three frontiers, Germany, Holland and Belgium converge. It would be easy from
there. The best time to make the attempt would be early in the
morning: the frontier guards would be sleeping and we could
walk across.

I told them I had no money to pay them but I could give
them the car.

'You must be crazy,' they told me. 'Where have you come
from anyway?'

'We are Jews. We have come from Russia.'

One of them ran to his truck and brought back some chocolate for Sonia.

'We don't want any money. You have suffered enough.'

So I took the car to the Adler garage in Cologne, saying I
wanted to complete certain repairs, hoping thus to cover my
tracks if there should be any hue and cry. The rest of the day
we spent with the drivers, then started off about midnight.

We crossed the frontier into Belgium near the Belgian town
of Hergenrath. It was in fact much easier than we expected. The
truck drivers kissed Sonia, said goodbye to us and gave us the
few Belgian francs they had. They asked us not to sell them out
if we should be caught. Several trucks were lined up in a yard
near a small house which was right on the frontier. We decided
to walk directly to the house using the trucks as cover. As we
came nearer I could see that the guards were not sleeping. They
were talking and even had a dog with them. I had to make an
instantaneous decision.

We just kept walking along the road. No one stopped us.
They had not even seen us. There were no barriers for us. Even
if they had stopped us we would have passed.

The first town along the country road was Hergenrath. The
local people all stared at us, and I knew that sooner or later
someone would stop us and question us. So I rang the bell at
the door of a small guest-house. A Flemish man came to the door
and asked us inside. I told him the story of how we had come to
be in the town, that we were Jews trying to get to Brussels. He

went to the telephone to call the police. As he lifted the receiver I put my hand on his arm and pushed it down.

'I would think twice before you do that.'

'But if I don't inform them I will be arrested myself,' he said. This was a general rule in frontier zones.

In my pocket I had the gold ten-rouble piece I had brought with me from Russia, sewn inside my jacket. When I saw that the man could not be swayed I tore open the seam and handed it to him. He asked for more but I told him that was all I had.

'You must be joking. Jews always have money. You will have to find some more.'

'The only way I can give you more is when I can get to Brussels. Then I can bring you more. But you must take us to the station and buy the railway tickets for us.'

He agreed. We all piled into his car. He drove us to Liège and bought the tickets. In a short time we arrived in Brussels. From the station I told a taxi driver to take us to a cafe called Gilbay between the Bourse and the Place de Brouckère, which I had heard was the regular meeting place of many Jews. And so indeed it turned out to be. They all gathered around us, kissed us, asked us question after question. One of them paid off the taxi. Another lifted Sonia high in the air and kissed her.

A new epoch began for us. Sometimes, you see, it is good to be a Jew. There are situations where one Jew competes with another and does not let him live – but he will not let him die either.

When we crossed the frontier only hours before, we had no money, no place to go, no work, and now we were surrounded by others who themselves had their own stories of survival. They were not rich but every one of them came up to us with offers of help.

That first night in Brussels we slept at the home of Max Bernstein, a Russian Jew of the old school, with a great Russian-Jewish heart. Since he was from Russia himself he was very interested to hear everything we could tell him. He let me have a thousand Belgian francs as a loan. I told him of our intention to leave Europe to go to the Belgian Congo or Venezuela and that I would need to borrow the fare money as I did not wish to apply to one of the several charity organizations for aid. He understood me. A Jewish organization applied for, and obtained, police permits for us to stay in Brussels until our emigration papers were ready. They obtained work for us too.

On our second day in the city we walked the streets gazing at the shops when suddenly Sonia saw a big window display of fruit. I had the thousand francs Bernstein had given me in my pocket, but we would need all that money to buy clothes. Sonia was particularly attracted by the oranges:

'Look, Papa! Oh look! Oranges!'

We went inside but they were very expensive and Luba said it was too much.

'You can't have one. They are too dear,' she told Sonia. When she was thwarted or dissatisfied with an answer Sonia would put two fingers in her mouth and hold her hand on her chin. She did it now. I bought her one orange. We had hardly crossed the Place de Brouckère before she had finished it and asked for another. Luba told her she could have no more.

'I will not buy you another one now because I do not want to go against your mother's wishes, but soon I will buy you one every day. One day when we come back to Belgium I will buy a shopful for you.'

'You promise?'

'Yes.'

It was during these weeks that Luba told me she was two months pregnant. I was not overjoyed but felt, all the same, that I would like to have a child. She had tried to rid herself of the child, but had been unsuccessful and wanted me to help her. I refused. When she asked why, I told her:

'You know I have never done that, and am against it on principle. If you were unable to have the child for reasons of health, I would do it for you.'

We had a violent quarrel over it. She reproached me:

'How can you expect me to arrive as a penniless immigrant in an unknown country and be pregnant?'

'Why not? It's perfectly normal. We shall be earning enough to raise a family. You should have it.'

But she was adamant. She said she would start the abortion and I would have to finish it.

'Forget it,' I told her.

I had one account to settle before leaving Belgium. One
morning, without telling Luba, I took a train to Hergenrath
and went straight to the guest-house to find the Flemish man
who had spoken against the Jews. I was told he was only on
duty at night and would not arrive until the evening. They
gave me his address. It was about lunchtime: he was already
up. He recognized me immediately.

'It's the *smerige jood*, the dirty Jew.'

'I've come to say good morning to you.'

He came up close in a threatening way. I held up my hand:

'Take it easy, take it easy. I came to repay you the money for
the train tickets.'

'Well, I never thought to see you again.'

'There is another reason I came: I want the ten-rouble piece
back.'

He laughed like an animal. 'I sold it.'

'Then get dressed, and we will go together and get it back.'

He grabbed a poker.

'*Got verdomme!* You can't just walk in here and tell me what
I should do!'

He came towards me, the poker raised. I grabbed his wrist
and twisted the poker out of his hold.

'Get dressed, or I'll call the police. You're a dirty Nazi!'

His wife and some other people had now gathered round. He
went out of the room and returned with the ten-rouble piece.

'I went to sell it. It is of no value at all, so take your ten
roubles, you dirty Jew and get out of my home.'

I took it and gave him 500 Belgian francs over and above the
price of the railway tickets.

'That money is for not selling me out to the police and for
taking us to the train.'

'So, you are a good Jew. Not like the others.'

This was an old song I had heard so often, and if the reader
is a Jew he will certainly have heard it too. I was relieved to get
the ten-rouble piece back. It had a greater significance for me
than its intrinsic value: I had kept it through so many vicissi-
tudes, in case of emergency. I still have it thirty-five years later,
and I hope one of my sons will keep it after me.

In Brussels, Luba started to become jealous of me again as

there were plenty of attractive girls although I gave her no reason to be jealous at this period. She was good to me, and looked after me, as well as being a beautiful woman. Sometimes I felt good with her but she also had the capacity to make me lose my temper with her jealous scenes. If I saw a lovely woman, God had given me eyes and I would look; and they, more often than not, would look at me. I have always been frank to the point of rudeness and I have often found that people are attracted by that. . . .

Now, as I write, Josephine my wife, who has been married to me for twenty years, is helping me with my English. She has her own opinion about my habit of looking at women. She has just laughed at me; I do not know what she is thinking about, but I do know that she believes in me, trusts me and loves me. The same goes for me.

It was different with Luba. I did not understand. In fact it took me nearly twenty years to begin to understand her.

We registered with two departments of immigration: one was at the Belgian Ministry of Health for work in the Belgian Congo, and the other was at the Venezuelan Consulate – for the Venezuelans were also advertising for doctors. I decided to take whichever came up first with a concrete offer. It was the end of September, the European summer holidays were over; we had been to the beach at Knokke a few times, but when we went Luba made such jealous scenes that I lost the desire to go there any more. The promenade and beach were full of women all hungry for men. They would come out from Brussels with their children, and their husbands would arrive only for the week-ends. So the rest of the week they were looking for sex. It is a windy resort on the North Sea, so they put up protective awnings against the wind, and sunbathed in their shelter. If a man walked past in swimming trunks they would look up, size him up, and invite him to sit down. Luba would not let me walk a hundred yards along the beach alone. So to oblige Luba I stopped going there.

Once, when we returned to Brussels from Knokke, we arrived at our flat in the Rue du Marche, to find a note for us inviting us down to the ground-floor flat where two brothers lived called Zarnik.

It was several seconds before they opened the door to my knock. The flat was in darkness, the curtains drawn. They both looked frightened: one held his finger to his lips.

I whispered: 'What's the matter?'

The younger brother replied:

'Doctor, we caught a *kapo** here in a cafe in Brussels. He was in our camp.'

I looked down. His clothes were bloodstained.

'Where is he?'

'We have him tied up in the next room.'

'And why did you ask me to share this secret?'

'Because you will know what to do. We don't know what to do next.'

'Well, you certainly cannot keep him here indefinitely. You will be caught and charged, and me too. Let me see him.'

They took me into the bedroom which was in complete darkness. He was hanging, head downward, from the ceiling, his hands tied behind his back. His face was badly cut, bruised and swollen. He had other external injuries. We lowered him down: he was breathing with difficulty and spat blood. He probably had kidney injuries too.

'He must be taken to hospital immediately.'

The younger brother took out a pair of long tailor's scissors.

'He's not going anywhere. I'll finish him now.'

'How did you manage to get hold of him?'

'Well, we saw him in this cafe called Le Palais. When he saw that we had recognized him he ran into the toilet. We went in after him and punched him and beat him. His shouts brought the other customers in, mostly Belgians, and when we told them he was a *kapo* they joined in too.'

Luba came into the bedroom. We examined him and gave him first aid, but it was clear that we must get him to hospital. The *kapo* started to cry and protest his innocence, but every time he swore that he had done nothing to harm his fellow prisoners the younger brother struck him across the face. I did my best to hold him back, but I could also understand his feel-

---

* Prisoner appointed by the camp authorities to supervise fellow prisoners.

ings: the brothers had lost both their parents in the camp. In most cases, the *kapos*, Jews too, had been recruited by the Nazis to collaborate with them and to help keep their fellow prisoners in subjection. The brothers pushed us out, and we could hear the blows and shouts continue. I was afraid they would kill him. We stopped a policeman and rushed back with him to force the door. The *kapo* was on the floor bleeding profusely from his nose which had been severed. They took him off in an ambulance and the two brothers went to the police station. The Belgian police had their own accounts to settle with the *kapos*. The brothers were released after two days after they had made a declaration that they would not attempt to leave the country.

Luba eventually found a fellow doctor who would help her with her abortion, a man called Dr Klebanov, her compatriot. When I spoke to him he expressed his reluctance to carry out the termination since in his opinion the case was too advanced. I told him I was against the whole idea. Nevertheless Luba had her way. He was a good specialist. I saw the foetus myself. It was a boy, about four months: he seemed to look like me. I did not feel on that occasion the sense of loss, misery and waste of human life that I was to feel later – perhaps because I had Sonia. But I never felt the same towards Luba again. There was always an element of hatred. Years later I understood: she was afraid that if she presented me with a child of my own I would never love Sonia as I had before. A mature, mentally stable woman would not agree with the logic of her thinking, but I suppose some women would agree with her. The divergence of opinion between us on this score resulted in my constant wish to have a child and in her determination to deny me. But at the time she pleaded unwillingness to arrive in a new country as a pregnant immigrant and gave me the impression that, once settled, we would have children. When Klebanov left, he realized how upset I was. He tried to apologize, explaining that he had simply given help to a colleague who had begged him for it.

I went off to Knokke to enjoy myself. . . .

Back in Brussels I found that I was scratched and bruised all over. I was lucky that Luba was out of action otherwise there would have been another hysterical scene. I suppose it was my way of paying her back for the abortion.

Towards the end of September we received an urgent message to present ourselves at the Venezuelan Consulate. The First Secretary of the Embassy informed us that the Venezuelan government was prepared to offer us a contract. The salary was high. We agreed to the conditions.

'There is a slight snag, though,' he said. 'I see from these documents that you are Jews and we do have certain laws limiting the numbers of Jewish and Chinese immigrants. If you were to put "of no religion" or some other religion I am sure your application will be acceptable.'

I grabbed the papers from the table.

'I have survived as a Jew and will die as a Jew. If your country has laws which discriminate against Jews I have no wish to go there.' I tore up the documents.

He tried to smooth it over.

'Oh no, it is not like that at all,' he said as he tried to salvage the papers, but we were already walking out of his office.

Two days later the same Secretary came to our home.

'Everything is arranged. You may emigrate to Venezuela as Jews. My country is certainly not anti-semitic. You will be proud and happy to live there.'

Our departure was fixed for two weeks later aboard the ss *Colombie* from Marseilles. There were more papers to be signed at the Embassy, then after a short wait we received the contract signed by the Ambassador. It stated that we were to be employed by the SAS (Sanidad Asistencia Social) of Venezuela to work as doctors wherever they found necessary for a period of one year and, after this period, we would have the right to revalidate our degrees and work where we wished. There were separate entry visas. We would have to make our own travelling arrangements to the ship. They wished us luck.

We reached Marseilles two days before the departure date and checked into a small hotel. At the dockside on the morning of departure we met many of the passengers – of all nationalities, but mostly Italians who, we could see from their appearance and bundles, were impoverished and anxious to make a new life for themselves in a new land. The ship had been used as a hospital and military transport during the war. We hurried aboard. Like me, the other passengers were waiting for the final blast of the ship's funnel. They searched for their bunk, left their bundles there, and came back on deck.

As we assembled we looked at each other, assessing what could have made this one or that one leave Europe. The trip would take up to three weeks. We none of us knew what Venezuela would be like. Even today many Europeans have no idea of where Venezuela is. The prospect held no fears for me. Looking back, I think how fortunate it was that Venezuela came up before the Belgian Congo – though it was just chance, or rather my lucky star, that decided that I was heading for South America rather than Africa.

As I stood on deck, many thoughts passed through my mind. The worst is over, I reflected. At least I have a government contract in my pocket. I will work and make money. A new life will open up for me. I was used to a life of action and problems and trouble of all kinds. The only point my conscience bothered me about was Sonia and her father. How would Venezuela treat me? I wondered what were the dangers I might encounter from tropical diseases: leprosy, malaria, cholera and many others. I was impatient to start work, but life had taught me that often it was necessary to control one's impatience.

The shrill blast of the ship broke through my thoughts, and passed through my body. Only a few people stood at the dock-side in scattered groups to wave us goodbye. Some of the passengers were crying: from grief, excitement, happiness. For whom should I cry? For my family – yes, for them, for they were with the forty thousand Jews in the cemetery in my mother's home town, all massacred. Is it possible that every one of them is dead? Perhaps one has survived, perhaps Mischa, my little brother.

The ship slid slowly out to the open sea. The coasts of Europe grew smaller. Darkness and distance obscured the lights.

Goodbye Europe, goodbye.